Victorian Countrywomen

Victorian Countrywomen

PAMELA HORN

Basil Blackwell

First published 1991

Basil Blackwell Ltd
108 Cowley Road, Oxford, OX4 1JF, UK

Basil Blackwell, Inc.
3 Cambridge Center
Cambridge, Massachusetts 02142, USA

British Library Cataloguing in Publication Data

A CIP catalogue record for this book is available from the British Library.

Library of Congress Cataloging in Publication Data

Horn, Pamela.
Victorian countrywomen / Pamela Horn.
p.   cm.
Includes bibliographical references and index.
ISBN 0-631-15522-8
1. Rural women—Great Britain—History—19th century. 2. Great Britain—Rural conditions.   I. Title.
HQ1593.H77   1991
305.4'0942—dc20   90-38582
CIP

Typeset in 11 on 13 pt Goudy
by Pioneer Associates Ltd., Perthshire
Printed in Great Britain by Billing and Sons Ltd, Worcester

Contents

Acknowledgements

I should like to thank all those who have helped in the preparation of this book, either by providing information or in other ways. In particular, my thanks are due to the Master and Fellows of Trinity College, Cambridge, for permission to quote from the Munby Papers, and to the staff at the Libraries, Record Offices and other institutions in which I have worked. I much appreciate the kindness and co-operation shown to me. These institutions include the Bodleian Library, Oxford, the British Library, the British Library Newspaper Library, Colindale, Dorset County Museum, the Fawcett Library, City of London Polytechnic, Hitchin Museum, the Imperial War Museum, the Institute of Agricultural History and Museum of English Rural Life, Reading, Lambeth Palace Library, Luton Museum, Oxford City and County Museum, Woodstock, Oxford Local History Library, Queen's College Library, London, the Queen's Nursing Institute, London, the Public Record Office, Roehampton Institute of Higher Education (for Whitelands College Archives), the Schoolmistresses' and Governesses' Benevolent Institute, Chislehurst, Somerset House, the Trustees of the Thomas Hardy Memorial Collection in the Dorset County Museum, Dorchester, Dorset, the University of Reading Library, the Library of the Wellcome Institute for the History of Medicine, London, and the Welsh Folk Museum, Cardiff. I have also received much efficient assistance from the County Record Offices for Bedfordshire, Berkshire, Buckinghamshire, Clwyd, Dorset, Essex, Gloucestershire, Hampshire, Northamptonshire, Oxfordshire and Wiltshire.

I am indebted to many individuals for the help they have given to me, including my brother- and sister-in-law, Mr and Mrs Ian Horn of Ivinghoe, Buckinghamshire, Mr Arthur Clifford of Sutton Courtenay for reminiscences of his mother, Mrs Howse, Mrs Wright and Mrs

Wiggins of Leafield, Oxfordshire, for information on the pre-1914 glove trade, the late Miss D. B. Dew of Lower Heyford, Oxfordshire, for life in the village before 1914, Miss M. Tyrrell of Marcham for life in Steventon (then in Berkshire) before 1914 and Mr Steptoe of Sutton Courtenay for details of Mrs Caroline Irons.

Finally, I owe a debt of gratitude to my husband, who has assisted in countless different ways. Without his help neither this nor any of my books could have been written. He has encouraged me throughout and his advice on the organization and content of the book has been invaluable.

Pamela Horn

Conversion Table

Shillings and pence and some illustrative decimal coinage equivalents:

	1d.	½p	
	2d.	1	p
	3d.		
	4d.	1½p	
	5d.	2	p
	6d.	2½p	
	7d.	3	p
	8d.	3½p	
	9d.	4	p
	10d.		
	11d.	4½p	
1s.		5	p
2s.		10	p
2s.	6d.	12½p	
2s.	9d.	14	p
2s.	10d.		
3s.		15	p
10s.		50	p
12s.	6d.	62½p	
15s.		75	p

She had the ornament of a meek and quiet spirit which is in the sight of God of great price.

1

Introduction:
Women in the Village Community

That which seems most to lower the moral or decent tone of the peasant girls is the sensation of independence of society which they acquire when they have remunerative labour in their hands either in the fields, or at home . . . All gregarious employment gives a slang character to the girls' appearance and habits, while dependence on the man for support is the spring of modest and pleasing deportment. . . . [T]he desolate appearance of the homes where the busy self-important women care nothing to please, and are anxious to sell every minute, is remarkable.

Seventh Report of the Medical Officer of the Privy Council, Parliamentary Papers 1865, Vol. XXVI, 'Inquiry on the State of the Dwellings of Rural Labourers by Dr H. J. Hunter'.

To outward appearance the world of the Victorian village was essentially masculine. Although females formed more than half the total population (in 1901 there were 3.75 m. of them living in rural districts, compared to 3.71 m. males), most visitors strolling along the lanes and byways saw merely the menfolk, labouring in field, forge and workshop, or travelling the highroad with horse and cart or delivery van. Only at the busiest seasons of the farming year – at haysel and harvest – did women work on the land in any numbers in most parts of England and Wales. Edwin Grey, in a typical comment, noted of his childhood home near Harpenden, Hertfordshire, during the 1860s that except when 'something out of the ordinary occurred, or on a Saturday or Sunday night, one saw little of the womenfolk about the place . . . So far as I can recollect, the housewives spent most of their time within doors, busy with their work.'[1]

This apparent male dominance of country life was particularly obvious in the economic sphere. Most of the land and many of the businesses were owned by men – a position which the lack of effective married women's property legislation reinforced for much of the period. Women rarely occupied responsible positions within the community, and it is significant that out of about 224,000 farmers in England and Wales in 1901, fewer than 22,000 were women; and most of these were doubtless the widows of farmers who had carried on after their husbands' deaths.[2] A mere one in six were spinsters. Women in fact formed a smaller proportion of the total labour force in rural areas at that date than they did in England and Wales as a whole. In 1901 they comprised under a quarter of the workers in country districts compared to almost a third of the total in the nation at large.[3]

The one significant area where female employment did advance in rural communities during the Victorian era was in school teaching. The heads of village schools were able to achieve a level of financial reward and a status available to few other working-class or lower middle-class girls at that time. One commentator claimed in 1872 that they had 'a sphere of Christian influence' as great in its consequences as that of the parochial clergyman.[4] At the end of the century about three-quarters of all elementary teachers were women, compared to just over half who were female in the mid-1870s. Nevertheless, gender differences persisted, with the most lucrative headships going to men — a situation examined in more detail in chapter 8.

But teaching apart, in most villages there was a growing tendency to stress the undesirability of women taking up any kind of employment outside the home. As Margaret Hewitt pointed out more than thirty years ago, it was with the spread of industrialization in the early nineteenth century and the consequent decline in domestic production that women workers in the countryside became the subject of comment and criticism.[5] For this two reasons can be advanced. First the long hours of toil in crafts and trades at home were easily ignored by society in the obscurity of a cottage in a way that proved impossible in large-scale factory production. At the same time, the industrial revolution itself, by marginalizing or destroying many of the women's former craft skills, also reduced their importance in the eyes of contemporaries. It is a token of changing attitudes that whereas the population censuses up to 1881 had included in the 'occupational' category such groups as shopkeepers' wives, shoe-makers' wives, farmers' wives and innkeepers' wives, thereby signalling that wives were seen as sharing in the running of the business, from 1881 that disappeared. Instead women without a specific occupation of their own were classed as 'unoccupied', with 94 per cent of all married or widowed women in rural areas so categorized by the 1911 census.[6] Even among *unmarried* girls and women aged ten and above, only 46 per cent in rural districts were classed in 1911 as employed. Admittedly, some part-time workers, especially in agriculture, may have failed to report their occupation to the census enumerator, but evidence from wages books and personal reminiscences indicates that even when these have been taken into account, the female work force in the countryside was shrinking.

The second factor to be taken into account was the technological change which occurred in agriculture as a result of mechanization and alterations in harvesting techniques. In consequence, the importance of women's contribution to land work was reduced and this made it easier for farmers to dispense with their services.

Yet, ironically, whilst these changes were under way, the passage of the stringent 1834 Poor Law Amendment Act, curtailing outdoor relief to the able-bodied and emphasizing the 'less eligibility' principle for recipients of parish assistance, increased the pressure on women to work in order to supplement an inadequate family income and avoid the stigma of pauperism. This was especially true up to the middle decades of the nineteenth century.

Hence, despite middle-class reservations, during the early Victorian period, the general stress on family self-dependence caused reluctant acquiescence to be given to female employment. Typical of this dichotomy of view was the comment of an assistant poor law commissioner on women land workers in south-west England in 1843:

I believe it would be much better for their husbands and children, if [they] were not engaged in such employment . . . but

... upon the fullest consideration, I believe that the earnings of a woman employed in the fields are an advantage which, in the present state of the agricultural population, outweighs any of the mischiefs arising from such employment. All direct interference in the employment of women in agriculture must be deprecated at present.[7]

At a time when male labourers in these counties earned around 8s. to 10s. a week, the 3s. to 5s. which a wife or daughter could secure made an important contribution to total family income.

Twenty years later a very different philosophy applied. Now the large-scale employment of married women was deplored as conflicting unacceptably with prevailing opinion that wives should remain at home to look after house and family. There was what Margaret Hewitt has called a 'deification of the home'.[8] As the purchasing power of most labouring families modestly advanced compared to earlier years and as middle-class social values became ever more pervasive, doubts about the validity of women's work outside the home strengthened. The proliferation of government reports and parliamentary debates on the subject in the 1860s is testimony to the mounting unease. One critic, writing of women land workers in East Anglia, claimed that the work 'almost' unsexed them, 'in dress, gait, manners, character, making [them] rough, coarse, clumsy, masculine'.[9] To another witness, agricultural labour was 'the certain ruin of the female character . . . They become bold, impudent, scandalmongers, hardened against religion, careless of their homes and children.'[10]

It was to counter such alleged deficiencies that agricultural and labourers' improvement societies began to offer prizes to householders who kept their homes in a spotless condition. They included the Romsey District Association for the Encouragement of Meritorious Labourers, set up in 1854. It offered annual prizes of £1 10s. to married couples who had maintained their cottages in a neat and clean condition. A winner in 1867 was Moses Silence 'and his wife'; ironically the wife, who presumably had been responsible for their winning the prize, is not even mentioned by name![11]

In the final decades of the nineteenth century such attitudes were to be further strengthened. The general report of the 1871 population census caught the popular mood, when it observed that wives and mothers had 'a noble and essential occupation'. On it, 'as much as on the husband's labour and watchfulness depend the existence and character of the English race'. The 'most useful of all [female] occupations', it concluded, was that 'of wife, mother, and mistress of a family'.[12]

Not all contemporaries, however, agreed with this exaggerated emphasis on domesticity. The barrister and diarist, Arthur Munby, who carried out his own interviews with mid-Victorian working women, angrily denounced the 'Mollycoddlers' who were trying to stop women exercising a free choice as to their employment.[13] In his accounts of meetings with female land workers he stressed the pride which many felt in their skills. And in a poem entitled 'Woman's Rights' (published in 1865) Munby expressed his opposition to the would-be reformers:

> Women, whose powers are so vast,
>   Are *children*, after all!
> They mustn't give, as men may give,
> Their sweat and brains, nor freely live
>   In great things and in small:
> They must be guided from above,
> By quips of patronizing love,
>   To do or not to do.[14]

This was a theme to which he returned on other occasions.[15]

George Sturt, writing in the 1890s, similarly applauded the strength and independence of many of the women in his hamlet of The Bourne, near Farnham in Surrey – women like old Sally Turner, who at the age of seventy-three supported herself by running a small laundry. 'She had been the equal of men all her life', wrote Sturt. 'She belonged (as I think of her) to two places: her cottage garden where the clothes were aired, and the high-road along which she took them home.' He contrasted her self-dependence with 'the typical old cottage woman of a certain order of books, who studies her Bible, keeps her spectacles among the geraniums on the windowsill, . . . and . . . can curtsey to her betters in a way to turn good children green with envy.'[16]

But such robust views on the female role in village society were already at a discount in the 1860s, and they became still more unpopular as the century drew to a close. Even working-class families themselves came to share the prejudice against female employment, especially on the land. Flora Thompson has recorded how, in her north Oxfordshire hamlet in the 1880s, the unsavoury reputation of earlier female agricultural gang members had given 'most country-women a distaste for "goin' afield"'.[17] A decade earlier the newly established agricultural trade union movement also declared its opposition to women on the land, regarding them, in part, as undermining the wages and employment prospects of the men.[18]

So strong had the reaction against outdoor employment become in parts of southern and midland England on the eve of the First World War that a researcher from the Women's Industrial Council referred to the 'morbid' seclusion which countless village women experienced as they sought to 'keep themselves to themselves'. She also pointed out that contrary to popular belief, the children of women who worked were healthier than the offspring of those who stayed at home, because a higher family income meant they were better fed.[19] But her findings had little effect. The majority of wives seemingly accepted the 'separate spheres' argument and saw their role as a domestic one, caring for husband and children.

Yet, despite the growing doubts about the desirability of female employment, throughout the nineteenth century women were expected to help on the land at the busy seasons of the farming year in most rural communities. However, outside a few selected areas, such as Northumbria, Cumbria, North Yorkshire, parts of East Anglia and Wales, the number so occupied on a permanent basis was relatively small. It was in being housewives, domestic servants and cottage craft workers that their main importance lay. This is confirmed by female employment patterns derived from mid-Victorian census returns. (See appendix 1.)

As appendix 1 indicates, opportunities for women to engage in employment on their own account were apparently greatest in villages where a predominant craft existed. The implications of this for the day-to-day lives of the women concerned will be examined in detail in chapter 7, when the cottage industries are analysed more closely. Suffice it here to point out that the economic independence thus bestowed was of major importance both to the financial security of the family and to the status of the women themselves. At Ivinghoe, Buckinghamshire, where there were thirty-one male agricultural

labourers and a groom recorded as unemployed in 1871, eighteen
belonged to families where plaiting by the female and child members
was apparently the only source of income. Alongside these were
widows and mothers of illegitimate children who relied on plaiting
for family support, while six single women living alone were also
plaiters. Similarly at Stonesfield, Oxfordshire, at least five households
seem to have been kept by the wife's earnings as a gloveress, while
four elderly widows maintained themselves from the trade. Overall
about three-quarters of the married women in this village were
glovemakers. In both Ivinghoe and Stonesfield, therefore, the
earnings of a wife either kept her family from pauperism or, where
the husband and other male adults were at work, gave a valuable
boost to household income. This was a bonus, since there is little
evidence that male wage rates were lower in the handicraft
communities than in those neighbouring parishes which were without
a trade.

The outlets for personal employment also encouraged greater self-
confidence and independence of outlook among the women
concerned. 'Many a house was bought on gloving', declared a present-
day worker from Leafield, Oxfordshire, an important glovemaking
village, and she was clearly proud of that record.[20]

Also important was the fact that where cottage industries flourished
there were opportunities for women not engaged in the main
handicraft to take up other occupations, perhaps providing services
the craft workers lacked the time to supply for themselves, or which
they could afford to buy. Dressmaking, laundrywork and shopkeeping
were often carried out by women in villages where there was an
important cottage industry.

Finally, many workers valued the companionship they gained
when they pursued a communal craft. At Cottisford in north
Oxfordshire, where there were nineteen lacemakers out of a total
female population of 125 in 1851, Flora Thompson recalled, years
later, her conversations with one of them, whom she called 'Old
Queenie', but whose real name was Mrs Eliza Massey. The old
woman described how in the winter she and her fellow workers met
together in one of the cottages, each bringing a faggot or a shovel of
coal for the fire. There they sat gossiping through the day as their
nimble fingers produced the delicate fabric. In summer they sat
outside in the shade of the houses, and each year they sold their

annual output of lace to a dealer at Banbury fair. They then purchased gifts for the family and for themselves before returning home with money in their pocket.[21] But when the lace trade collapsed in the late 1850s, this communal employment was lost.

Most accounts of village life undervalue or ignore this female contribution. It is the menfolk and their preoccupations which provide the focus of attention. Part of the reason for this may lie in the attitude of villagers themselves. Even in the late twentieth century Mary Chamberlain found women from Gislea in the fenlands reluctant to talk about their lives, considering them of far less interest than the men's.[22]

In Victorian times this male-centred approach was still more pervasive. Sons were regarded with greater favour at all levels of rural society than were daughters. As one aged countrywoman put it, 'she would sooner have seven boys than one girl: for the former, when they became lads, went out and earned their own living, but the girls, you never knew when they were got rid of – they were always coming back.'[23] In north Oxfordshire, Flora Thompson remembered that mothers always put sons before daughters: 'If there was any inconvenience, it must not fall on the boys.'[24]

Some girls resented the fact that they were expected to carry out household chores whilst their brothers were excused. 'I remember we had to knit father's socks. And make his flannel shirts', recalled a woman brought up in late Victorian Gislea. 'We all had to sit and sew. We didn't go out and play. The boys, they had a better time than we did.'[25]

The preoccupation with female domesticity was also apparent among educationists. In 1862, under the terms of the government's Revised Code, all girls attending grant-aided elementary schools were required to take plain needlework as part of the curriculum, along with religious instruction, reading, writing and arithmetic. No comparable bias was introduced into the instruction for the boys. And during the 1870s this approach was intensified when special government grants were offered for girl pupils learning domestic economy, and later cookery (from 1882) and laundrywork (from 1890). In 1882, one of HM Inspectors of Schools for the Newton Abbot district of Devon could even claim that it was a 'matter of common consent . . . that needlework' was 'by far the most important part of a girl's education'.[26]

PLATE 1 *The cult of domesticity. Grandmother is probably nursing the baby while mother operates the sewing machine, and other villagers queue up to have their turn upon it. At Plasbach, Cwmann, Lampeter, Cardiganshire, in 1894.*

(National Museum of Wales [Welsh Folk Museum])

A colleague reporting on pupils in the Northallerton district of Yorkshire shared this belief in the importance of domestic instruction, suggesting that girls should be trained to light the school fires, sweep the classroom floors, and dust the furniture.[27] Others suggested that half a girl's school life should be 'solely occupied with domestic training, and that some system of apprenticing girls to good housekeepers might be practicable'.[28]

School textbooks took up the theme, exhorting girls to work hard and to devote themselves to the needs of their family in a spirit of submission and self-sacrifice:

> Elder sisters, you may work,
>   Work and help your mothers,
> Darn the stockings, mend the shirts,
>   Father's things, and brother's.

(Book II, *Jarrold's New Code Reading Books* [1871])

Even failures in family life were blamed by textbook writers on the deficiencies of its female members. 'Of the men that are given to drink, how many are driven to it by the women that belong to them (be they wives or daughters) not enough studying to make home what it should be', warned the author of Book V of *The School Managers' Series of Reading Books*, also published in 1871.

At the end of the nineteenth century this anxiety to inculcate the virtues of female domesticity was reinforced by concern over the nation's health, aroused by a discovery of the poor physique of some of the men recruited to fight in the Boer War, and by continuing high levels of infant mortality. Although country children fared better in that regard than their urban counterparts, there was no cause for complacency: in the 1890s more than one baby in ten born in rural counties like Wiltshire, Dorset and Oxfordshire died before its first birthday.[29] Poor standards of infant care (including the injudicious administration of opiates like laudanum and Godfrey's cordial to quieten babies), as well as bad hygiene and impure water supplies, were blamed for these high rates. There was a widespread belief in government circles that one way of improving the situation was to include child welfare and care of the home in the school curriculum. Hence in 1905 the Board of Education issued its *Suggestions for the Consideration of Teachers and Others Concerned in the Work of Public Elementary Schools*, which required all courses in household management to cover cookery, laundrywork and practical house-wifery, so as to provide appropriate training in domestic skills.

Some rural education authorities responded by recruiting specialist peripatetic teachers to go round schools giving instruction in the relevant subjects. Others set up cookery and laundry centres to which the older girls were sent once a week. This solution was adopted in Oxfordshire, for example, and it is clear that many of the pupils took up the lessons with enthusiasm.[30]

Meanwhile, the general male dominance which had been established over the economic life of most Victorian villages was accompanied by an equal pre-eminence in political affairs. Although women began to offer themselves for election to school boards and poor law authorities in the towns from the 1870s, their contribution to similar bodies in rural districts was far smaller. Like their urban sisters, women in rural districts were, of course, excluded from the parliamentary franchise until 1918.

Opposition to the election of women as rural poor law guardians was particularly strong. In 1881, when Mrs Harriet McIlquham became the first married woman to be so elected (on account of ownership of land in her own right), her initiative led to appeals being made to her husband to stop her from standing. He was 'first entreated, and then abused in a public highway, for *allowing* his wife to be placed in what, it was prognosticated, would prove for her a most disagreeable and humiliating position'.[31] This did not deter the McIlquhams, and Harriet went on to become active in a variety of local government spheres, including membership of a school board.

Another exception to the 'derivative' political status of women was Miss Aldrich of Diss, Norfolk, a propertyless spinster, who in 1883 was able to exert sufficient influence on the local school board to prevent farmers lowering the school leaving age in order to obtain a cheap supply of juvenile labour.[32]

But most females who took part in local government owed their position rather to family connections than to their own merits. Mrs Broadhurst, a landowner's widow from Foston and Scropton, Derbyshire, only became a school board member when she took over her late husband's seat. After her death, the four other farmer members co-opted her brother, and when he resigned, his wife was chosen.[33] Elsewhere, a wife might serve alongside her husband, or a daughter with her father.

In 1894, however, a boost was given to the female role in rural politics by the abolition of property qualifications for those standing for election as poor law guardians, and by the setting up of parish and district councils, on which women could serve. As a consequence about 875 of them were elected poor law guardians throughout the country, with about 140 also serving on rural district councils. Norfolk, for example, had twenty-four female rural district councillors and thirty-one female guardians, while Suffolk had three district councillors and eleven guardians, and Cornwall five and eighteen respectively. It was in these circumstances that the journalist Richard Heath hailed the success of women and agricultural labourers at the elections as the 'emancipation' of 'two enslaved classes'.[34] But his optimism proved premature. Even in the mid-1890s counties like

Cambridgeshire, Huntingdonshire and Rutland still had no female representatives on their boards of guardians.[35] And women's participation in parish councils was even more disappointing, with only one or two hundred of them elected in the whole country in 1894–5.

Among those selected in Norfolk as both a district councillor and a poor law guardian was Charlotte Edwards, the wife of an agricultural trade union activist and fellow poor law guardian. Like many women members, she was concerned to expose the hardships and injustices experienced by paupers at the hands of unsympathetic poor law boards and officials.[36] As a result of pressure by her and her husband some improvements were secured in the amount of benefit paid by their own board. But these few pioneers apart, most village affairs remained in the hands of the traditional ruling classes. Women, for the most part, continued to depend for their status – or lack of it – upon the menfolk in their lives.

In such circumstances the position of those females, usually widows or elderly spinsters, who lived alone was particularly difficult, unless they had a private income. The census returns confirm the uncertain financial position of many of them. At Yarnton, Oxfordshire, where nine spinsters and widows headed households in 1871, five were paupers, a sixth ran a public house, one was a seamstress and the remaining two were farmers (probably running holdings inherited from another family member).[37] Likewise at Kilham, Northumberland, where four widows headed households in 1871, all were maintained by their family; none had an independent income.

In the early 1890s, Charles Booth's researches into the position of the aged poor revealed that almost twice as many women over sixty-five were dependent on parish poor relief in rural areas as were men in the same age group. Among elderly widows and unmarried women a mere 8 per cent were able to earn enough to maintain themselves, compared to just over 30 per cent who depended on parish relief and 37 per cent who relied on charity and the support of relatives. The rest had annuities or some other form of private income, such as a pension from a former employer.[38]

But most elderly widows and spinsters were without these scanty personal incomes. Instead they had to rely upon the vagaries of charity or the parish relief system. This latter included, if they were widows, undergoing investigation to ascertain the precise poor law

ASTOUNDING ANNOUNCEMENT FROM THE SMALL COUNTRY BUTCHER
(Who does not often Kill his own Meat).

Maid. "PLEASE, MA'AM, MR. SKEWER SAYS HE'S A-GOING TO KILL *HISSELF* THIS WEEK, AND WILL YOU HAVE A JOINT?"

PLATE 2 *Gossiping in the garden could be a pleasant way of spending the time.*

(*Punch*, 1857)

union where their late husband could claim a 'settlement'. For only when the parish of settlement had been established could long-term financial aid be arranged. Settlement could be gained by birth, property ownership or apprenticeship, but on marriage a woman normally took that of her spouse. Hence the problem of widows or deserted wives who found themselves despatched, like parcels, from one part of the country to another as their place of relief entitlement was established by the relevant poor law authority. (See appendix 6.)

Typical of the case studies quoted by Charles Booth was that of a 77-year-old widow from Satterly in East Anglia. She obtained 2s. 10d. a week in poor relief, but added to it by occasional earnings from 'sitting up with a sick person'. She also made 'several pounds every summer by taking in holiday children'.[39] In another instance an 80-year-old widow from Marsden, Leicestershire, received 2s. 6d. a week from the parish. This she supplemented, despite indifferent health, by carrying out a little 'seaming' for the local hosiery trade. Her niece, who kept one of the village shops, also gave her food.[40] In this precarious fashion she struggled by. It was women such as she who were particular beneficiaries when old age pensions were introduced under the legislation of 1908, for these guaranteed a weekly 5s. to all those over the age of seventy who had little or no alternative income – without the taint of pauperism.

The reaction of the elderly to the receipt of their first payments in January 1909 has been touchingly described by Flora Thompson, who as a former post office clerk was well placed to gauge the general response:

> When . . . the Old Age Pensions began, life was transformed for . . . aged cottagers. They were relieved of anxiety. They were suddenly rich. Independent for life! At first when they went to the Post Office to draw it, tears of gratitude would run down the cheeks of some, . . . and there were flowers from their gardens and apples from their trees for the girl who merely handed them the money.[41]

Press reports confirm the reaction. 'Many of the old women kissed the money', declared one postmistress. 'Others kissed the book of cheques when it was handed back to them.'[42] For such recipients the pension had removed fears that they would have to end their days in the much hated workhouse because they could not afford to support themselves outside.

The uncertainties and ambiguities in economic and political matters experienced by women living on their own were also carried through into the social sphere. As a recent historian has pointed out, Victorian spinsters were regarded by their contemporaries as human failures and were 'condemned to a lonely life of futility, ridicule or humiliation'.[43] In the upper ranks of society this probably meant dependence on the family for support and sustenance. In return, they were expected to care for ageing parents or to act as surrogate wives for bachelor brothers, and as child minders and nurses for other members of the family. Among the lower orders, their position could be still more unsatisfactory. In south-west Wales even at the end of the nineteenth century, they were frequently made the butt of jokes or were treated without consideration, as of little account.[44]

In Edwin Grey's small hamlet of Bowling Alley, Harpenden, a similarly dismissive attitude was adopted towards elderly unmarried women. According to Grey they were always referred to by their Christian names:

I remember many of these elderly spinsters: Polly Elmer, Polly Munt, Betsy Belcher, Sally Bonstead, etc. Polly Munt was an old lady who made and sold Vinegar Rock, a farthing a stick; Polly Elmer retailed bread, also doing a little mangling for a living; . . . A mother, finding herself short of bread, might say to her child: 'We are out o' bread, run to Polly Elmer's an' fetch 'arf a quartern loaf,' and thus were all the unmarried women alluded to whether young or old.[45]

Occasionally, at a time when superstition was still rife in rural parishes, the 'marginalizing' of these elderly women could take a more sinister turn, with a few being accused of having the 'evil eye'. The belief that to draw the blood of a witch broke her spell led to physical attacks being made on some suspects. Thus at East Deringham in Norfolk in 1879 a farmer was fined for assaulting the daughter of an old woman who, he claimed, had 'charmed' him by the use of a 'walking toad', which was her familiar.[46] Even when reactions to alleged 'witches' were less dramatic than this, there could be much unhappiness caused by communal hostility towards unattached women living alone; although a few of them may have got their revenge by taking a perverse pleasure in causing alarm among credulous fellow villagers by threatening to use their alleged supernatural powers.[47]

Happily, as the Victorian era drew to a close, these attitudes waned, but the uncertain social status of women living alone remained, unless they had substantial property and could afford to employ servants.

2

Family Life and Morality

Not a vestige of my grandmother's handwriting remains, and about the only worldly goods she left were a row of old books. Could any woman be more obscure? And yet . . . [she] wrote letters for her neighbours, helped them to cut out shirts, to whitewash their ceilings. Sometimes she would sit up at night with the sick. Little money passed, but her services were meticulously paid for. Her garden was dug, vegetables and rabbits brought, faggots of wood were stacked against her wall.

M. K. Ashby, *Joseph Ashby of Tysoe 1859-1919*
(Cambridge University Press, Cambridge, 1961).

As we saw in chapter 1, the contribution of most women to the externalities of village life was unobtrusive and restricted. But within the home, in the role of wife and mother, the position was very different. The agricultural trade union leader, Joseph Arch, was typical of many when he claimed that it was his mother's strength of character which had inspired his own efforts to lead the first National Agricultural Labourers' Union in the early 1870s:

When I look back to the days of my boyhood and live them over again in memory, I can see what a lot of truth there is in the well-known saying, 'The hand which rocks the cradle, rules the world.' . . . All her life [my mother] taught my sisters and myself by her precepts and her example; she educated us in the true sense of the word.[1]

16

He recalled, too, how her earnings as a laundress kept the family from starvation when his father, a Warwickshire farm worker, was unemployed during four difficult winter months.[2]

In other families it was the mother's role as carer and protector which most impressed her children. Kate Edwards, brought up in the Huntingdonshire fens, remembered how her mother kept the home together despite the drunken tantrums and irregular work pattern of a bullying father, and the physical attacks he made upon her:

> We were terribly afraid . . . that something 'ould happen to her, or that she'd run away and leave us, and after we'd gone to bed at night, we used to call to her and say 'Sing mother, so we know you're there.' Then she'd sit an' sing till her voice give out, an' after that, if we still wern't asleep, she'd whistle to let us know we were safe.[3]

Later, when Kate herself had married and her mother was suffering from a fatal illness, she repaid some of that debt of love by going backwards and forwards from her home as often as she could to look after the sick woman: 'It were a bad winter, and the droves were so bad you cou'n't hardly get along 'em at all . . . I really cou'n't do this terrible journey many times a day, so I used to do my own work at home first, and leave going to mother till the afternoon.'[4] She then stayed to cook her father's tea before setting off on the return journey. Often she was too exhausted to cook for her own family when she reached home, because 'I really cou'n't do no more.' Her mother died when she was just sixty-two.

Kate's experiences showed why women formed the essential core of family life. Not only did they carry out the basic tasks of cleaning, cooking, washing and mending clothes, but they nursed the sick and cared for the aged. Often, too, they were responsible for the weekly budgeting, struggling to make inadequate earnings cover necessary purchases. And when debts mounted at the shops, it was frequently their ingenuity which enabled these to be settled. A Devon shopkeeper, for example, accepted hens, ducks, turkeys, bushels of oats and even potatoes from smallholder customers in order to cover the sums due. But in the case of one family, who owed over £7 in 1901, the wife altered suits and made clothing for members of the shopkeeper's family in order to reduce the debt.[5] Still more common

PLATE 3 *Workhouse inmates, 1911: poverty and old-age unfortunately often went hand-in-hand for many countrywomen.*
(Institute of Agricultural History and Museum of English Rural Life, University of Reading).

was the practice of allowing debts to accumulate until harvest time, when the extra cash earned by the family in the fields could be used to pay off these sums and also to purchase such essentials as new boots or clothing. Nevertheless, such devices meant that what Joseph Arch called 'a little millstone of debt' was almost always hanging around the necks of labouring families.[6]

The battle to make ends meet had its darker side, too. Court records show a trickle of women convicted of stealing small items of food or fuel in order to supplement legitimate supplies. Thus in October 1854, Elizabeth Meads, a 35-year-old labourer's wife, was convicted by Oxford Quarter Sessions of stealing a peck of beans from a farmer at Rotherfield Greys, Oxfordshire. She was sentenced to fourteen days' imprisonment with hard labour in the House of Correction. Rosa Gater, aged twenty-eight, was punished still more severely when, in June 1868, she was sentenced by the same Quarter Sessions to three calendar months' imprisonment with hard labour for receiving five stolen tame rabbits. A year earlier two women were sentenced at Banbury to seven days' imprisonment for stealing turnip greens for use as vegetables.[7]

Of course, where a mother was slovenly or neglectful, the life of her family was made miserable. Equally, when she was over-severe, her children often became timid and nervous, and, especially in the earlier Victorian years, there were women who insisted on sending their children to work as soon as they could earn a few pence to contribute to family income. 'I heard one morning, before it was light, crying in the street', declared a surgeon from Whittlesey in Cambridgeshire, 'and looking out of the window I saw a child, whom I knew to be not six years old, running away, and the mother running after it, and heard her threatening it, saying that she would beat it if it did not go to work.'[8]

The majority of women, however, did not behave in this way. They tried to do their best for their offspring, despite all the odds, and they prided themselves on their domestic skills. Kate Edwards recalled the great care which most took of their possessions,

> even if it were only a few odd sticks of furniture and one bed. . . . [F]amilies with a lot o' child'en di'n't have enough chairs to go round, and nobody only the father and mother ever sat down to eat a meal. The child'en just stood round the table. The floors, always damp, 'ould be covered with rugs pegged from old coats and trousers etc. or with clean sacks, and perhaps a strip o' coco-matting when times begun to get a bit better. . . . The women washed their brick floors every day, and the hearths would get special attention . . . Every 'house-place' window had a plant or two in it . . .
>
> Women expected to work hard . . . They were forever making and mending and washing and ironing, and took a pride in doing it. They knowed very well that what they cou'n't or di'n't conjure up out o' bits and pieces, their families cou'n't have. . . . Children's clothes were made out o' their parents' old worn out ones.[9]

Where cottages were overcrowded or in a poor state of repair the housewife's task was particularly difficult. However, as appendix 2 shows, contrary to the claims of many contemporaries, the majority of households were not large. Even when families were substantial, the oldest children would frequently have left home before the youngest were born. In other cases, youngsters lodged with grandparents or uncles and aunts whose own children had moved away. Nonetheless, for that significant minority of homes which had five inhabitants or more there must have been serious discomfort, given the small size of most cottages.[10]

One of the fiercest critics of the inadequacies of rural housing was the Rev. James Fraser, writing in the late 1860s. He claimed that the majority of cottages in country parishes lacked

> almost every requisite that should constitute a home for a Christian family in a civilized community. They are deficient in bedroom accommodation . . . ; they are deficient in drainage and sanitary arrangements; they are imperfectly supplied with water; such conveniences as they have are often so situated as to become nuisances . . . Physically, a ruinous, ill-drained cottage, 'cribbed, cabin'd, confined,' and overcrowded, generates any amount of disease . . . The moral consequences are fearful to contemplate . . . Modesty must be an unknown virtue, decency an unimaginable thing, where in one small chamber . . . two and sometimes three generations – are herded promiscuously.[11]

Yet because labourers' wages were so low, rents had to be kept low also, and property owners had no financial incentive to improve their properties.

Even in Northumberland, where workers' earnings were higher, many cottages consisted of one room only. This applied, for example, at Lanton, where in 1871 over a third of the households had five members or more. (See appendix 2.) Yet, despite the lack of amenities, most Northumbrian wives, like their southern counterparts, took a pride in the cleanliness of their houses. Furniture was well polished, false ceilings of calico were rigged up to cover the bare rafters, and temporary partitions or box beds were used to give a little privacy for the sleeping arrangements.[12]

When it came to feeding their families, labourers' wives often displayed considerable ingenuity in making ends meet. One Norfolk girl recalled that in her home they took advantage of 'all the food that was for free; watercress from running streams, rabbits, pigeons, wild raspberries, wild plums and blackberries, crab apples, hazel nuts, chestnuts, walnuts. No squirrels hoarded these more carefully than we did.'[13] Elsewhere, as in Kate Edwards's fenland community, cheap and filling dishes like dumplings were a major staple in the diet.[14]

More difficult to overcome was the shortage of fresh milk which occurred in many villages, especially at the end of the nineteenth century, as farmers sold their output in bulk to the major centres of population or to neighbouring towns, and so had little surplus to

PLATE 4 *Elderly Somerset villager. She spent her entire life in this cottage.*
(*Country Life*)

retail locally. 'It pays the farmer better . . . and the children do not get it at all', declared one woman angrily.[15] However, in view of the heavy contamination of much of it with the tubercle bacillus, this omission may not have been all loss to the children.

The bitter struggle many mothers experienced in raising their families, especially in the middle years of the nineteenth century, was made very clear by a labourer's wife from low-wage Dorset. She and her husband had brought up ten children on a basic weekly wage of 8s., plus a rent-free cottage and garden:

We mayn't keep a pig, but instead of this master gives us 6d a week for the wash. . . . [W]e pay 1£ a sack for flour. We have it ground for 2s. Sometimes they let the miller take some of it for grinding. . . . We bake our own bread. . . . [I]f anything happens [that is, if an animal died from accident or disease] master's glad to sell us some of the meat. In the last three years we have got perhaps seven or eight bits in this way. We have bought a bit at Christmas, when the children are here. We buy a little pig meat;

we use it with the potatoes; we don't have a dish of pig by itself. At harvest we eat some cheese, but not at any other time. We don't often get potatoes. When we'd 10 at home we couldn't live on the bread we could buy. We'd get a little rice if the potatoes wasn't good. We could make a meal a day off rice. We'd buy a few peas; my husband could never eat barley.

My children never used to drink much tea. I'd mix them a little broth (bread, hot water, pepper, and salt).[16]

She, however, had an oven in which to do her cooking. Many wives lacked even that basic amenity. Instead, if they wished to bake bread, cakes and pies or to roast meat they had to take the uncooked food to the baker and pay a half-penny or penny for the use of his facilities. A few places, like Barnton and Davenham in Cheshire, had communal bakehouses, to which women could take the bread, each carefully pricking her initials on the top of her particular batch so that she could identify it when it was cooked.[17] Davenham also had three communal mangles for use on wash-day.

Some employers, as with the Dorset family quoted above, refused to allow their men to keep a pig or poultry because they feared fodder would be stolen from the farm to feed the livestock. But where hens, ducks or a pig were permitted, they provided a valuable supplement to household resources. In parts of the Vale of Aylesbury, cottagers even reared and fattened ducklings for the London market. Gardens were divided by planks into makeshift pens, and shedding was erected to protect the birds from inclement weather. The women fed and raised the birds whilst their husbands were at work on local farms. The only assistance they received was from fellow villagers who helped with the plucking, for 1½d. a duck. With the cash secured from this profitable sideline, thrifty families were able to purchase their own cottages, while a few moved into the ranks of smallholders or farmers.[18] In the Heathfield area of Sussex, it was the rearing of spring chickens for sale in the capital which provided a remunerative business for labourers and small farmers. In 1864 a single carrier alone took over 101,000 fowls from the three parishes of Heathfield, Warbleton and Waldron.[19]

But most livestock enterprises were far more modest than these. At Lanton, Northumberland, Mrs Ewart, wife of a local hind, regarded it as 'a grand thing' that she was able to keep a cow, even though farm wages in that county, paid in cash and kind, were among the highest in the country.[20] Elsewhere the family pig was the pride and joy of the household. In north Oxfordshire, Flora Thompson wrote of mothers spending

> hours boiling up the 'little taturs' to mash and mix with the pot-liquor, in which food had been cooked, to feed to the pig for its evening meal and help out the expensive barley meal. . . . Some-times, when the weekly income would not run to a sufficient quantity of fattening food, an arrangement would be made with the baker or miller that he should give credit now, and when the pig was killed receive a portion of the meat in payment. . . . [I]t was no uncommon thing to hear a woman say, 'Us be going to kill half a pig, please God, come Friday.'[21]

When the pig had been slaughtered, the wife would set about curing the hams and bacon flitches by immersing them in brine or applying salt direct to the carcase. Later these would be dried and hung on big hooks near the kitchen fireplace until ready for use. Pies and puddings were also made and chitterlings prepared. Fat was rendered into lard, to be eaten on bread instead of butter. 'You hadn't to waste a thing on a pig but the squeak!', declared a Yorkshire woman. A girl from Shotesham, Norfolk, similarly recalled the plentiful supplies of pig's fry, sausages and pork cheese (or brawn) her family enjoyed at pig-killing time. A substantial part of the carcase was also sold to the local butcher.[22]

Meanwhile, within country districts as a whole there was a general improvement in labouring families' living standards during the final quarter of the nineteenth century. Partly this was due to the advance in cash earnings secured by the trade union agitation of the early 1870s and, when that declined in the middle of the decade, to the subsequent sharp fall in consumer good prices. Food was perhaps 25 per cent cheaper in the mid-1890s than it had been twenty years before, as a result of growing imports of cheap grain, frozen meat and dairy produce, while mass production methods reduced the cost of clothing and footwear. Contemporaries commented on the change. 'On the clothes line, instead of rags, good linen is to be seen', said one; 'in the cottage there is more furniture, and lights are burning late into the night. . . . Butchers' carts go round the villages once at least every week on a Saturday ... At the village shops there is an increasing demand for tinned meats of all kinds.'[23]

At Otterbourne, Hampshire, the novelist Charlotte M. Yonge wrote in the 1890s of the improvement which had been secured in family comfort by the introduction of oil lamps. In her youth, half a century before, cottagers had gone to bed as soon as they had eaten their evening meal, in order to save on candles and firing. Now that was no longer the case. In Dorset, Thomas Hardy made much the same point.[24]

However, when prices began to move up again in the early years of the twentieth century this modest improvement was eroded. On the eve of the First World War the researches of Seebohm Rowntree and May Kendall revealed that sharp regional differences in earnings and in lifestyle still persisted in country districts. In areas remote from mining or industrial development, where there was little employment outside agriculture, conditions remained unsatisfactory for many labouring families, particularly those with young children. This was made clear in interviews which Miss Kendall carried out with labourers' wives. One such was Mrs Mayne of Oxfordshire, whose husband earned 14s. a week, plus a rent-free cottage and garden. They had three children living at home and one – the eldest girl – who had just gone to service. Five of their offspring had died in childhood. Mrs Mayne, a small, frail woman of forty, was described as an 'excellent manager':

> She will sometimes go a mile and a half and back, with her neighbour, to gather wood to eke out the coal. She also gathers crab-apples, which she boils, together with vegetable marrows from the garden, to make jam for the children. ... Mrs. Mayne has a sister in another part of the country, a trifle better off than herself, who sends her all the old clothing she can, and she 'makes all the clothes herself' ... But when all her skill has been brought into play, there are still shoes to consider, and clothes for the man, socks and stockings, and any incidental expense incurred.[25]

Vegetables from the garden were an essential part of the diet, to supplement the small quantity of chilled meat purchased each week for the daily dinner. But despite Mrs Mayne's valiant efforts, Rowntree and Kendall calculated that there was a deficiency of 21 per cent of protein in the family's diet, and it is clear from the specimen menus provided that there was a heavy reliance on tea and bread and butter or jam at most meals.

Even better-off families like the Walpoles from North Yorkshire had difficulty in keeping within their means, despite the fact that Mr Walpole was paid 17s. a week as a stockman, as well as having a daily three pints of 'old milk' as a perquisite. Part of their problem was that their four children were all under the age of eight and were thus unable to contribute to the family income. Their garden was also too small to supply all the vegetables they needed, and all of the children were sickly, so that a small sum had to be set aside each week to buy medicine for them. The family kept two pigs, which they sold in order to buy the clothes they needed. Mrs Walpole and her children rarely tasted meat, although the daily milk allowance was used to make cocoa for the youngsters' breakfast.[26]

As these cases show, there is little doubt that for many cottage wives budgeting remained a nagging worry right up to the First World War. Their dilemma was summarized by Mrs West of Oxfordshire who, when asked how she managed to feed her family, replied: 'I couldn't tell you how we do live; it's a mystery . . . *the thing is to get it past.*' Her husband's basic wage was 12s. a week, and even with extra payments for haysel and harvest the family was always in debt.[27]

In view of the heavy toil most cottage wives had to perform, as well as the financial problems they faced, and the large number of children they bore (at a time when contraceptive knowledge in country villages was very limited), it is not surprising that they came to value the quality of endurance above all others. 'If life were hard for the men, it were harder still for the women', remembered Kate Edwards. In consequence, during periods of illness or distress neighbours would rally round to help one another. In this way those who had few material resources to offer could support and sustain one another by giving practical help and sympathy when times were difficult. For some unfortunate wives that could mean enduring beatings and abuse from drunken or brutal husbands.

It was against this background, therefore, that the vast majority of countrywomen and girls – the wives and daughters of agricultural labourers, small farmers and village tradesmen – spent their lives. Cottagers' daughters were prepared for their domestic role from a very early age, with youngsters of seven or eight expected to care for younger brothers and sisters whilst their mother went out to work or was engaged in other household chores. Mrs Wrigley, born at Cefn Mawr, Wales, in 1858, the daughter of a shoemaker, was only about seven when she began to look after her brothers and sisters because her mother went out sewing for 1s. a day. Even when the mother was at home, she was expected to gather fuel, collect water and walk to a farmhouse two miles away to obtain buttermilk. On Saturdays she cleaned neighbours' floors and backyards for a penny a time and a piece of bread and butter. She also carried dinners and suppers to workers at a nearby iron forge for twopence a week.[28] At the age of nine she started work in earnest, as a nursemaid at the vicarage.

Mrs Wrigley was unusually young when she became a servant. Most girls would be thirteen or fourteen before they got their first position, probably in the household of a local farmer, shopkeeper or tradesman, who paid them a shilling or two a week. Later they would hope to move on to a better-paid post in a more prosperous household in town or country. Consequently, except in parishes where there was an important cottage industry or, as in parts of Northumberland, where there was widespread employment for girls on the land (in an area where young men could gain well-paid jobs in the expanding coal mines), the number of unmarried girls in most villages was relatively small. This is confirmed in the specimen parishes analysed in appendix 3.

Among those girls who remained at home, the daughters of well-to-do gentry, professional and farming families were, not surprisingly, most prominent. But in many communities, publicans' daughters and the offspring of the more substantial shopkeepers and skilled craftsmen also stayed at home, helping around the house or else engaging in one of the 'superior' independent trades, such as those of dressmaker or milliner. Of the communities examined in appendix 3, one of Ivinghoe's young dressmakers was the daughter of a land surveyor and postmaster, and the other of a shoemaker, while the Baptist minister's daughter was a milliner. At Ivinghoe Aston, the two dressmakers were the daughters of a dairyman and grocer.

However, in most villages, girls looking for work had to move away from home, and for a majority that break with their native community proved permanent. They might return for occasional holidays or between jobs, but they never again lived there for any length of time. Nevertheless, a substantial minority – amounting to perhaps a quarter or more of married women in some villages – did retain links with the place of their birth. Before marriage they perhaps worked as maids in houses within walking distance of their home, and in this way they kept up family contacts. They then often ended by marrying a boy from the parish of their birth. When this happened they enjoyed the support of kin and childhood friends after marriage.

In other cases, girls married men from the village where they were working, who might themselves be natives of that parish; or else important long-term marital links grew up between particular villages. (See appendix 4.) These were perhaps based on long-standing custom, or upon ease of communication. Thus at Wilburton and Haddenham in Cambridgeshire, census returns reveal that of eighty-seven wives living in the former village on census night in 1881, twenty-nine had been born in the parish; but thirteen of the rest came from Haddenham. There was no comparable relationship with any other parish in the Wilburton census, and an examination of the returns for 1851 reveals a similar pattern.[29] Similar connections were identified by P. J. Perry in his survey of the Dorset villages of Chetnole and Yetminster. These two parishes accounted for about a quarter of the marriages of both communities between 1837 and 1886, while other neighbouring villages showed no such close linkage.[30]

It is clear that inter-village prejudice or rivalry had a part to play in this situation. Even at the end of the nineteenth century, when greater mobility of labour and better transport had broken down some traditional community barriers, a girl from Needham Market in East Anglia, who was walking out with a man from a nearby parish, was told firmly by her father: 'You must not do it! I can't have a daughter o' mine a-courting one o' those owd Creeting *jackdaws*.' Creeting lay less than half a mile away, on the other side of the river. Likewise in the Ceiriog valley in North Wales, the men regarded a girl's interest in an outsider as a personal affront which they must avenge by verbal (and sometimes physical) attacks upon her or upon the young man concerned.[31]

Nevertheless, by the end of the nineteenth century, the population decline which was occurring in many rural areas meant that most women and girls who moved away to work in the towns married there. In the early 1890s there was widespread comment that the large-scale migration of village girls to posts as maids in the urban areas was encouraging the men to move also. They were acting as 'magnets to the lads they [left] behind them'.[32]

Inevitably, given the limited knowledge of contraceptive techniques at the time, a few of these migrants 'got into trouble', and returned home to have their baby. This was probably then left to be brought up by grandparents whilst the mother went away to work once more. But in other cases, girls who remained in the villages to work on farms, in cottage industries or around the home also bore illegitimate children. At Chatteris in Cambridgeshire, where many females worked in agricultural gangs, the vicar complained that 'Fornication and bastardy are so common that I seriously question whether any girls or boys are pure or chaste in mind or body beyond the age of 17 or 18 years . . . I seldom marry any of them without being obliged to see the bride to be of larger dimensions than she ought to be.'[33] Although this is exaggerated, it is significant that the overall level of illegitimate births was higher in country districts than in either towns or mining communities. However, as appendix 5 shows, within this broad pattern there were sharp regional differences.

Part of the blame for high rural illegitimacy was placed on overcrowded cottages, which were considered to encourage promiscuity and even incest among the inmates.[34] One Dorset clergyman referred to the 'unbecoming and pernicious nearness, not to say openness of sex to sex in their bed rest'.[35] But the problem proved most severe in counties like Shropshire and Cumberland, where small farms were common and there was much living in by servants, both male and female. Combined with the isolated location of many holdings and the lack of varied leisure pursuits, what one commentator delicately labelled 'the temptations to immorality' were high. 'Unchastity . . . is not regarded in a very serious light by the class from which farm servants are taken', he observed of rural Cumbria:

No disgrace, scarcely any discredit, attaches to a girl who has had one illegitimate child, . . . the event being merely spoken of as a misfortune. . . . I heard of young female servants having had as many as three, four, and even five illegitimate children by different men, but the notorious fact did not in any way affect their prospects of future employment. The children are either put out to nurse or taken care of by the mothers' relatives.[36]

Significantly, bastardy levels in the Longtown district of Cumberland in the mid-1880s were nearly four times the national average.[37]

Even at the end of the nineteenth century, marked differences remained, with the illegitimacy rate in Herefordshire and Shropshire about 75 per cent above that for England and Wales as a whole, and for Cumberland and Westmorland around 50 per cent above the average. Possibly the practice of delayed female marriage, which was common in many of these counties (see column 3 of appendix 5) and was itself perhaps caused by the men waiting to succeed to a holding or saving up to rent a farm, aggravated the problem. Another important factor was the tolerant attitude towards bastardy shown by society at large in these districts. This attitude was also found in Norfolk, another high-rate county. 'I find cleanliness on the increase in the parish, but no diminution of illegitimacy', ruefully commented the vicar of East Dereham in his diary in 1857. 'The girls see nothing sinful in it, and their mothers, apparently, connive.'[38]

In parts of rural Wales, where illegitimacy rates were also high, local courting customs were blamed – notably the practice of 'bundling', whereby couples made love clandestinely at night, often in the girl's bed, while the rest of the household slept. The Archdeacon of St David's claimed that in his area during the late 1860s, not only was bastardy widespread, but 'unchastity in the youth of both sexes the rule rather than the exception'. The Baptist minister of nearby Narberth attributed the difficulty to the practice of local farmers' accommodating their male servants in outhouses, barns, and haylofts rather than in proper bedrooms. 'Hence . . . they prowl about in the night, about neighbours' houses, seeking and obtaining intercourse with the girls through the night.' Employers were said to be aware of what was taking place but to be reluctant to curb it in case this discouraged servants from working for them. Significantly, similar complaints were still being voiced in the 1890s.[39]

Such laxity was very different from the attitude which was displayed in estate villages like Helmingham, Suffolk or Ketteringham,

Norfolk, at the time. Here the respective squires threatened families with eviction if a daughter became pregnant out of wedlock or was guilty of other misconduct.[40] Court records, too, reveal a sad trickle of cases where girls attempted to conceal the birth of an illegitimate child, or even to murder the baby.[41]

Economic pressures ensured that the daughters of most agricultural labourers had to take up paid employment as soon as they left school. But their counterparts in small farming families or in those of more prosperous artisans often remained at home. Farmers' daughters would assist around the dairy and farmyard as well as carrying out household chores, while village tradesmen frequently required their daughters to combine domestic duties with writing business letters and keeping the accounts. This was true of Ann Staight, a blacksmith's daughter from Dumbleton, Gloucestershire. She and her elder sister, Sarah, assisted their mother in the house, with Sarah performing the skilled tasks as well as looking after the poultry, and Ann acting as maid-of-all-work, cleaning, scrubbing and washing. When members of the family were ill, both girls shared the nursing duties, sometimes going away from home to look after sick relatives living at a distance. They also wrote letters for illiterate neighbours. Ann was expected to help her father by drawing up bills and letters in connection with his blacksmith's business. She was especially busy around quarter day: 'I began Mr. Smithin's [Cullabine Farm] and Rector's bills, finished them before dusk', reads one entry in her diary.[42]

Other tradesmen's daughters assisted in a similar fashion. Mary Ann Hearn, who was born at Farningham, Kent, in 1834, helped her father with both his shoemaking and his postmastering, especially after the death of her mother when the little girl was twelve. She sorted the letters in the post office and learnt to bind the shoes. In return, she was allowed to resume her education on a part-time basis, and eventually became a teacher. She also wrote a number of improving books for young people.[43]

Even more active was Mary Smith, the daughter of a boot- and shoemaker and small grocer from Cropredy, Oxfordshire. She, too, lost her mother at an early age, and since Mrs Smith was a far better business organizer than her husband, the family soon ran into financial difficulties. Eventually Mr Smith was appointed a poor law relieving officer, and he then handed over the running of his other enterprises to one of his sons and to Mary. Although still in her early teens, she managed the grocery and provision shop, which her mother had originally started, and also kept the books for both businesses. She took up dressmaking and sold poultry and eggs as well, while her brother combined shoemaking with beekeeping and pig-rearing. As a result of these efforts, the family finances were restored. But then her brother married. His wife took over the shop and Mary had to return to the parental home, without either cash or prospects. As she later wrote bitterly: 'I had worked hard, but had had no wages . . . [and] as is often the case with women, even the most capable and energetic, the one small event of my brother's marrying had stranded me without occupation.' Shortly afterwards she moved to Westmorland with the local Baptist minister, his wife and baby, as a companion to the wife, and whilst there was invited to conduct a school in the small town where they were living. With some trepidation she accepted, and was soon embarked upon what proved to be a lifelong teaching career.[44]

Both Mary Ann Hearn and Mary Smith left their respective family businesses whilst they were still young, after having made an important contribution to their success. Both then embarked on careers as teachers. But many other tradesmen's daughters followed the example of Ann and Sarah Staight and continued to help at home until they married or, as in Ann's case, they died.

In status terms all of these girls clearly regarded themselves as superior to the labourers' daughters in their respective villages. They looked for social contacts among the families of fellow tradesmen and small farmers, or among the upper servants of gentry households. The Staight girls were also on visiting terms with the clergyman's wife and attended sewing parties at the rectory.[45] Mary Ann Hearn and Mary Smith both came from nonconformist families, but they, too, were on friendly terms with the ministers of their churches and played an active role in the religious life of their communities.

Class distinctions of this kind applied even more strongly when it came to marriage. It was rare for members of farming or substantial tradesmen's families to marry into labouring households. Jean Robin, in her survey of Victorian Elmdon, discovered that marriages between the smaller farmers and shopkeeping families were fairly common, while those who had prosperous businesses as shopkeepers, publicans or village craftsmen married spouses of equivalent status. Of twenty-two marriages involving farmers or farmers' sons and daughters in Elmdon, nine were to members of other farming families in the locality. In two cases, schoolmistresses married the sons of small farmers, while one farmer married an assistant in his uncle's grocery store and two others married bakers' daughters.[46]

The marriage registers of parishes like Cottisford, Bloxham, Lower Heyford and Sydenham in Oxfordshire confirm this picture. At Sydenham, all three farmers' daughters who married between 1850 and 1880 married grocers and provision dealers from outside the village. At Bloxham, where there were three weddings among farmers' daughters during the 1850s, the grooms were respectively a farmer, a bailiff (who was himself a farmer's son) and a maltster. At Lower Heyford, where only one farmer's daughter married between 1850 and 1869, her groom was a grocer. Among tradesmen's families, a butcher's daughter from Sydenham married a builder; a wheel-wright's daughter, who was also the village schoolmistress, married a London saddler; a mason's daughter married a carpenter; and a shopkeeper's daughter married a miller.[47] Most of the other marriages were of a similar kind, although a few tradesmen's daughters did marry 'beneath them'. Thus at Cottisford between 1851 and 1890 a blacksmith's daughter married a labourer and a greengrocer's daughter also married into a labouring family. But these were more than matched by four labourers' daughters who married respectively a blacksmith, a shoemaker, a mason and a tailor, and who thus modestly moved up in the world.

The general tendency for 'like to marry like' was based not merely on status and a desire among aspiring members of the lower middle classes to maintain a social distance between themselves and labouring families, but also on grounds of property. As Jean Robin notes of Elmdon, when a farmer's son married a shopkeeper's daughter this might be partly because there was no room for him on the family farm, and his wife's shopkeeping expertise could provide him with an alternative way of earning a living. Or else the running of a small farm and a shop could go hand-in-hand, as was the case with one Elmdon family.[48]

Property considerations were always important among farming families, and this was especially true in parts of rural Wales, where marriage and the securing of a holding were normally closely linked.

A farmer's son would not usually contemplate matrimony until he could get his own property, and he would then choose a bride who could help him finance the venture, with the aid of her family. For this reason, marriages between cottagers' daughters and farmers' sons were extremely rare. And if a farmer's daughter married a labourer, the most that she could expect was that her family would assist them to set up in a tiny subsidiary holding, to which a farm worker could aspire anyway.[49]

Family resources were also supplemented in the principality by the common custom of organizing 'biddings' when a couple became betrothed. These took the form of gifts in cash and kind made by friends and neighbours, whose own families had benefited in a similar fashion in the past, or hoped to do so in the future. Each contribution was carefully recorded, and when the giver or one of his or her children married, the 'debt' would be redeemed by an equivalent donation. Printed invitations were issued to the 'biddings', and these displayed a shrewd mixture of business and pleasure. One typical example involved Thomas Lewis and Anne Davies of Llandilo, who issued their invitation on 5 November 1869 for a bidding to be held on their wedding day, 3 December. It was to be conducted at their new house in the parish of Llandlo-fawr,

> when and where the favour of your good and agreeable company is humbly solicited, and whatever donation you may be pleased to bestow on us then, will be thankfully received, warmly acknowledged, and cheerfully repaid whenever called for on a similar occasion . . . The Young Man with his Father and Mother, John and Sarah Lewis, Pante, and his Brothers, William, David, and John Lewis, and his Sister, Anne Lewis, desire that all Bidding Debts due to them be returned to the Young Man on the above day, and will be thankful with his Uncles and Aunts, for all additional favours granted.
>
> Also the Young Woman with her Father and Mother, John and Jane Davies, White Square, and her Brothers, Thomas and Daniel Davies, desire that all Bidding Debts due to them be returned to the Young Woman, on the above day, and will be thankful with her Brothers and Sisters, for all additional favours conferred.[50]

Such arrangements not only reflected the strong kinship ties which were a feature of rural life in Victorian Wales, but provided a way of overcoming the chronic shortage of capital which prevailed in the Welsh countryside at that time. Even the wedding feast itself could be turned into a fundraising event. At a wedding in south-west Wales in the 1840s guests were given details of the feast: 'They shall have good beef and cabbage, mutton and turnips, pork and potatoes, roast goose or gant, perhaps both if they are in season, *a quart of drink for 4d., a cake for a penny*, clean chairs to sit down upon.'[51]

Sometimes as many as five or six hundred people attended a 'bidding', contributing between 6d. and 2s. 6d. apiece. At the wedding of Thomas Thomas of Llwynhelyg in 1866, there were 202 contributions, yielding a sum of £22 11s. 6d. – sufficient to stock a small farm. Thomas carefully recorded the amount received from each donor and by October 1880 he had repaid £8 6s. of the debt. In at least three cases the cash was given to members of the donor's family rather than the giver him-or herself.[52]

Apart from weddings, however, there were many other opportunities for villagers to enjoy social contacts and entertainment. Most women welcomed a gossip with a friend over the garden fence or in the street, and there were weekly shopping trips to be made by many to the nearest market town. The more energetic clergymen's wives organized sewing parties or mothers' meetings for those who cared to attend, and church and chapel offered both spiritual consolation and social contact for women as well as men. Tea meetings were regularly held in connection with both, though in parts of rural Wales (and doubtless elsewhere) the duties associated with them were carefully graduated according to class. The cottagers' wives and daughters tended the fire, boiled the water and washed the dirty dishes, whilst the farmers' wives and daughters waited at table and carried out the less laborious chores.[53] For the younger women, attendance at a religious service on the Sabbath was also often combined with a little surreptitious courting.[54]

Even the agricultural trade union movement of the 1870s, although primarily concerned to raise the wages and improve the working conditions of its mainly male members, had a flourishing social side in which women could join. Typical was the tea meeting organized by the Horndean branch in Hampshire during September 1873. It

PLATE 5 *Washing up outside a Devon cottage doorway. Water was a scarce commodity in many rural areas and had to be husbanded carefully.*

(*Country Life*)

was attended by about 150 men, women and children, and was preceded by dancing and other entertainments, carried out to the music of a brass band from a neighbouring village.[55] Tea meetings particularly appealed to the temperance-minded leaders of the union movement.

Many villages held dances in the schoolroom or a large barn during the winter months. These were particularly popular among the farm servants of Cumberland and Westmorland. 'A day labourer with a large family may declare that he is too poor to pay the weekly pence for his children's schooling', commented one critic sourly, 'but he seldom fails to find money enough to pay for the lessons of the itinerant dancing master.' As for the womenfolk, a passion for dress was universal among them:

> no inconsiderable part of the wages of a . . . girl is expended on her person. At church it would be difficult to distinguish a farm servant from the daughter of a . . . substantial tenant farmer, and a girl whose ordinary costume is a coarse petticoat, pinned close round her body, and wooden clogs, will appear at a dance in a white muslin dress, white kid gloves, and with a wreath of artificial flowers on her head.[56]

Elsewhere, as at Lower Heyford, Oxfordshire, a dancing booth formed a regular part of the celebrations. 'Last Sunday was Lower Heyford Feast', wrote the young George Dew in his diary, '& on Monday night as usual there was a dancing booth in "The Square". There it is again this evening & many of the labourers & their wives & sons & daughters are dancing as merrily as possible.'[57]

In the north of England, where farm servants were still widely recruited through hiring fairs, maids seeking a fresh place could combine business with pleasure. Once they had agreed terms with a new employer they were free to spend the rest of the day at side-shows and merry-go-rounds or in mild flirtations with some of their young male colleagues. At Alston in Northumbria the Martinmas hiring in 1870 was such an occasion, with what the local newspaper called 'an abundant supply of music'. Dances were held in the evening or, for those of a soberer disposition, a coffee supper and service of song was arranged in the Primitive Methodist Chapel.[58] 'Many a match was made at a hiring fair' was a common saying, although others, less charitably, blamed the fairs for encouraging immorality.[59] Partly on these moral grounds, but also because registry offices and newspaper advertisements offered alternative ways of recruiting farm staff, the hiring fairs fell into disfavour at the end of the nineteenth century.

In a few villages, friendly societies were organized for the women, to match those more commonly available to men. Although their ostensible purpose was to provide benefits during sickness or at death, their annual feast day was an occasion for celebration. Drayton, near Langport, Somerset, was the home of one such society, which held its annual feast in the middle of June:

> What a washing of white finery went on the week before. What a goffering of the many frills under and on top. For it used to be the custom to wear a white frock adorned with a rose-pink sash worn cross-wise. Knotted at the waist, and . . . the smart bonnets that made their appearance.[60]

Tea was arranged in a large marquee and, as with the men's feast day in this village, there was also a fun fair. Club members began the festivities with a procession to church, headed by a band and with the marchers bearing appropriate banners. There they attended a service before starting their celebrations in earnest.

Of course, when all other entertainment failed, there were always casual flirtations with members of the opposite sex to add spice to the lives of younger villagers. Elizabeth Otter, born at Southwell, Dorset, in 1866, remembered the meetings of girls and youths in her parish on moonlit evenings:

> The old folks would get angry at us sometimes, as we made so much noise. One would say to the other: 'Do you know whose bwoys and maids 'tis then?' . . . 'Get along whome where you belong, time for you to go to bed. Ought to have a good hiding, all of you.' . . . Then we had to run some other place or go home.[61]

It was this light-hearted spirit which the Dorset clergyman and dialect poet, William Barnes, captured so engagingly in his poem, 'Woodcom' Feast':

> Come, Fanny, come! put on thy white,
> 'Tis Woodcom' feäst, good now! to-night.
> Come think noo mwore, you silly maïd,

O' chicken drown'd or ducks a-straÿ'd;
Nor mwope to vind thy new frock's täil
A-tore by hitchen in a naïl; . . .
Come, let's goo out, an' fling our heels
About in jigs an' vow'r-han' reels;
While all the stiff-lagg'd wolder vo'k,
A-zitten roun', do talk an' joke
An' smile to zee their own wold rigs,
A'show'd by our wild geämes an' jigs. . . .
Come-out, you leäzy jeäde, come out!
An' thou wult be, to woone at leäst,
The prettiest maïd at Woodcom feäst.[62]

3

Wives and Daughters of
the Country House

[Lady Lufton] liked cheerful, quiet, well-to-do people, who loved their
Church, their country, and their Queen, and who were not too anxious
to make a noise in the world. She desired that all the farmers round
her should be able to pay their rents without trouble, that all the old
women should have warm flannel petticoats, that the working men
should be saved from rheumatism by healthy food and dry houses,
that they should all be obedient to their pastors and masters — temporal
as well as spiritual. . . . She desired also that the copses should be full
of pheasants, the stubble-field of partridges, and the gorse covers of
foxes.

Anthony Trollope, *Framley Parsonage* (Oxford University Press World's Classics,
London, 1957 edn). First published in book form in 1861.

Despite the influence of strong-minded dowagers like Lady Lufton in
Anthony Trollope's novel, *Framley Parsonage*, or such real-life
counterparts as Frances Anne, widow of the third Marquess of
Londonderry, and Mary Elizabeth Lucy of Charlecote Park, Warwickshire, nineteenth-century landed society remained essentially male
dominated. Nowhere was this more clearly demonstrated than in the
matter of ownership itself. When, in 1878, John Bateman undertook
an analysis of *The Great Landowners of Great Britain and Ireland*, he
discovered that out of 1,644 individuals with holdings of at least
3,000 acres (some of which were in England and Wales), fewer than a
hundred were women.[1] An updating of the work in 1883 revealed

little change. Only one woman – Lady Willoughby d'Eresby – was among the sixty-six major holders with landed incomes of £50,000 a year or more.[2]

Almost within the £50,000 range was the Hon. Mrs Meynell-Ingram of Hoarcross Hall, Staffordshire, with an annual income of over £45,000 and a land holding of more than 25,000 acres in Yorkshire, Staffordshire and Shropshire. When she died in 1904 her estate was valued at over half a million pounds.[3] But for the most part primogeniture and patrilineal descent ensured that women were of little importance where landownership was concerned. Only when a male heir failed did the property pass to, or through, a woman. Thus between 1840 and 1880, a mere 8 to 10 per cent of transfers of landed property were made directly to women. If seats transferred *through* women were taken into account the estimated total rose to 12 to 15 per cent.[4]

In these circumstances females rarely exercised influence over the running of estates, although, as we shall see, there were exceptions to this. Often daughters were regarded with anxiety by hard-pressed fathers and brothers as a potential drain upon family resources; for sooner or later portions would have to be provided to enable them to marry well, or, failing that, to provide them with a sufficient income to mitigate the stigma of spinsterhood. Barbara Tasburgh (later Charlton) of Burghwallis Hall, Northumberland, wryly recalled that although she was her 'mother's favourite I certainly was not my father's'. He thought 'a third daughter a superfluous addition to his family'.[5] Likewise Lady Maud Cecil, eldest child of the third Marquess of Salisbury (and a future Countess of Selborne) was 'very much offended' at the age of three by overhearing people say after the birth of her eldest brother: '"It is a good thing it *was* a boy this time."' From that time, she 'began to look at life from a feminist standpoint'.[6]

Wives who produced daughters rather than an heir often felt guilty about their failure. The formidable Mary Elizabeth Lucy's daughter-in-law was reduced to tears after the birth of a third daughter, sobbing, 'Oh! What will Spencer [her husband] say to me for having another girl?'.[7] Even villagers sometimes shared this dismissive attitude towards daughters. Rosalind, Countess of Carlisle, recalled that when her first child was born, she was staying at her old home in Cheshire. The village people wanted to celebrate the event by ringing the church bells. 'But the word came . . . that it was a girl which had been born, and [the bellringers] left the Church, saying, "It is nowt but a lass!"'.[8]

In such cases the birth of a son became a cause for special celebration. Lady Carrington, who had already borne five daughters, wrote with triumph in her diary on 24 April 1895: '*A boy born* at 11 today. Many kind telegrams from the dear family & others. C. [her husband] & I overjoyed.' Early in June the baby was christened amid general rejoicing at the parish church at High Wycombe, where the family mansion was situated: '4,300 schoolchildren afterwards came in procession past the Abbey [her home] & into the Park where we regaled them with *tea*', noted Lady Carrington happily. By contrast, the christening of her eldest daughter in 1880 had been a very modest affair, conducted in London in the presence of family and friends only.[9] Small wonder that Consuelo Vanderbilt, from a transatlantic perspective, condemned the way daughters were 'sacrificed to the more important prospects of the heir'.[10]

Yet, paradoxically, when landed families were in financial difficulty they often saw marriage to a wealthy wife as the way out. Lord Monson was not alone in repeatedly urging his son to marry a girl with a fortune so as 'to rescue the house of Monson from its predicaments, which were mainly caused by the prolonged burden of two dowagers until 1851 and one survivor until 1891'.[11] A particularly desirable candidate was recommended because she had an income of £9,000 a year – later upgraded to £15,000 on closer investigation. In the event William Monson did not marry until 1869, seven years after his father's death, and his choice then fell upon the widow of the Earl of Yarborough.

Frances Maynard, who succeeded to her grandfather's fortune and estate at Easton Lodge, Essex, when she was only three, was regarded as an especially valuable 'catch' by prospective parents-in-law and by the popular press. She seems even to have been considered as a possible spouse for Prince Leopold, Queen Victoria's youngest son, while *The Referee* newspaper, commenting on her presentation at Court in 1880 and her generally attractive appearance and personality, added: 'Fancy a disposition like that *and* thirty thousand a year! Where lurks the lucky man?'.[12] The 'lucky man' proved to be Lord Brooke, heir to the Earl of Warwick, whom she married in 1881.

PLATE 6 *Frances Maynard, the future Countess of Warwick, at the time of her wedding in April 1881. She subsequently became involved in various social reform movements and by the end of the 1890s had been converted to Socialism. Her intimate friendship with the Prince of Wales during that decade was also a subject of much comment and speculation.*

(From Frances, Countess of Warwick, *Life's Ebb and Flow* [1929])

As a consequence, Frances herself was omitted from the 1883 edition of Bateman's survey of *Great Landowners*. Her substantial estates now appeared under the name of her husband.[13]

The policy of overcoming financial problems by taking a wealthy bride was applied with particular force at the end of the nineteenth century, when a number of aristocratic families were hit by falling rentals and declining agricultural incomes. Many turned their attention to American heiresses, selling their family name and title for a much-needed injection of cash.[14] So it was that Minnie Stevens, 'the Belle of Newport', became Lady Paget, and Mary Leiter was transformed into Lady Curzon. Mary Leiter brought £140,000 into the marriage settlement, compared to her husband's £25,000, and interest on her investments yielded the substantial annual income of £6,300. This sum rose to £30,000 on her father's death. It was her money which provided Curzon with the funds he needed to become Viceroy of India.[15]

Another notable American heiress was 18-year-old Consuelo Vanderbilt, with a dowry reputed to be in the region of two and a half million dollars. She bowed to maternal pressure and married the Duke of Marlborough in 1895, although she had little affection for him. Earlier the Duke's father had also married an American – the widowed Mrs Hammersley – as his second wife. Her wealth, Consuelo tartly observed, 'had been freely spent installing central heating and electric light at Blenheim'.[16] Another critic, writing in 1905, was far less restrained in describing aristocratic motives: 'there is always . . . some decayed or degenerate or semi-drunken peer, whose fortunes are on the verge of black ruin, ready and willing to devour, monster-like, the holocaust of an American virgin, provided bags of bullion are flung, with her, into his capacious maw.'[17]

For the daughters of landed families, too, matrimony was a serious matter, only to be entered into after careful thought and negotiation. In the eyes of most parents, the securing of a husband was the main object of a girl's entry into society, and the value of the prize she won, in terms of her spouse's material possessions or social status, was the criterion of her success. On marriage, a woman was seen as leaving her parental family in order to be incorporated into that of her husband.[18] In this way, the break with her past was made very clear.

On occasion, discussions over settlement terms could become acrimonious, with both partners aiming to bring into the marriage as much money as their parents could afford, or could be persuaded to find. The fifth Earl of Onslow was not alone in finding the quite 'absurd wranglings' which took place over his engagement to Miss Violet Bampfylde highly distasteful. He considered that 'every sort of difficulty was made over settlements', because 'to get the full fun out of it everyone had to raise objections'.[19]

Equally, a daughter desiring to marry a man deemed unsuitable by her family was expected to bow to their wishes and relinquish him. Thus Barbara Tasburgh's first choice was a young army officer but, as he was only a second son of limited means, he was rejected as unsuitable. Shortly afterwards, in the late 1830s, she married the dull but worthy William Charlton of Hesleyside, who was heir to an estate of over 21,000 acres.[20]

Mary Glynne, who stoutly refused to marry the eligible Lord Gairlie on the grounds that she did not love him, was chided by her aunt over the frivolity of her conduct.

> Women are not like men, they cannot chuse, nor is it creditable or lady-like to be what is called in love; I believe that few, very few, well-regulated minds ever have been and that romantic attachment is confined to novels and novel-readers, ye silly and numerous class of young persons ill-educated at home or brought up in boarding-schools.[21]

Fortunately for Mary, in 1839 she was able to satisfy both her own wishes and those of her family by marrying the witty, slightly eccentric, George, fourth Baron Lyttelton, to whom she was devoted and who was devoted to her.

For the sons and daughters of the lesser gentry or the younger members of great families, suitable partners might be found among the ranks of the professional classes, such as bankers, barristers, solicitors, military men and the more prosperous clerics. Cecilia and Mary Parke, daughters of James Parke, a prominent member of the judiciary, married respectively Sir Matthew White Ridley, owner of an estate in Northumberland, and Charles Howard, fifth son of the sixth Earl of Carlisle. At a humbler level, one of the sons of Robert Wilkes, owner of the Lofts Hall estate at Elmdon, Essex, married a clergyman's daughter, and a second, the daughter of a Saffron Walden solicitor. The eldest daughter also married a clergyman.[22]

Essentially these girls, like their working- and lower middle-class sisters, derived their status from the male relatives upon whom they depended, and an unwise match could easily jeopardize their standing. Lady Charlotte Guest, a daughter of the ninth Earl of Lindsey, certainly attributed her exclusion from polite society to her mother's unfortunate second marriage to a drunken clergyman cousin, contracted whilst Charlotte was still a child.[23] Her own marriage in 1833 to the leading ironmaster Josiah John Guest, of Dowlais in south Wales, compounded these problems. Such an association with 'trade' was not considered respectable, and it was some time before she gained sufficiently elevated patrons to enable her to return to the upper ranks of 'society' which she considered her birthright.[24] In her quest for social acceptance she refused to allow her frequent pregnancies to get in the way of her ambitions – she was to have ten children in thirteen years. Her first major concert was, in fact, arranged on 13 June 1834, about three weeks before the birth of her first baby. And the following season she underwent a formidable round of calls, afternoon parties and the like, despite feeling ill before the birth of her eldest son in August.[25]

It was partly to prevent the formation of undesirable friendships and alliances that the daughters of most landed families were isolated from contact with social inferiors. For many, the only 'outsiders' they encountered were servants, tenants, villagers and various members of the 'deserving' poor whom they visited with soup, blankets, medicines and religious tracts, and who were conditioned to accept meekly the social order as it then existed.

But if women's *economic* contribution to country house life was often calculated in terms of what they were likely to bring in to the family by way of a dowry, or what they might take out through portions and jointures, in social matters their influence was far broader. It was their prime responsibility to ensure that the household ran smoothly. A woman's 'first duties are to her own family, her own servants', pronounced the Rev. Charles Kingsley, in typical vein, in a volume of *Lectures to Ladies on Practical Subjects*, published in 1855. They must dispense charity to the poor, oversee the children's education, and entertain guests. In their capacity as 'Lady Bountifuls' they could reinforce the landed classes' traditional authority over the rural poor by demanding deference in return for their largesse. And through the careful exercise of charity they could contribute to the

Old Woman (to young Lady Bountiful). "Yes, Miss, Nellie do grow. She skips out of 'er shoes in no time. 'Er feet are tremendous. I should think a pair of yours would just fit 'er, Miss!"

PLATE 7 *The 'Lady Bountiful' role was assumed by many wives and daughters of the country house.*

(*Punch*, 1903)

stability of village society. Thus, early in 1877, at a time of labour unrest in Norfolk, Lady Suffield and her eldest daughter, Cecilia, visited local cottagers to dispense charity but also to impress upon the wives that they 'ought not to allow their husbands to strike'. According to Cecilia, the women promptly answered 'that it was quite against *their* wishes' that the menfolk were taking this action. What particularly offended the Suffields was that the strikers had each been given an allowance of 2 cwt of coal 'the night before they . . . left, besides the labourers' Xmas dinner'. However, they took comfort from the fact that 'more than half of the men who have struck only do it out of cowardice, just because one or two really bad men laugh at them.'[26] Clearly Lady Suffield intended to get the wives on her side and in this way to exert pressure to end the dispute. Her daughters, meanwhile, continued to distribute clothing and wine to the 'deserving' poor.[27]

Some cottagers may have secretly resented this kind of interference, but many genuinely appreciated the interest taken in them. Mrs Flinton of Burgh-on-Bain, Lincolnshire, years later recalled with gratitude the gifts bestowed by Lady Fox of Girsby Manor:

> one year, her lady's-maid, set to and made all us girls 'red riding hoods' to go to school in, in winter. My word, wasn't they warm! . . . Oh, they were very, very good, were Girsby Manor. Burgh's been going down ever since they left. We thought a lot of Sir John and Lady Fox, and they did of us; we were *their* people. We didn't need no sick club to look after us, not with having Sir John.[28]

Even greater devotion was displayed in Lord and Lady Wantage's estate village of Lockinge, by an inhabitant who told the rector that it seemed 'as if Mother [was] out of the house' when Lady Wantage was away.[29]

At Christmas generous doles of beef, plum pudding, bedding, coals and clothing were widely distributed among estate families.[30] On a humbler level, as at Otterbourne and some other Hampshire villages, St Thomas's Day (21 December) was spent by the poorer women in what they called 'gooding', going from house to house among the well-to-do to receive something towards the Christmas dinner.[31] Elsewhere thrift was encouraged by the establishment of coal, clothing and boot clubs, whereby the contributions of the members were supplemented by the subscriptions of the better-off. At the end of the century the rural district nursing service was initiated largely as a result of the efforts of gentry families in Gloucestershire and Worcestershire.

But some women, confident that they knew what was best, combined their giving with insensitive authoritarianism. Charles Kingsley warned against any temptation to treat the poor

> as *things*: . . . A lady can go into a poor cottage, lay down the law to the inhabitants, reprove them for sins to which she has never been tempted; tell them how to set things right, which, if she had the doing of them, I fear she would do even more confusedly and slovenly than they. She can give them a tract, as she might a pill; and then a shilling, as something sweet after the medicine; and she can go out again and see no more of them till her benevolent mood recurs . . . Clubs, societies, alms, lending

libraries are but dead machinery . . . without the smile of the lip, the light of the eye, the tenderness of the voice, which makes the poor woman feel that a soul is speaking to her soul.[32]

Sadly his strictures were often ignored. Susan Sitwell, for example, arrogantly ordered that all the girls attending her school must have haircuts, while Lady Greene of Nether Hall, Suffolk, sent her groom with sheets of brown paper to a family short of bedclothes. With them came a message that they would 'keep the children warm and when the warm weather comes they won't need washing but can be burned'.[33] Ironically the mother of this family had acted as a wet nurse to Lady Greene's first child. Even the well-meaning Rosalind, Countess of Carlisle, in her zeal for the temperance cause had no hesitation in closing licensed premises on the family's estates in Yorkshire and Cumberland.[34]

Far more common, however, was the businesslike attitude adopted by Mrs Wroughton of Woolley, Berkshire, who considered it her duty to watch over both the spiritual and the physical well-being of the cottagers. If they failed to attend church on Sundays she paid them a visit; when they were ill she supplied soup, rabbits and camphorated oil; and when they were short of clothing, flannel and calico were provided from the 'Poor Persons' cupboard' kept specially for the purpose. Her granddaughter described how almost every afternoon

> she drives to visit the sick, with cans, bottles and bundles. The footman knocks on the door and inquires if the person is at home. Then Grandma enters the cottage . . . She settles down for a lively chat before reading the Bible, the chapter she has chosen beforehand to suit each person to be visited . . . Next they expect Grandmama to pray, which she does very well from long practice and great faith.
>
> Then Grandmama takes out her pocket-book and writes what chapter she has read and what is needed, such as sheets, jelly or castor-oil, and how the person seems.[35]

It is clear that villagers who might have wished to escape her attentions had little opportunity to do so.

A similarly forceful approach was adopted by Lady Wilbraham, a daughter of the Earl of Fortescue. Each Saturday she drove round most of the cottages on the family estate in Cheshire in a pony

PLATE 8   *Ladies out for a drive in a pony cart, c.1910.*
(National Museum of Wales [Welsh Folk Museum])

carriage, with gifts of red flannel, soup, puddings and the like. But the basket also contained a bottle of castor oil, and this, too, was frequently administered, to the consternation of the recipients.[36]

Little girls began to learn their charitable duties from an early age, accompanying their mothers on visits and helping to distribute soup and religious tracts. They also learnt to sew baby clothes and make flannel petticoats.[37] When they grew up such girls often taught in Sunday or night schools, inspected the needlework in the village day school and perhaps gave occasional lessons, as well as playing an active role in church affairs.

This was true of Charlotte M. Yonge, daughter of a minor landed family from Otterbourne, Hampshire. Not only did she help in the village schools, which her mother had established, but in 1838 she began her literary career by publishing a story to help finance an extension to the girls' school. Despite the disapproval of her grandmother, who considered authorship an unladylike pursuit, she continued to write novels, history books and religious tracts for the next sixty years. Her purpose was to bring before her readers a model of Christian behaviour based on her own brand of high Anglicanism.[38]

That her efforts bore fruit is confirmed by the reminiscences of Rose Fane, the youngest child of the Earl of Westmorland. It was under the influence of the writings of Charles Kingsley and Charlotte Yonge that she embarked upon charitable work in the small village of Apethorpe, where she was living. With the help of the vicar's daughters, she started a night school for farm lads, conducted a Bible class on Sundays and organized a lending library, which continued long after she had left the village.[39]

In return for dispensing their favours, most Lady Bountifuls looked for outward displays of gratitude from the recipients. At Great Missenden, also in Buckinghamshire, the squire's four sisters expected the women to come to their doors in clean aprons and to curtsey as they drove through. On one occasion when two women in the street failed to offer the required mark of respect, they were asked 'whether their knees were stiff'.[40] Again, at Helmingham, where the Tollemaches provided much charitable aid in the form of coal, clothing and boot clubs, and also kept the cottages in good repair, girls attending the school were expected to curtsey whenever they met Lady Tollemache. One who failed to do so remembered being caned at school next day for the omission.[41] It was on these grounds that the Countess of Warwick, writing in 1931, condemned the whole system as 'something akin to serfdom':

> The landowning classes expected a certain fealty, a certain acceptance of the view of those who gave the 'dole.' Blankets, soup, coals, rabbits, and the rest were all paid for, though not in cash – because the recipients were the poorest of the poor – but in subservience, in the surrender of all personality, and in a certain measure of humility from which there could be no escape.[42]

However, she was writing at a time when such attitudes were already under question. In the Victorian years, perspectives were very different. Many of those living in estate villages welcomed the attentions of the lady of the manor. They enjoyed boasting to neighbours in less favoured communities that 'Her Ladyship' had called that afternoon and had enquired after the health and welfare of their family.[43] Indeed, in 1843, Cecilia Ridley complained that whenever she went into Plessey, near to Blagdon, her Northumbrian home, she was 'obliged to make a visit to all the people or they are quite jealous'. About a year later she went to Newcastle-on-Tyne to spend almost £50 on her club: 'Some of the people have begged me to give a £ a pair for blankets', she told her mother wryly.[44]

Where such charitable initiatives were neglected by landed families, through either indifference or cash shortage, it is clear that the omission sometimes caused local resentment. Lady Dashwood was firmly reproved by the treasurer of the High Wycombe Lying-in Charity when he acknowledged her one guinea subscription to the fund – seemingly because she was thinking of discontinuing it. 'The Committee cannot but express their *astonishment* and *regret* that as it is the *only aid* Lady Dashwood affords to the poor of this place so small a sum should be *intended* to be withdrawn.'[45] Not all critics were so outspoken, but the attitude displayed was widespread.

Charitable activities also provided wives and daughters with opportunities to exercise their personal initiative at a time when many aspects of their lives were circumscribed by family duties or tradition. Thus Lady Charlotte Guest used educational developments at Dowlais as a way of expressing her own ideas. She turned her attention to infant and adult education, opening an evening class for girls from her husband's ironworks in October 1848.[46] Other women, like Anne Sturges Bourne of Testwood House, Hampshire, and the Countess of Macclesfield in Oxfordshire, established servant training schools. The Countess's catered for about a dozen girls in a purpose-built property at Watlington, where they were instructed in laundry-work, cooking, and housework.[47] Miss Sturges Bourne's venture was less ambitious, with the daughters of local cottagers taken into her own home for training. By the beginning of the 1860s she had eight girls aged between ten and fourteen in residence, together with their mistress. Many letters to her friend, Marianne Dyson, at around this time includes details of their progress or of the efforts she was making to find them a situation.[48]

A number of other ladies, like Mrs Henley at Waterperry, Oxfordshire, considered it their duty to secure suitable employment for young villagers, and spent much time and effort to that end. In 1850/1 Mrs Henley was able to supply Lady Dashwood with both a kitchen maid and a page for West Wycombe Park. As she carefully informed Lady Dashwood, the page had lived with them for two years and was aged 17½: 'He is very willing and good temper'd. His friends live in our village and our reason for parting with him, we

wish to take another of our village boys in – we generally keep them
till we can get them a situation, and he will be very fortunate if you
are kind enough to take him.' Lady Dashwood decided to employ
him, and a mutual friend of the two ladies jokingly commented:
'Waterperry . . . I think at last . . . will be in the geographical
dictionaries as a place famous for its servants.'[49]

For many women, therefore, the exercise of philanthropy was a
means of escape

> from the isolation, self-abnegation, and conformity of domestic
> roles. It was a means of expressing their personality, fulfilling
> their abilities, and gaining satisfaction from their achievements.
> These activities were indeed real work, demanding a sacrifice of
> time, considerable effort, and a whole range of skills. Their
> competence in counselling, teaching, planning, organizing, and
> public speaking gave them greater self-confidence and self-
> esteem . . . They gained a sense of usefulness and worth,
> especially important for unmarried women.[50]

A minority went on, in the late Victorian and Edwardian years, to
combine these charitable duties with service in local government, as
poor law guardians, district and parish councillors and members of
school boards. A few, like Mrs McIlquham and her friend, Mrs Elmy,
saw this as a way of demonstrating women's competence in
administrative matters and, therefore, as a vital precursor to full
female political equality.[51] Shortly after the first parish and district
council elections were held in December 1894, Mrs Elmy expressed
her satisfaction at the way this wider role was opening up: 'I believe
that – when "the tale is fully told" – of women on School Boards,
Boards of Guardians . . . Vestries, & District Boards, Urban District
Councils & Parish Councils, – there will prove to be nearer 2,000
than 1,500 women now actually engaged in great administrative
work – as against not 220 last year.'[52]

In January 1895, the *Parish, District and Town Councils' Gazette*
reported approvingly that one of the most 'pleasing features of the
recent elections' was the 'comparatively large number of lady
members of the Aristocracy who have been chosen to take a share
either as Councillors or Chairmen – in the government of the villages
where their family estates are situated'. It singled out for particular
mention the Dowager Countess of Lovelace, who had been elected

to the parish council of East Horsley, where she resided. She had long played an active role in the county's philanthropic and social work, and had also taken an interest in the political life of the neighbourhood, being a leading figure in the Conservative Party's Primrose League. For women such as she, local government provided still wider opportunities for the exercise of political influence and organizational abilities.[53]

Charitable duties apart, much of the leisure time of country house wives and daughters was spent within the family circle or among a narrow range of socially acceptable neighbours. 'Most ladies', wrote Edith Olivier, 'played whist, consequences, and the piano. If they were tall and graceful, they shot with bows and arrows.'[54] Croquet matches, too, were a popular feature of country house life, while photography beguiled the leisure hours of a few. At the end of the century some of the more daring also took up bicycling. The Marchioness of Londonderry considered that this, and lawn tennis, had contributed more to the freedom and happiness of women in late Victorian England than almost any other factor. 'The fact is that sportswomen of . . . fifty years ago, had to be very strenuous, exceptional creatures', she wrote in the late 1930s, 'as in everything they did they were hampered by their clothes and petty conventions. . . . Before the advent of lawn tennis, badminton was played in garments which would have been impossible even in a restricted game of lawn tennis.'[55]

On fine days, younger women would exercise in the garden and go for country walks, or, at the appropriate season, ride to hounds. Cecilia Harbord, eldest daughter of the fifth Baron Suffield, described a 'capital' coursing expedition she undertook with her brother early in 1877. She was riding a new horse, which jumped 'beautifully . . . They did not get many hares, but except for the farmer's sake . . . I was delighted, because the poor things deserve to get away.'[56] For Lucy Lyttelton, the future Lady Frederick Cavendish, her first day's hunting was 'the most glorious exciting enjoyment I have ever had': 'I saw the fox break away, I heard the music of the hounds, and horns and halloos, I careered along to the sound of the scampering hoofs . . . I flew over 2 or 3 fences, too enchanted to have a moment's fright; in short, I galloped for ½ an hour in all the glory of a capital run.'[57]

By the 1890s a number of women were hunting regularly and a few

A NORFOLK DUMPLING.

Young Hodge (in expectation of a Copper). "OI'LL OPEN THE GATE."
Lady. "YOU ARE A VERY CIVIL LAD. YOU DON'T COME FROM THESE PARTS?"
Young Hodge. "YOW'RE A LIAR. I DEW!"

PLATE 9 *Riding was a major leisure interest of country house ladies, especially in the mid- and late-Victorian years.*

(*Punch*, 1877)

were being appointed Masters of Hounds. Of Miss McClintock, who in 1899 became the first Lady Master of a subscription pack, *Country Life* approvingly observed that she was 'one of the hardest riders the country [had] ever known'.[58] Earlier, Lady Willoughby de Broke, who shared her husband's passion for the chase, had ridden with him at the head of the local hunt for several seasons.[59]

During inclement weather the hours were occupied with books, needlework, and sketching, or in practising on the piano. Cecilia Ridley, who spent much time when her husband was hunting 'poddling about the garden and making little arrangements therein', welcomed the company of her sister, Mary, and the latter's new husband, Charles Howard, when they came to stay in October 1842. 'We have had some charming mornings, Charles reading aloud to us whilst we worked or drew in my little room, for the weather has not allowed us to go out much.'[60]

Afternoon calls and extended visits to friends and relatives were other diversions widely adopted, especially by those with a large network of kin. Admiral Montagu, whose mother was a Paget, recalled their house at Uxbridge filled with 'numberless uncles and aunts . . . and to this goodly array were added numerous progeny until to my juvenile mind the world seemed to consist of nothing but Pagets'.[61] Likewise, in the early years of the nineteenth century the widowed Lady Glynne and her young children spent more than half their time on visits to the homes of uncles, cousins and grandparents. Later her daughters, Mary Lyttelton and Caroline Gladstone, continued the practice. 'Great cavalcades of nurses and babies were for ever travelling between Hagley, Hawarden and London', writes Catherine's biographer, 'and [that] winter of 1849–50, when the Gladstone family were staying at Hagley [the Lyttelton family seat], the big nursery at the top of the house was crammed to overflowing with children under the age of ten, presided over by the Lyttelton nannie'.[62]

For the mothers of marriageable daughters such country house gatherings provided a useful opportunity for matchmaking, to supplement the opportunities of the London season – though the girls themselves probably regarded them simply as opportunities to enjoy themselves. Adeline de Horsey, later the Countess of Cardigan, recalled the round of country house visits which had followed her 'coming out' in 1842:

After . . . the innumerable balls and parties . . . we went to Cowes, where we spent a delightful month. . . . From Cowes we went to stay with the Ailesburys at Savernake, and then to Badminton, where the Beauforts had a large family party. . . . From Badminton we went on a visit to Lord Forester at Willey Park, Shropshire, where I met Lady Jersey and her daughter, Lady Clementina Villiers.

Lady Jersey was the greatest *grande dame* in London Society, and her house in Berkeley Square was the centre of the Tory party. She knew all the artistic and literary celebrities of the day . . .

We usually spent Christmas at Beaudesert, Lord Anglesey's lovely old place. . . . There was no hunting or shooting at Beaudesert, and our amusements were very simple ones. After lunch we walked over Cannock Chase, and those ladies who did not care for walking rode sturdy little ponies. We returned to tea, and after dinner there was music, cards or dancing . . . nobody was bored.[63]

With the improvement in transport in the later Victorian years came a growing tendency to substitute 'week-end' visits for some of these more lengthy stays, at a time when London society was itself ceasing to be the 'large family' that Lady Dorothy Nevill, for one, had enjoyed in the 1840s and 1850s.[64] Early in the twentieth century, Lady Cynthia Asquith, a daughter of the Earl of Wemyss, remembered weekend visits arranged during the season, or in the winter for shooting and hunt ball parties. Much time was spent in changing clothes according to accepted social ritual, and this meant travelling with a large amount of luggage, especially during the winter months.

> You came down to breakfast in your 'best dress,' . . . and after Church changed into tweeds. Another 'change' for tea . . . However small your dress allowance, a different dinner gown was considered essential for each evening. Thus a Friday to Monday party involved taking your 'Sunday Best,' two tweed coats and skirts, three garments suitable for tea, your 'best hat' – usually a vast affair loaded with feathers, fruit or corn – a variety of country headgear, as likely as not a billycock hat and riding habit, numerous accessories in the way of petticoats, stoles, scarves, evening wreaths and what not; and a large bag in which to carry about the house your embroidery – then the almost universal 'work' of the idle, for 'reading aloud,' . . . was still much in vogue, and while one member of the house-party read nearly all the Shes would ply their needles.[65]

Dinner normally consisted of seven or eight courses and then, while the men sat over their port, liqueurs, and cigars in the dining-room, the ladies retired to the drawing-room. The first evening was usually spent in conversation and playing games, or, for those so inclined, in the pursuit of discreet flirtations. But these activities still left ample time for members of the party to follow their own inclination, be it going for walks with a chosen companion or reading in the bedroom. Only when shooting parties were in progress was the routine more circumscribed, since it was difficult, without being labelled eccentric, to avoid 'going out with the guns'. 'Hours spent in dripping woods, watching men slaughter birds was not my idea of fun', wrote Lady Cynthia. 'It was dreadful to be all the colours of the rainbow from cold and yet expected to stand stockstill.'[66] Towards the end of the nineteenth century some of the more daring women joined in shooting parties on their own account, though this was still considered highly unconventional. *Country Life* stressed that women who chose to share in the sport must expect no special privileges; they must wait for the rabbit to bolt or the bird to rise on equal terms.[67]

Alongside these more active pursuits, most ladies devoted much time to letter writing.[68] Such correspondence covered not merely the major events of family life, but the choice of a place for a holiday, the merits of the sermon heard in church on Sunday, or the hiring and firing of servants. Ellen Fane, writing from Waterperry in 1851, sent three letters to her friend, Lady Dashwood at West Wycombe Park, concerning the desirability of the latter recruiting a kitchen maid who had come to Ellen's attention.[69] And Anne Sturges Bourne, as we have seen, spent a good deal of time writing to her friend, Marianne Dyson, about the merits of the girls she was training for domestic service.

Meanwhile, Anne herself had grown discontented with the emptiness of her social round:

> it is a bad thing to have no objects in life . . . I suppose no people in this Babel have less of fuss or interruption, but it is not like pursuing a study or an art, perfecting or finishing anything, & this lazy sort of life seems to unnerve the mind for any exertions . . . when I hear what others are doing, I cannot fancy in myself the same power.[70]

'Good works' among local cottagers were clearly no substitute for a more purposeful routine.

The long periods which family members spent in one another's company, perhaps inevitably, also led to ill-feeling and disagreements in many households. Mary Berkeley, eldest daughter of Sir John Dashwood King, was not alone in experiencing difficulties with an intimidating mother-in-law. In a letter to her brother's wife, Mary confided the problems which were likely to arise when arrangements were made for her daughter's wedding:

> Milady Berkeley I fear will torment us to death. I had rather the wedding had taken place any where but Cranford [Lady Berkeley's residence] for she is sure to come out with something

coarse . . . She (Lady B.) is going to give Georgina all her Linen
. . . now this is kind, but if you knew, when she gives a thing,
how dearly she makes one pay for it, I would rather go without
the above than suffer what I see is preparing for us . . . It is
certain all Berkeleys live upon tormenting others.[71]

Barbara Charlton was equally disillusioned with her in-laws at
Hesleyside, complaining, soon after her marriage, about the
discomfort of the house and the low standard of the family's table
manners.[72] So appalled was she by their behaviour that she learnt to
eat with downcast eyes.

Even the London season was not without its tensions. This was
especially true of a girl's first entry into society. Cynthia Asquith
remembered the rituals associated with 'Coming Out':

> The metamorphosis . . . was supposed to be effected when you
> were presented at Court, where the wand was officially waved
> over your head. The picturesque rites of this social baptism were
> preceded by weeks of trepidation – weeks busied with long
> lessons in deportment . . . and panic-stricken rehearsals of my
> curtsey . . . then there were endless wearisome hours of trying-
> on.[73]

Likewise in 1877, when Florence Sitwell and her mother, the
widowed Lady Sitwell, came to visit friends and relatives, the frivolous
conduct of those they met offended their strong religious sensibilities.
Lady Sitwell was especially anxious that their relations were

> going to make a set at us, to try and bring us into the vortex of
> London life; and that she does not wish for me, nor do I wish it;
> we came up to town to see our friends and relations, and get, if
> possible, among a good and interesting set of people. Mother
> said she would prefer Grace [Florence's cousin] and me sitting a
> good deal by ourselves, as she so disliked us hearing the kind of
> talk that went on.[74]

Lady Sitwell need not have worried. Florence's principal enjoyment
seems to have been attending church services and bible classes,
rather than in going to dinner-parties and balls. It was with relief that
she and her mother returned to their quiet Scarborough home on 8

June. 'I have been quite home-sick, and was so glad to get back that I just sat down and cried', she noted in her diary.[75]

However, it was Florence Nightingale who perhaps most clearly expressed the frustrations many women experienced within the confines of a too closely knit family circle. Mr Nightingale owned estates in Derbyshire and Hampshire, and the family also made regular visits to London and to the continent. But for long her attempts to strike out on her own account were thwarted. 'The family uses people, *not* for what they are, not for what they are intended to be, but for what it wants them for − its own uses', she wrote on one occasion. In her youth, Florence had wished to study mathematics, but her parents had firmly refused to provide a tutor, Mrs Nightingale arguing that it was her daughter's duty to concentrate on domestic affairs in preparation for matrimony: 'what use were mathematics to a married woman?'[76]

So, like other country house daughters, Florence had to confine herself to worsted work, carriage drives, quadrilles and similar trivia. 'What is my business in this world and what have I done this fortnight?', she wrote despairingly in July 1846. 'I have read the "Daughter at Home" to Father and two chapters of Mackintosh; a volume of Sybil to Mama. Learnt seven tunes by heart. Written various letters. Ridden with Papa. Paid eight visits. Done Company. And that is all.'[77] She had been given responsibility for the still-room, pantry and linen-room by her mother, and twice a year she checked their contents, as well as supervising the making of preserves in the still-room.[78] Mundane though these tasks were, she preferred them to many of her other occupations, although 'in the middle of my lists . . . I cannot help asking in my head, "Can reasonable people want all this?"'[79]

Florence's harshest condemnation of the sterility of female existence was reserved, however, for her *Suggestions for Thought to Searchers after Religious Truth*, written in the 1850s but unpublished in her lifetime:

Why have women passion, intellect, moral activity . . . and a place in society where no one of the three can be exercised? . . . Women are never supposed to have any occupation of sufficient importance *not* to be interrupted, . . . and have trained themselves so as to consider whatever they do as *not* of such value to

the world or to others, but that they can throw it up at the first
'claim of social life.' They have accustomed themselves to
consider intellectual occupation as a merely selfish amusement,
which it is their 'duty' to give up for every trifler more selfish
than themselves . . . [A] woman cannot live in the light of
intellect . . . Those conventional frivolities, which are called her
'duties,' forbid it. . . . What are these duties . . . ? – Answering a
multitude of letters which lead to nothing, from her so-called
friends, keeping herself up to the level of the world that she may
furnish her quota of amusement at the breakfast-table; driving
out her company in the carriage. . . . The actual life is passed in
sympathy given and received for a dinner, a party, a piece of
furniture, a house built or a garden laid out well, . . . in devotion
to your guests . . . in schemes of schooling for the poor, which
you follow up perhaps in an odd quarter of an hour, between
luncheon and driving out in the carriage . . . and the rest of your
time goes in ordering the dinner, hunting for a governess for
your children, and sending pheasants and apples to your poorer
relations . . . The time is come when women must do something
more than the 'domestic hearth'.[80]

Fortunately most country house ladies shared neither Florence
Nightingale's bitter dislike of these household duties nor her
determination to escape from them. The majority accepted that the
'domestic hearth' was to be their future sphere, albeit interspersed
with visits to London for the season (between April and the end of
July) or lengthy stays with relatives and perhaps prolonged tours to
the cultural centres of Europe. Some, like Lady Randolph Churchill,
were able to share vicariously in political life by campaigning on
behalf of their husbands during elections, or acting as hostess at
dinner parties attended by their husbands' parliamentary colleagues.[81]
A particular enthusiast was Rosalind Howard, who spent many
hours canvassing for her father-in-law during the 1874 general
election.[82]

Lady Selborne, the former Maud Cecil, was, as befitted a prime
minister's daughter, another who was deeply interested in political
matters. Whilst her eldest son, Roundell, was at school and at Oxford
she wrote him long letters of advice on politics, and was anxious that
he should 'go early into the House of Commons' – advice which he

took. She, too, canvassed on behalf of friends and members of the family who were standing for Parliament and was considered an effective organizer of female electoral workers. She was a shrewd judge of character as well. 'I don't feel sure that George Curzon will be a help in spite of his great ability', she wrote to Roundell in June, 1908:

> He is such an egoist, it will be very difficult to make him play for the side. . . . I want one of his rich relations to put Philip Kerr [the future Marquis of Lothian] into Parliament . . . As far as I can gather he holds the proper opinions for a modern young Tory. Imperialist with a mild dash of Socialism.[83]

Not surprisingly, she also became involved in the women's franchise battle, becoming president of the Conservative Women's Suffrage Society in 1907.

But most country house wives, unlike Lady Selborne, confined their political activities to offering help and support to their husbands', brothers' or fathers' political ambitions, rather than engaging in campaigns of their own.

Once married, a woman was expected to organize her life in accordance with her husband's wishes. Lady Boileau of Ketteringham, Norfolk, was not alone in anxiously examining her conscience to see how well she had performed in this regard. She submitted all her household accounts to her husband for vetting, and he personally audited the contents of the house. When he found fault with the children, his wife tried to stop herself opposing him, although sometimes her emotions got the better of her and she was outspoken in their defence. Occasionally she fell back upon the legendary armour of Victorian wives, and resorted to tears and hysteria to get her way. But in the main, she tried to keep herself 'modest and meek, and though keeping her opinion, not setting it up against his'. Her eldest daughter compared her timid yet determined efforts to protect her children from her husband's wrath to the actions of a peahen caring for its chicks.[84]

As well as accepting her husband's wishes and opinions, and thereby confirming his God-given masculine superiority, it was a wife's duty to superintend the running of the household. This was not easy when much entertaining was done. Occasionally thirty or forty guests assembled at house-parties, many of them with their personal maids and valets, so that a household might comprise more than a hundred people. 'One never knew where one's duties as hostess would end', wrote Consuelo, wife of the ninth Duke of Marlborough. 'It was not astonishing that at the close of my first London season, on going to the seaside to recuperate, I slept for twenty-four hours without waking.'[85]

Supervision of the servants could be a particular problem, especially in the largest houses where they might number as many as fifty. Although the housekeeper normally controlled the female staff and the steward or butler the male, most ladies interviewed their housekeeper each day to decide upon menus, make arrangements for prospective guests, discuss the running expenses of the household and similar matters. At Blenheim a French chef presided over a staff of four in the kitchen and the Duchess of Marlborough recalled the frequent quarrels which broke out between him and the housekeeper over the breakfast trays.[86] It was the mistress's task to pacify the warring factions.

Small wonder that Lady Cynthia Asquith considered the role of any woman who ran a large country house an arduous one. 'The châtelaines I knew', she wrote, 'seemed so very seldom free really to live in the immediate *present* . . . They were too distractingly preoccupied by plans for the future. Indeed, what with the cares of family, household and tenants; incessant village duties; the trickiness of parochial politics and the perpetual coming and going of guests, they seldom had a disengaged hour in which to read, let alone follow any pursuit of their own.'[87] These were sentiments with which Florence Nightingale would have heartily agreed.

The worries to which 'the servants' gave rise are confirmed in letters and diaries of the day. Even Cecilia Ridley, who was in general well served, had problems in persuading her housekeeper to air the bed of a prospective guest. Not until Cecilia warned her of the man's delicate health and pointed out that if he died it would be the housekeeper's fault did she do as she was required. Ironically, Cecilia's own premature death from tuberculosis seems to have been due to contracting the disease from the butler.[88]

Lady Frederick Cavendish, at Chatsworth in November 1866, also bewailed the difficulties she was experiencing because her new lady's maid was 'turning out dreadfully huffy with the Duke's household, and unmanageable when I tell her to show my gowns to other people. . . . It perplexes me sadly how all I say and do, though it is not without prayer, seems to fail utterly with one maid after another.'[89] Shortly after, this 'odious little maid went off', to be replaced by 'gentle, pleasant-looking, quiet little Mrs. Parry', who soon revealed that she was pregnant and thus had to leave almost immediately. In July 1867, Lady Frederick reported a further 'miserable catastrophe' in her household: 'the housekeeper drinks, and has wretched health. . . . I gave her warning. My life feels shortened by these things.'[90]

A third victim of 'servant troubles' was Louisa Yorke, who became mistress of Erddig near Wrexham in 1902, when she was almost thirty-nine. She found her new responsibilities a marked contrast to life as the daughter of a Wiltshire country clergyman. 'I have I think, undertaken more than I can accomplish', she wrote anxiously in her diary about a month after returning from her honeymoon. 'The management of this huge house with 6 female & 3 male servants is no joke.' A few days later she resumed her complaints. 'I am having great trouble with the numerous servants. Some are too noisy, some too grand, some find the work too much. I wonder if I shall ever be quite settled.'[91] Even when she was in hospital, undergoing an operation and already pregnant with her first child, domestic problems pursued her. 'Oh! the trouble of Servants at Erddig. It is sad to contemplate', she lamented on 11 November 1902. There were also skirmishes with William Hughes, the agent, whom Louisa suspected of negligence and extravagance. On one occasion she spent two and a half hours with him, trying to disentangle the accounts.[92]

Although she, from a relatively modest background, doubtless found the transition to country house life a bigger challenge than the daughter of a landed family would have, there is little doubt that for all newly-weds there were many organizational problems to overcome as they commenced what Lady Frederick Cavendish called a 'chapter of household cares'.[93]

Another hazard, especially in the early and mid-Victorian years, was the frequency with which pregnancies occurred, at a time when the use of contraceptive techniques was widely regarded as immoral and against the will of God. Recent research suggests that the years 1760 to 1850 represented the period of the highest fertility in the

history of the English aristocracy.[94] Although nursemaids and
governesses took over the care of the children, the physical toll
exacted by the pregnancies was considerable. Queen Victoria
doubtless spoke for many when she wrote to her newly-married
eldest daughter in 1858:

> if you have hereafter (as I had constantly for the first two years of
> my marriage) – aches – and sufferings and miseries and plagues
> – which you must struggle against – and enjoyments etc. to give
> up – constant precautions to take, you will feel the yoke of a
> married woman! . . . one feels so pinned down – one's wings
> clipped – in fact, at the best (and few were or are better than I
> was) only half oneself.[95]

Many less fortunate women succumbed to puerperal fever or to
the effects of a serious miscarriage; others were fatally weakened by
too rapid pregnancies. Cecilia Ridley, who had two children in the
first three years of marriage, died from tuberculosis little more than a
year after the birth of the second. Her sister, Mary Howard, had died
shortly before, during her first confinement. Although Catherine
Gladstone had six children during the first ten years of marriage, she
survived; but her sister, Mary Lyttelton, was not so fortunate. She
had eleven children in quick succession, as well as one miscarriage –
wryly calling these regular pregnancies her 'yearly penance'. After
the eleventh confinement her sister was told that another pregnancy
would almost certainly prove fatal. A twelfth child eventually arrived
in February 1857 and six months later, Mary, then aged forty-four,
was dead. She had borne twelve children in less than twenty years of
married life.[96] The diary of Mary's second daughter, Lady Frederick
Cavendish, mentions several similar cases – like that of Lady
Fortescue, who died in December 1866, whilst being confined. She
left behind thirteen children, the eldest of whom was only eighteen.
Lady Curzon, the former Mary Leiter, became dangerously ill with
peritonitis and phlebitis in 1904, about a month after her second
miscarriage. She survived two operations, but died two years later at
the age of thirty-six – ostensibly from heart trouble.[97]

Sometimes, as with Lady Boileau, who had nine children in rapid
succession, repeated pregnancies led to chronic invalidism. Even the
formidable Rosalind, Countess of Carlisle, suffered heart trouble
after she had had eleven children.[98] In other cases, as with Mabel

Morrison, wife of the wealthy Wiltshire landowner and businessman Alfred Morrison, over-frequent child bearing led to temporary illnesses – though these may have been seized on by some women as a way of avoiding further unwanted pregnancies.[99] By the 1880s, however, birth-control methods were being slowly accepted, and average family size gradually declined in all classes of society.[100]

Whilst their children were growing up, few country house mothers spent much time with them. The youngsters – especially the girls – were the responsibility of the nanny and later of the governess. The vast majority of daughters of landed families were still educated at home even at the end of the Victorian era, though a few were sent to expensive day schools in London or, from the 1860s, to a growing number of exclusive boarding schools, like Cheltenham Ladies' College.[101] By the 1890s, Cheltenham was aiming to attract 'the daughters of gentlemen' and to that end was requiring 'references in regard to social standing' before girls were admitted.[102] Other schools followed in its wake, but on the eve of the First World War, Loelia Ponsonby, whose father had been Equerry to Queen Victoria and later became Head of the Royal Household, recalled that her parents' decision to send her away to school was still considered self-consciously 'modern'.[103]

Most families, therefore, relied upon governesses, perhaps supplemented by religious instruction given by their mother, and instruction in dancing and in music from itinerant specialist teachers. 'Till I was 10 I had very little education', remembered Lady Selborne. 'Daily governesses of a transitory character, & a few classes like dancing & gymnastics . . . Boys went to preparatory schools & then on to public schools, just as they do now, but it was not at all usual for girls of the upper class to go to boarding schools. Queen's College [in London] was just beginning its work, & when I was older I went to a German class there.'[104]

The instruction provided by governesses was usually confined to reading, writing, scripture and embroidery, with a smattering of French, German and music. Blanche Dugdale considered the most important part of her family's education was to learn 'by heart metrical versions of certain Psalms', to read Scott's Waverley novels, and to practise 'the "principles of good conversation"'.[105] At Hagley, the Lyttelton children's schooling was divided into distinct compartments: Monday and Thursday were devoted to Italian, Tuesday and

Friday to French, and Wednesday and Saturday to English. There was also dictation practice, music, some arithmetic, a little geography and drawing.[106] This programme was drawn up in the 1850s, but half a century later the curriculum had changed little in many families. Joan Poynder, born in 1897, the daughter of Sir John Poynder Dickson-Poynder of Hartham Park, Wiltshire, recalled that she always had French governesses. Her life was particularly lonely because her mother was unable to have other children and yet her parents refused to send her away to school.[107]

Most parents considered that the traditional 'female' accomplishments were essential if a girl were to find a husband. Too much learning would mark her out as an unattractive blue-stocking. Needless to say, some intelligent girls bitterly resented this. As one young woman commented acidly, the object seemed to be: 'Keep your daughter's intellect back. Let her draw, sing, study botany, languages, etc., etc., but do not urge her to think . . . [or she may] desire to find a husband to whom, in strict justice, she can look up, instead of doing so as her duty . . . whether he deserves it or not.'[108] This was written in 1846, and it is not surprising to learn that she never married.

However, the subordinate position of women in landed society was nowhere more clearly demonstrated than in financial matters. Although about 10 per cent of all married women in the mid-Victorian years were protected by settlements, any wife who was without this safeguard lost control of her property upon marriage. Not until the passage of the Married Women's Property Acts between 1870 and 1882 was her right to control her personal property, earnings and income confirmed. And it was 1935 before wives gained the same rights and responsibilities in regard to contracts and property as had single women and men.[109]

Even the appointment of trustees under the terms of a marriage settlement might not protect a wife's financial position. Much depended upon the zeal and probity with which they carried out their responsibilities, as well as upon the care with which the relevant legal documents were drawn up, and the wife's own attitude. Negotiations over marriage settlements frequently stressed the need to provide adequate protection for a wife's property and money.[110] Lady Selborne, hard-headed as ever, expressed concern about the engagement of her daughter to Viscount Howick, eldest son of Earl Grey, in 1906. She was anxious about Howick's idea of getting 'something in the city' in order to boost his income, adding sourly: 'I never saw anyone more certain to fall a victim to the first designing Jew he tries to do business with . . . The only thing to do is to tie up all the money we can as tightly as the law will allow us, so he won't be able to completely ruin himself.'[111]

One of those less fortunate in the mid-nineteenth century was Anne Dashwood, wife of the Rev. Henry Dashwood, and daughter-in-law of Sir John Dashwood King of West Wycombe Park. She eventually persuaded her trustees (one of whom was Henry's brother) to extract £2,000 from her marriage settlement of £20,000 so that her husband's debts might be settled. Various other avenues for securing cash had been explored without success and she decided that this was the only way in which her husband could be kept out of debtors' prison.[112] Subsequently, when her father-in-law died in 1849 she had great difficulty in obtaining the £200 annuity provided for in her marriage settlement. Even before Sir John's death, the annuity had been £120 in arrears and by April 1851 the sum owing had mounted to £500, despite her repeated appeals for payment. She was forced to borrow money at high interest in order to maintain herself and her daughter, since an added complication was that she and her profligate husband had now parted.[113]

Alongside those who had inherited their wealth, however, there were a few strong-minded wives like Lady Charlotte Guest who not only persuaded husbands to acquire a landed estate but decided how it was to be developed. After an unhappy childhood caused by her mother's unfortunate second marriage, Charlotte married the Welsh ironmaster, John Guest, in 1833. Fifteen years later, she began to remodel their newly acquired property at Canford, Dorset. The estate had cost the vast sum of £335,000, with a further £19,000 spent on acquiring additional land from the vendor. Between 1848 and 1852 the size of the house was approximately doubled, at a further cost of £30,000, with Lady Guest determined to use her husband's great wealth to establish the family's social position.[114] As early as October 1845 she confided in her diary her desire 'for a quiet happy place in which to bring up my children respectably as everybody else does'. In February 1849, when the alterations were under way, she noted that her husband felt 'bitterly' the heavy expense 'which he has been almost unconsciously led into', but she considered it would be worthwhile because it would enable her children to enjoy 'fitting consideration with their neighbours'.[115] Significantly, when the High Church tendencies of the Canford rector offended her Evangelical sensibilities, it was she rather than her husband who tackled him on the subject. She even called in the aid of the Dowlais rector to persuade him of the error of his ways. By December 1850 her efforts seem to have been successful, for a diary entry praises the 'excellent sermon' preached by the rector.[116]

Towards the end of her husband's life and for a short time after his death in 1852, Lady Guest was also involved in the management of the Dowlais ironworks, aided by a loyal and experienced professional management team which John Guest had already built up. At that time, as her recent biographers point out, she was mistress of the world's largest ironworks. But although initially she took an active part in the business, the strain of her isolated position – and her plans to marry again – brought about a change. In 1854 she withdrew from what had become a thankless duty. Significantly she now described the community of Dowlais, which she had once called 'a dream of Lotus land' as 'more dull and dirty and dismal than I ever saw it'.[117]

A still higher level of organizational ability was displayed by Frances Anne, Dowager Duchess of Londonderry, who assumed control of the family's collieries around Seaham in County Durham in 1854, following the death of her husband. Benjamin Disraeli, who visited her at Seaham Hall in 1861, has provided a vivid pen portrait:

> our hostess is a remarkable woman. . . . Twenty miles hence she has a palace (Wynyard) in a vast park, with forest rides and antlered deer, and all the splendid accessories of feudal life. But she prefers living in a hall . . . surrounded by her collieries and her blast furnaces and her railroads and the unceasing telegraphs, with a port hewn out of the solid rock, screw steamers and four thousand pitmen under her control. . . . In the town of Seaham Harbour, a mile off, she has a regular office, a fine stone building with her name and arms in front, and her flag flying above; and here she transacts, with innumerable agents, immense business – and I remember her five-and-twenty years

ago a mere fine lady; nay, the finest in London. But one must find excitement if one has brains.[118]

It was at her personal instigation that blast furnaces were built near to Seaham Harbour, and throughout the latter part of her life she kept a ruthless grip on the whole enterprise.[119]

A third strong-minded female administrator was Alice de Rothschild, who inherited her brother's estate at Waddesdon, Buckinghamshire, in 1898, when she was already a spinster of fifty-one. She immediately showed her determination to run things her own way. According to her niece, she looked after every detail of the estate, undeterred by any opposition, and soon became a familiar figure in the surrounding villages as she drove about in a low phaeton.[120] Although she spent October to April each year away from the estate at a villa in the south of France, she seldom allowed it to slip out of her thoughts. A constant flow of instructions, enquiries and exhortations was despatched to underlings at Waddesdon. On a broader front she improved amenities in the village and its environs by building schools, a nursing home and recreational clubs.

Rosalind, Countess of Carlisle, similarly seized the opportunity to manage her husband's estates as a way of developing her administrative talents at a time when a political career was barred to women. As she wrote in May, 1888, 'Though politics are denied to me still I have got hold of the reins of government in estate matters.'[121] When she first assumed direction, the estates were mortgaged heavily. She cleared off these liabilities by land sales, and then judiciously built up the Naworth estate in Cumberland, as well as managing about 13,000 acres in Yorkshire around Castle Howard, the family seat. The burden of the work was heavy, entailing much travelling from one estate to another. Small wonder that on one occasion she wrote of the 'bottomless morass of work' in connection with the estates. But under her careful supervision, their net annual income rose from just over £15,000 in 1892–4 to almost £25,000 by 1911–13.[122]

Only a few women possessed the energy and the wealth to exercise authority in the way Miss de Rothschild, the Countess of Carlisle, Lady Londonderry and Lady Guest were able to do. Nevertheless, by the end of the century an increasing number of women were growing impatient with the emptiness of their lives. Like Florence Nightingale half a century before, they sought a career of their own. Among them was Lady Florence Dixie, youngest daughter of the seventh Marquess of Queensberry and wife of Sir Alexander Beaumont Dixie, Bart. She acted as a war correspondent for the *Morning Post* during the South African War of 1879, and also engaged in exploration, particularly in South America. She was a tireless opponent of blood sports – a view unlikely to commend her to most members of her class – and a keen champion of women's rights. Her advocacy of birth control, then an unpopular cause, was just one aspect of her controversial life. When she died in November 1905, at the early age of forty-eight, her career as author, explorer, war correspondent and propagandist was widely recognized.[123]

Other women, like Eglantyne Jebb, the daughter of a Shropshire landed family, elected to attend university, feeling that their life 'must be one of service'. Eglantyne, after three years at Oxford, emerged in 1898 determined to become a qualified elementary school teacher.[124] To this end she spent a year at Stockwell Training College in London before taking a post in Marlborough. Although the stresses of teaching proved too great and she resigned after little more than a year, her desire for independence and a career was unabated. Eventually she became the founder of the Save the Children Fund.

Some country house wives and daughters who sought a broader and more fulfilling existence were inspired by a fervent religious faith, considering that God had called them into the world to carry out a mission. As Joan Burstyn has commented, such girls watched with envy as their brothers trained for useful work while they sat idly at home waiting to get married.[125] A few took advantage of the local government reforms of the 1890s and began to serve on parish and district councils, hoping thereby to improve the health and welfare of villagers. One of them was Mrs Barker of Sherfield-on-Loddon, near Basingstoke, who became chairman of her parish council in 1894 when her husband, the chief landowner, declined to be nominated. She soon turned her attention to the reorganization of the parish charities, as well as taking in hand such matters as the local footpaths and village sanitation. She believed that women could tackle what she called these 'small things' more effectively than men:

A polluted well, an overcrowded cottage, a barrier across a footpath, are too trivial for men to make a stir about . . . but an independent woman, knowing that 'trifles make the sum of human things', . . . will be earnest for frequent meetings; her cry will ever be, 'Look for work, make work, never . . . stand still till all the good you have the power to do for the poor of your parish is an accomplished fact.[126]

Elsewhere, a tiny minority of women, seeking independent careers in agriculture or horticulture, took advantage of training facilities offered by institutions like the Lady Warwick Hostel. This began a course of instruction in association with Reading College (later Reading University) in 1898, at a time when, as *Country Life* suggested, farming was beginning to be seen as an appropriate occupation for educated girls.[127] After four years the Lady Warwick Hostel severed its connections with Reading and moved to Studley, Warwickshire, where it provided its own classes and lectures. Although many students were the daughters of professional men rather than of the landed gentry, the first warden, Emily Bradley, stressed that the intention was to cater only for 'gentlewomen by birth and education'. In a letter to Viscountess Cranborne in February 1899, Miss Bradley emphasized that although the venture needed the support of women of 'all ranks and classes . . . it is our great English Aristocracy . . . who can throw in their weight if they will, & lift the whole movement into the realms of Patriotism'.[128]

In the event, these ventures appealed to a very small minority of the female members of landed families. And many who did embark upon them had to overcome considerable opposition and scepticism. Not until the First World War was there a general relaxation of attitudes and an acceptance that the daughters of the aristocracy and gentry, like their humbler sisters, should be allowed to develop their talents, instead of having them confined within an exclusive but cramping social straitjacket of etiquette and custom.[129]

4

Professional Families

She was for 16 years the light of her husband's eyes and the wise and tender Mother of his eleven Children.

Epitaph on Charlotte Christiana Money, wife of the Rev. James Drummond Money, rector of Sternfield, Suffolk, who died at Romsey, Hampshire, on 19 December 1848 and is buried in the Abbey there.

Although the professional classes increased in numbers and importance in Victorian England, within the rural areas they remained, with one major exception, of limited significance only. That exception was provided by the clergy of the Church of England and their families. An Anglican cleric was present in virtually every parish throughout the land, whereas doctors, solicitors, bank managers, surveyors, auctioneers and the like were rarely resident outside market towns. Nor, as table 4.1 suggests, were they particularly numerous within them.

Consequently, although these 'professionals' formed a distinct social group within most towns, enjoying what George Eliot called 'nice distinctions of rank' among them, their overall impact upon country life was modest.[1] Even their exact composition was uncertain. Doctors and attorneys were normally included among the elite, at any rate from the 1870s, whereas dentists and chemists were not. This remained true even though the Pharmaceutical Society, the chemists' professional body, had obtained state registration for duly qualified chemists in 1852, and the speciality of dentistry was officially recognized in 1859 with the institution by the Royal College of

TABLE 4.1   *Specimen male professional occupations in rural districts in 1901*

Occupation	Total
Clergy of the established church	12,127
Roman Catholic priests	534
Ministers, priests, of other religious bodies	2,824
Barristers and solicitors	3,063
Physicians, surgeons, general practitioners	3,786
Engineers and surveyors	2,579

NB With the exception of twenty-six female physicians, surgeons and general practitioners, there were no *women* members of any of these professions in rural England and Wales in 1901.

Source: 1901 Census of Population (England and Wales), PP 1903, vol. LXXIV, p. 220

Surgeons of a licence in dental surgery.[2] As the wife of an Edwardian country clergyman, herself a member of a cadet branch of an aristocratic family, acidly observed: 'I know today it is quite the custom to ask the doctor into your house, but of course never the dentist. They are trade and should go to the back door.'[3]

So it was that by the mid-Victorian years, the lawyer and the GP could 'with some conviction make a claim to gentility in the High Street of Middlemarch . . . if not in the mess of a fashionable regiment, . . . or in the drawing-rooms of great country houses'.[4]

The advance in attorneys' social status was the subject of particular comment by mid-nineteenth century writers like W. Johnston, who saw them as ranging from 'the low rapacious pettifogger, who grasps at three-and-sixpenny fees, and is something between the common cur and bulldog of the law, up to the finished gentleman, who has in his hands the most important affairs, and is professionally acquainted with the most delicate secret histories of the first families of the land'.[5] Twenty or thirty years later, their position was a great deal more secure, with Richard Jefferies describing the average country solicitor as taking a leading role in the promotion of 'athletic clubs, reading-rooms, shows, exhibitions'. His wife and daughters shared in this change of fortune, and would now be carried to and fro in a brougham as they made their social calls.[6] Although they might still be called upon occasionally to witness wills and to copy documents, especially in the smaller partnerships, country solicitors' daughters were beginning to marry into the lower reaches of landed families and were thereby becoming assimilated into the ranks of the traditional rulers of rural society.[7]

Medical men, too, had by then largely overcome their initial status problems. Early in the century they were still seen, in many cases, as 'on the border of tradesmanship' and as suffering from 'the taint of services rendered'.[8] In *Wives and Daughters*, set in the first half of the nineteenth century, Mrs Gaskell suggested that although they might receive occasional invitations to dine with members of the gentry, they were rarely considered appropriate partners for the daughters of such families. In her novel, the widowed doctor, Mr Gibson of Hollingford, wished to remarry. He had a 'few thousands well invested' and a good professional income, yet he had difficulty in finding a suitable spouse: 'Among his country patients there were two classes pretty distinctly marked: farmers, whose children were unrefined and uneducated; squires, whose daughters would, indeed, think the world was coming to a pretty pass, if they were to marry a country surgeon.'[9] Eventually he chose Mrs Kirkpatrick, a former governess to the children of Lord and Lady Cumnor, the principal landowning family in the area.

This was symptomatic of the general situation. Lionel Tollemache of Helmingham, the son of a landed Suffolk family, at the beginning of the 1900s could look back to a time, half a century earlier, when the doctor 'used to come in at the back door, and sometimes (there being no steward's room) to take refreshment in the housekeeper's room'.[10] And in the late 1820s, Sir Anthony Carlisle, a member of the council of the College of Surgeons, and later its president, argued that medical practitioners should allow their womenfolk to train as midwives, since this would secure their practice against competition from newly emergent man-midwives and obstetricians. It would also provide their dependants with 'a respectable maintenance' should they die prematurely. However, as midwifery was held in low esteem at this time, such a suggestion seemed like an 'invitation to social suicide', at a time when most medical men were concerned to advance their standing in the world.[11]

After the passage of the Medical Act of 1858, which established a system of registered practitioners, qualified doctors became distinguished from the 'quacks' who still clung on the fringes of the profession. From that point doctors' status in the community gradually improved. And although many, in rural areas, remained relatively poorly paid compared to some urban colleagues – £600 was considered a good annual income for a country GP in East Anglia as late as 1905 – by that date they had become part of the social elite in both villages and market towns.[12]

Turn-of-the-century advertisements for the sale of practices confirm the aspirations of the more prosperous practitioners. Thus one man offered a 'Pleasant Practice' in

> one of the finest Hunting localities, where there is excellent society. The vendor is retiring from the profession, in which he has been engaged more than thirty years. A complete introduction can therefore be given. The actual receipts average £700 a year, including valuable transferable appointments. No opposition within five miles. Working expenses light. Railway station within one mile. Patients middle and upper class. Excellent house, with large gardens and paddocks at a moderate rent. To a gentleman . . . accustomed to good society, the practice presents an unusually safe investment, with pleasant occupation.

This appeared in Dr Langley's List of Selected Partnerships and Practices in the *British Medical Journal Advertiser*.

Obituaries in the medical press confirm the growing importance of the GP and his family in rural society. One typical example was a report in *The Lancet* of the death of Dr Fox of Broughton, Hampshire. At one time he had been medical officer to three districts in three separate poor law unions, and through his death, *The Lancet* observed:

> The country gentlemen have lost a skilful practitioner, and one of the brightest ornaments of their society. The yeomen will mourn one whose wise counsel they often sought in matters medical and non-medical; while the poor will regret their friend, philosopher, and guide, whose genial smile and timely pleasantry robbed sickness of half its terrors.[13]

The wives and daughters of these men shared in their upward social mobility, although, as was shown by the experiences of Molly Gibson in *Wives and Daughters* and of Mary Thorne, niece of Dr Thorne in Trollope's novel of that name, gentry families still had reservations about their sons marrying into medical households.[14] Even at the end of the century, doctors' daughters rarely married into the aristocracy.[15]

Nevertheless, a few doctor's wives began to make a mark on their own account. One such was Mrs Milner, whose husband had a practice in Shipdham, Norfolk, and who was elected to the parish council in the 1890s. Once there she took a leading role in the provision of allotments for villagers, as well as in registering footpaths and common land, acquiring additional burial ground and reorganizing the local coal charity, of which she became a trustee. She was also concerned at the fire hazard offered by thatched cottages and persuaded the parish council to purchase a fire engine. Unfortunately, her energy was not appreciated by the ratepayers. In particular, her involvement with the coal charity proved unpopular, with disputes over its administration soon occurring. When fresh council elections were held later in the decade, only thirty electors attended the parish meeting, and Mrs Milner tied for bottom place. The chairman gave his casting vote against her, and she was deposed.[16]

If growing numbers of doctors and lawyers were able to climb the social ladder, members of other professions, however, like chemists, veterinary surgeons, schoolmasters and nonconformist ministers were not so fortunate. Chemists were 'never able to escape the taint of retail trade', and it is notable that the 1,853 male and 111 female chemists and druggists recorded within rural areas in 1901 were included in the manufacturing section of the population census rather than among the 'professionals'.

Dissenting clergymen, too, were almost always categorized as belonging to the lower middle classes, along with clerks, tradespeople and small shopkeepers (the sections of society from whom they were largely recruited), rather than with the more prestigious professionals. Poor remuneration often reinforced their status problems. Even in 1879 about a third of all Wesleyan circuits were paying their ministers less than the prescribed minimum salary of £150 a year for married men and £80 for the unmarried. Six years earlier a Baptist Union official had estimated that the average salary received by men in the sect's English churches was about £75 a year; and in Wales it could be as little as £25 a year. For this reason, some men were driven out of the profession by their lack of means, and others had to take up additional occupations. At Ivinghoe, Buckinghamshire, one long-serving, locally born Baptist minister combined his office with employment as a registrar of births, deaths and marriages, while his wife and eldest daughter worked as milliners.[17]

Inevitably the worry of making ends meet in such households fell with particular force on wives. A Congregationalist minister's wife wrote to a denominational newspaper in 1895 complaining that she could not manage on her husband's annual income of £75: 'I feel sometimes heartbroken, and with the dreadful strain of pinching and saving, of having to do the family washing, sewing, housework with not a soul to help, I am so tired at night that I just sit down and nearly sob my heart out.'[18] Earlier in the century the position was still worse, particularly among the families of Primitive Methodist ministers. William Clowes and his wife received so little in their first pastorates that they dined 'when by ourselves on a little suet and potatoes, or a piece of bread and a drink of water'. Financial difficulties caused them to sell their only luxury – a feather bed – for 'it was a maxim with us . . . never to go into debt.'[19] Like other Methodist preachers, Mr Clowes spent much time travelling around his large circuit, and this added to the pressures on his wife. In the end Mrs Clowes died whilst he was away at the farthest end of the circuit, and he admitted that her death had been hastened by the stress of their repeated separations.[20]

Such women were expected to help their husbands in their pastoral work, visiting members of the congregation, distributing charity, organizing meetings and the like. Small wonder that a contemporary suggested that a minister's wife must not possess 'a woman's wants and weaknesses', but be 'an angel with an angel's energies and excellencies'. For this reason, too, ministers were encouraged to marry within their own denomination.[21]

Although chapels were often located in villages, particularly those associated with the Primitive Methodists and Baptists, the main body of nonconformist ministers resided in towns.[22] In *Felix Holt*, George Eliot described one such man, Mr Lyon, who lived with his daughter in a small house 'not quite so good as the parish clerk's'. Needless to say, the more prosperous members of the congregation soon made him aware of his financial inferiority. So although 'tears were shed into best bonnets at his sermons', when he visited his flock in their homes, hostesses deemed 'the weaker tea . . . good enough for him'. His daughter, compelled to earn a living as a private teacher, was only too painfully aware that dissenters in general were looked down upon by those whom she regarded as 'the most refined classes'.[23]

Outside the pages of fiction these feelings of social uncertainty among ministers' families were common. Mary Thompson, the daughter of a Norwich stationer, was warned by her mother to take care to run her household efficiently, soon after she married a Methodist minister in 1837:

> You have often heard me say . . . that a good servant would never stop in a Methodist preacher's family for this reason – they have so much running about and their errands are so unjudicially planned . . . It is a common remark that Met. preachers wives are never good mistresses because they dont know how to manage them nor their work, dont let this be said of my dear Mary.[24]

A little earlier she had stressed the need for her daughter to employ a full-time maid. Clearly she feared that, like many other ministers' wives, Mary might be tempted to economize by dispensing with that essential mark of middle-class respectability, a resident domestic servant.

Nevertheless, unlike the established church, nonconformity also offered a few women of determination and religious zeal the opportunity to act as preachers in their own right. At Fritwell, Oxfordshire, during October 1868, the Wesleyan chapel was crowded to excess when a Miss Ghostley preached for the first time. According to a male member of the congregation, except for 'some provincialisms in her pronunciation & some peculiarity of voice at the end of each clause she was very satisfactory indeed. Her sermon was very good & to the point.' He was unsure whether women ought to be allowed to assume such a role and on the whole concluded it 'would be better for them not to do so'.[25]

Another female Methodist preacher was Caroline Boileau, one of the unmarried daughters of the squire of Ketteringham in Norfolk. In 1872, three years after her father's death, she began journeying round the country with a Methodist minister. She led prayer meetings, preached to holiday-makers on the beach and ministered to the dying and the drunken. In June 1873, she returned to Ketteringham and held a great evangelistic gathering in the village hall, attended by about 250 people from the surrounding area. But soon the strain proved too great and in 1877 she died, at the early age of forty-eight.

She was buried in her home parish to the accompaniment of a hymn of her own composing.[26]

A third female preacher, this time with the Primitive Methodists, was Elizabeth Bultitude, who began her thirty-year career as a travelling minister in 1832 in Norfolk and ended it at Faringdon in Berkshire. According to an historian of Primitive Methodism, during those thirty years she only missed two appointments, both because of bad weather, and often preached five or six times a week, as well as on the Sabbath. 'Female travelling preachers required to be extremely circumspect, and even in her later years Elizabeth Bultitude would not allow any man to speak to her in chapel in her own pew: she would request him to go into the next seat.'[27]

At a time when the female religious role was regarded as essentially subordinate and derivative, preachers like Miss Bultitude showed what could be achieved by women of perseverance and determination. Yet it must be stressed that they were always a tiny minority even among Primitive Methodists. The Bible Christians, another small group, made rather more use of them, with about seventy-one female itinerant preachers listed between 1819 and 1861 in the connection's Conference *Minutes*. But by 1860 only five were still active, and twelve years later this had declined to one.[28]

So, for the most part, women in the nonconformist churches, like their Anglican sisters, found themselves confined to Sunday school teaching, missionary collecting, organizing entertainments and similar matters: '[they] played a larger role in Primitive Methodism than in the parish church', writes James Obelkevich, 'but it was still recognizably a "women's" role, extended from the home to a new setting'.[29] The prestigious offices of local preacher and society steward were almost always held by men.

Unlike the socially ambiguous status of nonconformist ministers, the standing of Anglican clergy and their families was never in doubt. By tradition they were associated with the elite of rural society, even though the income they commanded and the style in which they lived varied considerably from parish to parish.[30]

In communities where there was no resident squire, or where landownership was too widely dispersed to permit of one man exercising a predominant influence, the Anglican clergyman and his wife or daughter usually took the lead in village affairs. Many clerics were also landowners in their own right, as well as being justices of the peace. Others were the younger sons of landed families, who, whilst not inheriting property themselves, were yet presented to a remunerative benefice by relatives or friends possessing powers of patronage. This was true of the Rev. Charles Thomas Moore, rector of Appleby Magna, Leicestershire, from 1877 to 1922, whose brother was the local squire. Three years after his presentation to the living, Charles married Mabel Byron, daughter of the Hon. Augustus Byron, rector of nearby Kirkby Mallory. According to their son, it was Mrs Moore who was the real 'tower of strength. She did a large amount of the parish work, chose the hymns etc., and conferred with the organist . . . as to the Church music in general as father was not musical.'[31] To carry out the domestic duties of the Moore household, she kept a resident indoor staff of four.

Another comfortably placed clerical household was that of George Sumner, son of the Bishop of Winchester, who became rector of Old Alresford, Hampshire, in 1851. Both he and his wife were well-to-do and by the early 1860s employed a French governess and five maids, as well as a footman, to look after themselves and their three children.[32] Within the rectory, life followed an orderly routine. The family breakfasted at 8 a.m. each day and followed this with prayers for themselves and the servants. Dinner was at 3 p.m. or a little earlier, and the rector and his wife then spent the afternoon visiting cottage families until 5 p.m. or 6 p.m.[33] Mrs Sumner, as befitted her secure financial position, undertook no domestic duties herself.[34]

Charles Kingsley and his wife, Fanny, enjoyed similar standards at their Eversley parsonage, also in Hampshire. Fanny was the youngest daughter of a Cornish tin magnate and former MP, and only married Kingsley after overcoming bitter family opposition. The wedding took place early in 1844, shortly before Kingsley was offered the Eversley living, but by the middle of the nineteenth century they, too, had five resident maids, plus a stable boy, to look after themselves, their two small children and a sixteen-year-old pupil, John Martineau, whom Kingsley was coaching. Even before the wedding, Charles had laid down a timetable which the couple should follow:

Let us rise at 6.0 and have family prayers at 7.30. We will breakfast at 8. From 8.30 to 10.0 must be given to household matters, and from 10.0 to 1.0 we will study divinity together, having our doors open for *poor* parish visitants. At 1.0 I must go out in all weathers and visit the sick and poor and teach in the school. . . . We will dine at 5.0 and then draw and feed our intellect and fancy all evening . . . Then family prayers and bed at 11.0.

Fanny accepted this programme submissively, managing the household with quiet efficiency, although she was unable to abandon the attitudes of her wealthy background and remained 'a very *grand* lady' to the end of her days, according to her family. This did not preclude her taking a practical interest in the welfare of her husband's pupil, who remained with them from January 1850 to June 1851.[35]

Where families were larger or incomes smaller, however, clergy wives and daughters had to adopt a far more stringent regime. William Henry Whitworth, who married in 1836 and then held a series of ill-paid curacies, including one which yielded £80 a year only, was never able to afford to keep more than one servant. As a consequence Mrs Whitworth 'wore herself to the bone' in trying to make ends meet, and died from tuberculosis in 1876.[36] Again, Harriet Tyrwitt-Drake, wife of the vicar of Great Gaddesden, near Hemel Hempstead, soon found herself short of money after her marriage in 1872. She lost her first baby at the age of one in 1874; early in 1876, already pregnant with her third child and ill, she referred despairingly to the doctor's insistence that they have more heating in the vicarage: 'It is an expense we cannot afford, and if done, it must be left unpaid for, and we are unable to pay for other things.'[37] Her baby was born a month later, but by December 1876 she was pregnant for the fourth time. Once again, she became ill, but on this occasion her husband's mother came to the rescue by giving the family a much-needed break in Eastbourne during the following May: 'we were only too thankful to accept her kindness', wrote Harriet in her diary, 'as otherwise we could not have afforded going to the sea.'[38]

A number of wives acted as teachers of their own children, at least until they were old enough to go away to school or until a governess could be afforded. One such hard-pressed mother was Georgiana Thompson, whose husband was incumbent of Aldeburgh in Suffolk. As one of her daughters recalled, they had a large family, with 'four boys and girls living before the eldest boy was fourteen'. Often the

Thompson daughters relied on gifts of second-hand clothing sent by an aunt for their wardrobe. And their mother engaged in a formidable programme of baking, jam-making, sewing and darning in order to keep her household fed and cared for. 'Her work in the parish was considerable; almost every afternoon she was out visiting houses.'[39] Yet, despite these efforts, poverty 'continued to knock at the vicarage door' and led to even greater economies. After eighteen years' service, the nanny was dispensed with, along with a laundrymaid, who had served the family for twelve years. The washing had now to be done more cheaply, despite the fact that Mrs Thompson was catering not only for her family but for paying guests as well. These were taken to provide an additional income, and included boys from the schools where her sons were educated, as well as summer holiday visitors. Even the family's pet pigeons were sacrificed in order to save the cost of the corn used to feed them.[40]

In the last quarter of the nineteenth century many of the smaller clerical livings faced particular difficulties as a result of the collapse of grain prices during the years of agricultural 'depression'. Not only were tithe rent-charge incomes undermined, since these were calculated on the basis of corn prices, but it was often difficult to secure tenants where glebe land had to be let. By 1887 more than a third of the 13,000 beneficed clergy in England were receiving stipends of less than £200 a year. It was at this time that the custom of an Easter offering, as a gift to the parson, spread rapidly in country parishes.[41]

In these circumstances, some clergy wives followed Mrs Thompson's example and supplemented their husband's income with ventures of their own. In *Hodge and His Masters*, Richard Jefferies described a parson's wife who took up poultry-keeping, market gardening, and beekeeping, admittedly without much success, in order to earn a little cash. She even tried to turn her 'accomplishments' to commercial account by undertaking 'difficult needlework of various kinds, in answer to advertisements which promised ample remuneration for a few hours' labour. Fifteen hours' hard work she found was worth just threepence, and the materials cost one shilling; consequently she laboriously worked herself poorer by ninepence.'[42]

But those under greatest strain were impecunious clergy families living in rural Wales. From the mid-1880s to the early 1890s a powerful anti-tithe movement developed in the principality, as

farmers, hit by agricultural depression and mostly nonconformist by
religion, refused to pay to support what they deemed an alien church.
In such parishes, servants had to be dismissed, household furnishings
and fittings sold to pay debts to local shopkeepers, and 'wives and
children . . . sickened from sheer want of food'.[43] The isolation of
these small Welsh communities added to their distress, since it made
contact with clerical neighbours difficult. Often families saw scarcely
anyone other than those who had been induced to join in the anti-
tithe agitation of which they were the victims, and their self-respect
was wounded by the debts incurred at village shops. Occasionally
events took an uglier turn, with effigies of unpopular clergymen
burned by hostile mobs of farmers, or acts of vandalism committed
against church or parsonage.[44] Families shrank in upon themselves,
and the female members, in particular, experienced much unhappiness
as they spent their days in a drudging effort to make ends meet. Not
until the 1891 Tithe Rent Charge Recovery and Redemption Act
made landowners responsible for the payment of tithes did the
position ease.

But even without the special anxieties of late-Victorian Wales, life
on a small stipend in an isolated community could be a narrow and
depressing experience. Mary Paley, whose father was rector of Ufford
cum Bainton, Northamptonshire, remembered that when she and
her sister were in their teens even illness in the village was 'hailed
with satisfaction' as it gave them 'something to do. Now and then we
might be asked to an evening party or a dance, but my father
accompanied us and made a rule of carrying us off in the pony
carriage at nine o'clock, just when the fun was beginning.' (Indeed, so
strict were Mr Paley's religious views that he even confiscated their
dolls when they were children and burnt them, because he said the
little girls were 'making them into idols'.)[45]

Another sufferer from the loneliness of clergy families in the
remoter villages was Emma Gifford, later the first wife of the novelist
Thomas Hardy. In 1867 she came to live with her sister, Helen, at St
Juliot rectory in 'darkest north Cornwall'. Helen had recently married
the elderly Cadell Holder, incumbent of the parish, which yielded a
gross income of about £125 a year and had a population of 226.[46]
According to Emma, only her brother-in-law, her sister, the parish
clerk and herself took an active part in the Sunday services. Traditions
were deeply rooted and 'strange gossipings' and 'evil-speaking' the

order of the day. Newspapers seldom penetrated and, when they did, were usually 'thrown aside for local news'. New books rarely appeared, and 'seeing few strangers we all had a vivid interest in every one who came – a strange clergyman, . . . a school inspector, a stray missionary, or school-lecturer – all were welcome, even the dentist from Camelford who called regularly and . . . dined with us at our mid-day dinner'.[47] Emma spent much time riding along the cliff tops on her pony or helping her sister run the household, but she also engaged in parish visiting and played the harmonium in church on Sundays. Not surprisingly, her interest was aroused by the arrival in 1870 of the young assistant architect, Thomas Hardy, who was to carry out restoration work on the church.

Dissatisfaction with the limitations of rural life was expressed in still stronger terms by Mrs R. L. Ottley, wife of the rector of Winterbourne Bassett, Wiltshire, from 1897 to 1903. When she and her husband first arrived they had little idea of what to expect. Their notions of rural life had been gained chiefly from literary sources, like Crabbe, Wordsworth and Oliver Goldsmith's *Vicar of Wakefield*. The reality proved very different from their romantic imaginings:

> Great wide patches of unfenced land constitute our fields . . . After a day's rain, the whole place is transformed into a quagmire of whitey-grey, clogging, clinging mud, which is unconscionably slow a-drying. The use of a bicycle for four months of the year is out of the question and a drive is a luxury not to be contemplated. Thus it comes about that through the winter we never go out of the place, and often, for months together, we see no single face from the world outside. Our nearest visiting neighbour lives six miles from us over hilly roads . . . The doctor is ten miles away. We seldom see him . . .
>
> The village itself boasts of one shop . . . The remnant of the village consists of the labourers and milkers on the three farms, with their families. . . . The very sound of wheels is a surprise to us, and a ring at the door bell is as startling as a sudden thunderclap. . . . [I]n the dark, long winter evenings . . . we . . . read again and again, Dickens, Thackeray, Stevenson – books which transport us as it were, into a theatre bright with lights and teeming with life, where we can forget for the time being what and where we are. Our blessed books, what should we do or become without them?[48]

Not surprisingly, Mrs Ottley's relations with the parishioners were often strained. She complained, in particular, of their ingratitude. 'You may save a child's life, you may sit up with it, nurse it, nourish it slowly back to life, but you will not have touched a soft spot in the mother's heart.' The Ottleys were chronically short of cash, and the cost of running the large, straggling vicarage, with its stables, outhouses, greenhouse and gardens was a perpetual worry.[49] It was doubtless with much relief that they left their remote Wiltshire parish in 1903 for the lusher pastures of Oxford University.

Lower down the financial scale, the struggle for existence was even more acute, as the experience of the Brontë family at Haworth demonstrated. When the Rev. Patrick Brontë became perpetual curate of the high moorland parish in 1820, his stipend was £200 a year. For the rest of his life the living was a poor one, and by the late 1830s his three daughters were having to take temporary posts as governesses. When they were at home they carried out most of the domestic chores themselves, aided by an old servant, Tabitha. In December 1839, for example, whilst Anne was away working, Emily and Charlotte ran the household. 'I manage the ironing, and keep the rooms clean', Charlotte told her friend, Ellen Nussey:

> Emily does the baking, and attends to the kitchen. . . . I excited aunt's wrath very much by burning the clothes, the first time I attempted to iron; but I do better now. . . . I am much happier blackleading the stoves, making the beds, and sweeping the floors at home, than I should be living like a fine lady anywhere else . . .

She also confessed that she must suspend her subscriptions to charity because she had no money, and that she intended to force herself 'to take another situation when I can get one'.[50]

On a more prosaic level, the Scotts of Marksbury, Somerset, and later Chilton Foliat, Wiltshire, shared many of the Brontës' financial difficulties. Mr Scott had spent a quarter of a century in various poorly paid posts before he and his wife and five daughters settled in Somerset in the spring of 1885. The living was in the gift of the Leyborne-Popham family of Littlecote on the Berkshire/Wiltshire border, and it was through the influence of friends that Mr Scott secured the benefice. Unfortunately his stipend was only £250 a year, but at least it offered a secure base, which the family had hitherto lacked. At first they rejoiced in their good fortune. 'Now we have a prospect of a settled home after so many years of wandering', wrote the second daughter, Louisa, optimistically in her diary, '& . . . with economy & care we hope to make two ends meet.'

Unfortunately, that proved more difficult than she anticipated. In May 1887, Mr Scott even wrote to the Archbishop of Canterbury to protest against proposed legislation designed to alter the method of collecting tithes, since this would have reduced his income still further. In the event, the changes were not introduced, but in his letter he detailed his straitened circumstances. Out of £250 a year, including the rent of his glebe, he had to pay almost £17 in taxes, more than £29 in poor rates and £3 4s. to cover the school rate and the insurance of the rectory and chancel.[51] Happily, after six years the Leyborne-Pophams presented him to the more lucrative living of Chilton Foliat, which had a stipend of around £500 a year. There he remained until his death in January 1907.

Soon after the move, two of the daughters were married, and by the mid-1890s only Louisa and her youngest sister, Helena, were still at home. Throughout her youth, Louisa had learnt by bitter experience the need to economize and to make do and mend. In the more relaxed surroundings of Chilton Foliat those habits were hard to break. Surviving accounts also show that her personal income remained small. She appears to have received an annual allowance of £20 from her parents and to have supplemented this with a small dividend income, occasional birthday and Christmas gifts from wealthier relatives, and earnings from carrying out odd jobs for her parents and sister.[52] Despite the large size of Chilton rectory, the family often had only one servant, and sometimes none at all. Inevitably the girls and their mother had to carry out most of the household chores. On 19 August 1899, Louisa ruefully commented that because they were reduced to two charwomen, her mother was having to rise at 5 a.m. each day to 'open windows etc.' while she herself was getting in practice to 'become a skilled parlourmaid'.

Like other clergy daughters, Louisa played an active part in parish affairs, organizing concerts and charities, teaching at the Sunday school, and helping her father with routine administration. On 29 July 1897, the Cottage Garden Show was held: 'A most successful day . . . I gave away the prizes. The sports were most entertaining and I enjoyed myself immensely . . . Mother & I judged the bread, boiled potatoes and wild flowers. All the children who picked bunches got 2d. each.' Later, on 13 December in the same year, she distributed funds from the parish savings club, '2½d. in the 1/– interest', and went to read to a sick villager. On 14 January 1902, she went to a neighbouring hamlet to see about confirmation classes. 'I also interviewed half the village maidens and later the boys in the Church Room'. She then added sourly: 'I do not love the Proletariat.'

Other clergy daughters shared her reservations about parish work. 'Another Sunday has come & no school to my joy', noted Caroline Smith, daughter of the rector of West Stafford, Dorset, in September 1881.[53] Sunday school instruction was a regular Sabbath ritual for most female members of parsonage households in the second half of the nineteenth century.

Far more to Caroline's taste were tennis parties, musical evenings, balls in Dorchester Corn Exchange and the like. Louisa Scott shared her preferences, paying visits to neighbouring clergy and gentry households and spending holidays with relatives in London, Oxford, Somerset and Denmark. However, by the mid-1890s, at the age of thirty-three she was beginning to feel 'too old for dancing'. The principal opportunity she had to demonstrate her independence was through her hobby of cycling. Apart from the pleasure it bestowed, this had another, even more important, influence on her life. For it was an enthusiasm shared by her future husband, Philip Yorke, squire of Erddig in Denbigh. Her marriage to Yorke in the spring of 1902, when she was almost forty, and her consequent elevation into the ranks of the landed gentry was a fate aspired to by many impecunious clergy daughters, although few achieved it.[54] Most, if they married at all, found a partner in the ranks of the clergy, or, as with two of Louisa's sisters, among members of the medical and legal professions.

As Louisa Scott's experiences demonstrate, a clergyman's wife or daughter was expected to do more than care for home and family. Like her counterpart in the country house she was expected to assume the role of a 'Lady Bountiful'. This meant taking part in various parish duties, such as visiting the poor, organizing the distribution of charity, holding mothers' meetings and ensuring that food was sent from the parsonage kitchen to the sick and needy. Mabel Moore at Appleby Magna provided a weekly supply of soup

A SAVING CLAUSE.

The Vicar's Daughter. "GOOD MORNING, MRS. TAYLOR. IT'S A LONG TIME SINCE I SAW YOU AT CHURCH! YOU REALLY OUGHT TO ATTEND MORE REGULARLY!"

Mrs. T. (guiltily). "YES, YES, MISS. IT *IS* A LONG TIME SINCE I WAS AT CHURCH! BUT"—*(cheerfully)*—"I *NEVER* GOES TO CHAPEL!"

PLATE 10 *Checking up on the church attendance of their father's flock was a task often undertaken by female members of the vicar's family.*

(Punch, 1885)

for the poor and aged, who came to the rectory door with cans to collect it. She visited all the mothers with newly born babies, taking with her a gift for mother and child, and occasionally she helped the village midwife with a confinement. She attended christenings and, according to her son, was, as a result, godmother to about half the parish.[55]

Mary Gladstone, too, after her marriage to the Hawarden curate Harry Drew early in 1886, distanced herself from the political circle of her prime minister father, William Gladstone, and became involved in parish activities. A typical diary entry, for 5 March 1888, reads: 'Sandycroft at 3, reading at Mothers' Meeting & from there to the

THE BUMP OF LOCALITY.

Vicar's Daughter (meeting one of her class). "WELL, JANE, I HEAR YOU'VE JUST BEEN TO LONDON. YOUR FIRST VISIT, WASN'T IT?"

Jane. "YES, MISS."

Vicar's Daughter. "AND WHERE DID YOU STAY?"

Jane. "AT MY SISTER'S, MISS."

Vicar's Daughter. "AND WHAT PART OF LONDON IS THAT?"

Jane. "NEXT DOOR TO THE DOCTOR'S, MISS!"

PLATE 11   *Vicar's daughter and a member of her Sunday school class.*

(Punch, 1905)

PLATE 12 *Pitstone branch of the Mothers' Union meeting, c.1900. The Mothers'*
Union was first established by Mary Sumner, wife of the rector of Old
Alresford, Hampshire, in 1876. It was concerned to promote Christian virtues
among the nation's mothers.

(Pitstone, Bucks., Local History Museum)

school for our first Children's work party . . . Such a lot of children –
all so happy, industrious & delighted & the helpers so good & kind
& able.'[56] Sunday school teaching, the organizing of a local flower
show, and parish visiting were other regular features of her pastoral
routine.

There were also disappointments, when parishioners failed to
support the church in the way expected. 'Greatly grieved lately by
the falling back into drinking of many who had taken the teetotal
pledge', wrote Harriet Tyrwitt-Drake at Great Gaddesden, in her
diary. 'The hay season has caused so many to fall back into their old
evil ways.'[57] Again, in November, 1875, she had expected to begin a
class for men and boys: 'I was all ready, notice had been given in
Church and I quite expected a good number, but to my greatest
disappointment *not one came*.'[58]

Some women, like Mrs Sarah Joyce, wife of the vicar of Dorking,

Kent, took an interest in the education of the girls of the parish. Early in the 1840s she organized a Girls' Friend Society to encourage parents to keep their daughters at school to the age of fourteen.[59] In other cases, as with Mrs Palmer, wife of the rector of Mixbury, Oxfordshire, instruction was given to the girls attending the village day school in needlework and knitting, and sometimes in other subjects, too. Mrs Palmer also provided female pupils with pinafores, dresses and bonnets.[60] Elsewhere the Sunday school movement was linked to the temperance cause by enthusiastic clergy families. At Ilmington, Warwickshire, the rector's eldest daughter started a temperance movement for young people by hiring a room and selling soft drinks.[61]

One of the keenest supporters of the educational cause within country districts was, however, Mary Simpson in the East Riding of Yorkshire. She opened evening classes and Sunday Bible classes for ploughboys working in her father's scattered parish of Boynton and Carnaby with Fraisthorpe. On visits to the local farms she had discovered that many of the ten or a dozen young men employed on each of them could neither read nor write, and had little to do during their leisure hours. It was to meet this need and to arouse their interest in religion that she embarked upon her programme. Often she walked to the fields where the youths were at work in order to make contact with potential pupils, and would keep pace 'alongside the different ploughs and harrows, trying all I can by exhortations (which from being so heartfelt, seem to make some impression) to induce them to come on Sunday and hear some of the Bible read and explained'.[62] Frequently she stood at the gate of a field, trying to summon up courage to aproach one of the lads; at other times she was unable to eat her breakfast on Sunday mornings because of nervousness about teaching in the school later in the day. Yet, despite this, she readily admitted that her evening class had become 'and I hope and pray may continue to be, the one absorbing interest in my life'.[63] She subsequently established a village library, and formed friendships with several of the young men which lasted long after they had left the district. The scheme only ended with her father's death at the end of the 1860s. She and two of her sisters then moved to Leicestershire, and there she died in 1884 at the age of sixty-four.[64]

The wife and daughters of William Marsh, the Evangelical rector of

St Peter's, Colchester, from the 1820s likewise found an outlet for their energy and piety in good works. Not only did they teach at the Sunday schools, which were held in a converted carriage house next to the rectory (the family having given up keeping a carriage to save money for charity), but they 'counselled the poor, distributed soup from the kitchen, provided refreshment between services on Sunday for parishioners who came from afar in the laundry place behind the house, and "heartily aided" husband and father in the Bible, Missionary, Conversion of the Jews, Prayer Book, Homily, Religious Trust, Anti-Slavery Societies and other endeavours, often leading separate ladies' committees'.[65] 'Working parties' were arranged for the young ladies of the parish, and religious instruction provided for the servants. Mrs Marsh would pray individually with any of them who had been found guilty of wrongdoing.

Mary Sumner at Old Alresford was even more ambitious. Not content with organizing classes, meetings, choir practices, parties, concerts and theatrical performances, in the late 1870s she went on to found what became the Mothers' Union.[66] It started when Mary invited thirty or forty village women to attend a meeting at the rectory in 1876. Simple cards were prepared, which the women signed, promising to train their children for a life of Christian service. For the next nine years, the organization remained purely parochial, until in 1885 the Church Congress was held at Portsmouth. Mrs Sumner was asked to give an address on her Mothers' Union gatherings at Old Alresford, and in it she called on mothers to raise the nation's moral standards. Within two days, the movement had won the support of the Bishop of Winchester and his wife, and had developed into a diocesan society, with Mary as president. Soon support was coming from outside the boundaries of the Winchester diocese as well, with seventeen other dioceses joining in by November 1887.[67] Tracts were issued on the training of children and on practical household problems, such as the importance of purchasing warm clothing and the need for high standards of hygiene in the home. A quarterly journal appeared in 1888, and by the end of 1896 was claiming a circulation of 60,000. Not only did it detail branch meetings, many of which combined religious services or addresses with a tea, but it gave advice on a variety of issues – including the avoidance of debt.[68]

PLATE 13 *From parsonage to country mansion. Louisa Yorke (née Scott) shortly after her marriage to Philip Yorke, squire of Erddig, near Wrexham, in 1902. Her father was rector of Chilton Foliat, Wiltshire.*

(Clwyd Record Office)

Although the tone was often uncomfortably patronizing and always carried an 'improving' moral message, it was the first attempt to recruit working women into a nationwide social organization. It also gave them an opportunity to meet together to discuss their problems and to enjoy a friendly gossip. Later the idea was to be extended and developed in a different way with the Women's Institutes established during the First World War and after. At the same time the *Mothers' Union Journal* offered a means by which branches could keep in touch with one another and could also learn what was going on in other parts of the country. By the 1890s the organization was even setting up branches overseas.[69]

Throughout the early years, the Winchester diocese retained its predominance within the Mothers' Union in terms of numbers and strength of organization.[70] By 1912, national membership had reached 278,500, nearly all recruited from working-class mothers. Mary herself, meanwhile, continued to take an active interest in union affairs almost until her death in 1921, at the age of ninety-two. In her later years she was particularly involved in campaigns to uphold the sanctity of marriage and to resist an easing of the divorce laws, arguing that divorce had already undermined 'many of the homes of England' and was 'contrary to the Divine Law'.[71] But this proved a cause where her efforts were unavailing.

Most clergymen's wives and daughters, however, operated on a far more limited scale than Mary Sumner, although many – like Harriet Tyrwitt-Drake – devoted much time to developing the Mothers' Union in their own area.[72] Others followed a routine like that at Juniper Hill, Oxfordshire (the community on which Flora Thompson's fictional *Lark Rise* was based). In the 1880s Flora remembered the rector's daughter providing baby clothes for new-born infants, to save mothers the cost of having to supply them. They were 'made, kept in repair, and lent for every confinement', and were sent out, when requested, in a box which contained gifts of sugar, tea and patent groats for gruel. She also tried to obtain suitable places for cottagers' daughters wishing to enter domestic service, advertising in the *Morning Post* or the *Church Times* when necessary. And when she died in 1923, Grace Harrison (to give her her real name) bequeathed £100 to the parish, the income from which was to be used 'for the benefit of six of the oldest and most deserving poor'. Her emotional links with the area clearly remained strong, even though her father had ceased to be rector more than a quarter of a century before. She is commemorated by a brass plate in the parish church.[73] Yet, despite the many kindnesses she showed during her father's incumbency, she was not popular among cottage wives.[74]

Flora attributed this latent hostility to the fact that the women subconsciously resented the contrast between her lot and their own. 'Her neat little figure, well corseted in; her clear, high-pitched voice, good clothes, and faint scent of lily-of-the-valley perfume put them, in their workaday garb and all blowsed from their cooking or water-fetching, at a disadvantage.'[75] Their ambivalence towards someone whom they recognized as coming from a different social background from their own was shared by villagers elsewhere. Sometimes this was because, as members of the parish 'elite', clergy wives and daughters insisted that they should be treated with subservience by 'their' parishioners. Joseph Arch, who, as a nonconformist local preacher and agricultural trade union leader, was an admittedly hostile witness, nevertheless recalled the ill-feeling engendered in his home parish of Barford:

> I can . . . remember the time when the parson's wife used to sit in state in her pew in the chancel, and the poor women used to walk up the church and make a curtsey to her before taking the seats set apart for them. They were taught in this way that they had to pay homage and respect to those 'put in authority over them,' and made to understand that they must 'honour the powers that be,' as represented in the rector's wife. You may be pretty certain that many of these women did not relish the curtsey-scraping and other humiliations they had to put up with, but they were afraid to speak out. They had their families to think of, children to feed and clothe somehow; and when so many could not earn a living wage, . . . why, the wives and mothers learned to take thankfully whatever was doled out to them at the parsonage . . . and drop the curtsey expected of them, without making a wry face.[76]

Even at the end of the Victorian era, 'Michael Home' recalled the gulf which existed in his village of Great Hockham, Norfolk, between the well-to-do parson and his flock. To 'Home', the private life of the Hall and the vicarage was as far removed from our own as that of Her Majesty . . . when we passed the Vicarage and saw tennis-parties in progress on the courts, . . . or . . . saw the traps or dog-carts and their smart coachmen arriving for some call or garden-party, we even felt in some vague way that the village was being honoured by such things.[77]

Inevitably the vicarage family appeared remote, with the vicar's wife regarded as 'a terrifying figure and very much of a *grande dame*' by the youthful 'Home'. 'Never do I remember to have seen her smile . . . when I met her I could do no more for the life of me than scrape off my cap and mumble a something which I trust she took for a greeting.'[78]

This social separation applied equally to the children, for the sons and daughters of the clergy rarely mixed with the offspring of cottagers on terms of equality. Phyllis Bottome, whose father was, in the 1880s, successively incumbent of Great Fawley in Berkshire and Over Stowey in Somerset, recalled that she and her sisters and brother were allowed to play only with the children of the respective squires of these two parishes. Phyllis secretly befriended one of the village children, a little girl named Hannah, whom she met behind the tombstones in the churchyard. Hannah warned her friend not to tell anyone that they were playing together, 'or they'll stop we sure-lye'. Somehow the truth about their meetings leaked out, and Phyllis was promptly forbidden to have any contact with her new playmate.[79]

Yet, whilst such social strains existed, as Joseph Arch's reminiscences underline, the charitable aid dispensed by clergy families was welcomed in most labouring households. Equally, the majority of parsonage wives and daughters felt it their duty to give such assistance as they could. Even Mrs Ottley, at Winterbourne Bassett, although disillusioned with clerical life in a remote rural community, still felt obliged to give help. On her parochial rounds she dispensed castor oil and other medicaments, and when a new baby was born she was quickly informed, 'as I am regarded as the natural purveyor of "puddens" and "sops" . . . and of tiny garments, too'.[80] Yet, given the superior air with which she seems to have dispensed much of this help, it is not surprising that she should complain of the lack of trust and affection with which parishioners regarded her.

In the matter of education, clergy daughters normally relied for instruction upon their mother or an older sister, or a governess. At Ufford cum Bainton, Mary Paley and her sister had a German governess from 1859 until 1863, when Mary was thirteen. History lessons consisted chiefly of learning dates, and geography of the names of towns and rivers. But they were taught French and German thoroughly and the family spoke German at meals. 'Science we learnt from *The Child's Guide to Knowledge* and *Brewer's Guide* ... We did a little Latin and even Hebrew with my father and some Euclid ... On Sundays we learnt the church catechism, collects, hymns and Cowper's poems.'[81] However, many girls, like Mary herself, developed their own intellectual interests. Brought up in households where books were readily available and highly valued, and where, often enough, brothers were attending public school or university, they were anxious to raise their educational standards, too.

Emily Davies, who went on to found Girton College, Cambridge, and was a major pioneer in the promotion of women's education, was the daughter of a clergyman and schoolmaster who became rector of Gateshead. Although chiefly instructed by her mother and older sister, she began to learn Latin for pleasure, 'because the boys were doing it', and also wrote what she called 'Themes, i.e. bits of English composition, once a week'. These were 'looked over by my father'. However, she bitterly resented the fact that unlike her brothers, she had to pick up an education at home as best she could:

> Probably only women who have laboured under it can understand the weight of discouragement produced by being perpetually told that, as women, nothing much is ever to be expected of them, and it is not worth their while to exert themselves ... that whatever they do they must not interest themselves except in a second-hand and shallow way, in the pursuits of men, for in such pursuits they must always expect to fail.[82]

It was a desire to change this situation which led to her efforts to promote girls' higher education and to press for recognition of the intellectual equality of men and women.

Mary Paley was more fortunate than Emily Davies in that when, at the age of nineteen, she began to study for the newly established

Cambridge Higher Local Examination for women, her father acted as tutor. Her former governess, who had married a local farmer, also coached her in French and German.[83] Despite this help, she failed in 1870 and 1871, although in the latter year, on the strength of a distinction in Divinity and German, she was offered a scholarship to the newly opened Newnham College, Cambridge. Mary was one of Newnham's first five students, entering in October 1871. In 1874 she took the Tripos examination in Moral Economy with such success that two of the four examiners awarded her a first-class pass and two a second.[84] After returning home for a few months, she was invited to become a tutor in economics at Newnham. Subsequently she married Alfred Marshall, one of the leading economists of his day.[85]

Monica Bell, daughter of the vicar of Henley-in-Arden, Warwickshire, was able to develop her talents in another direction. At the end of the Victorian era she attended for what she called 'one blissfully happy year' at the Royal College of Music in London. At the end of this the College principal suggested that she could pursue a career as a professional accompanist. But her father refused to consider this, commenting coldly that 'Monica must not be allowed to go about London alone in hansom cabs.'[86] So she returned home and in 1903, to parental disapproval, married Orlando Wagner, whom her parents dismissively referred to as a 'penniless schoolmaster' and who had taught at a private school in Henley. Shortly afterwards the Wagners established a successful pre-preparatory school for boys, with Monica as chief organizer and music teacher.

Another diligent seeker after knowledge, although this time within her own family circle, was Emily Shore, the eldest child of an unbeneficed Bedfordshire cleric. Emily was born in 1819, and in 1832 she and her family moved to Woodbury. Within a few years the household included not only her father, mother, four brothers and sisters and several servants, but a number of young male pupils whom Thomas Shore instructed in order to supplement his income as a part-time curate for a neighbouring rector.[87] Emily herself received an education which, in those days, would have been considered more appropriate for a boy than a girl. On 21 January 1833, when aged almost fourteen, she described the strenuous daily routine:

I rise as soon as I can wake, which is usually . . . [at] half-past seven, and employ myself in doing my Greek and Latin, and learning whatever I have to get by heart. After breakfast I feed the birds with bread-crumbs, and from about that time till twelve o'clock I am usually employed in teaching the children [her brothers and sisters], and in some of my own lessons. At twelve we go out till dinner; after dinner I amuse myself for half an hour; then I read to mamma, and do my needlework; then we go out again for about an hour and a half; then I and Richard [her brother] finish our Greek or Latin for papa, and I read Fuseli's *Lectures* to mamma. This employs me till tea, after which I and R. do our lesson with papa, and then we amuse ourselves till bedtime.[88]

She supplemented this formal instruction with a formidable programme of self-education in natural history, architecture and a study of the development of manufacturing industry – this last an interesting choice for a country clergyman's daughter at a time when Britain was establishing itself as the 'workshop of the world'.[89] As well as teaching Greek, arithmetic, geography and history to younger members of the family, she accompanied her mother on afternoon calls, visited the poor, and taught in Sunday school. However, her prodigious energy and talent were tragically cut short by the onset of tuberculosis, and she died in July 1839.

Emily was able to develop her academic interests by studying at home. But for many daughters of impecunious clergy families, financial pressures were such that they had to seek outside employment. Often this meant a post as governess or companion, which in theory did not involve a loss of social caste. But at a time when idleness was the mark of middle-class female respectability, the fact that they were earning a living of any kind inevitably undermined their standing in society. In December 1848, the *Quarterly Review* defined the governess as 'a being who is our equal in birth, manners, and education, but our inferior in worldly wealth. . . . There is no other class which so cruelly requires its members to be, in birth, mind, and manners, above their station, in order to fit them for their station.'[90] The *Christian Lady's Magazine* likewise referred to the sad fate of clergymen's daughters 'driven to the situation of governess'. So common had this apparently become that Tennyson in 'The

Northern Farmer – New Style' (1870) could claim: 'Parson's lass 'ant nowt, an' weänt a nowt when 'es dead, / Mun be a guvness, lad, or summut, and addle [earn] her bread.' In practice, many governesses were recruited from the daughters of businessmen, solicitors and medical men rather than of clerics, but a considerable number did come from the clergy's families, as advertisements in the press make clear.[91]

The uncertain social position occupied by the average governess has been summarized by Rita McWilliams-Tullberg, and most of her comments are equally applicable to paid lady companions as well:

> She was neither a guest nor a member of the family with whom she worked; by birth a lady, she was economically in the position of a servant. Rarely did she gain the respect of her employers, her pupils or even the lowest chambermaids, since all too often she was manifestly bad at her job. Her own education would have consisted, beyond learning to read and write, of the cultivation of 'accomplishments'. An ability to recite a few simple sentences of French, to sing, to embroider, to walk and dance gracefully and to ornament the drawing-room was all that was necessary for a girl who wished to capture a husband.[92]

Not until 1848, with the establishment of Queen's College in London, was there an attempt made to train girls professionally for a career as governess. The venture enjoyed the backing of the Governesses' Benevolent Institution, itself formed five years earlier to provide applicants with financial help during periods of unemployment and in old age. Queen's was an Anglican college and a year later a similar body, Bedford College, was created to cater for nonconformists. At Queen's, classes were provided in modern languages, theology, history and geography, natural philosophy and astronomy, principles and method of teaching, drawing and music.[93] By mixing academic instruction with 'accomplishments' it met a growing need among aspirant women teachers and governesses in the capital, but its provincial impact was small. Interestingly, of thirty-five entrants who came to the college in Michaelmas 1882, only two were the daughters of clergymen, compared to nine who came from medical families; many of the remainder were from a business or commercial background.[94] It is clear that even after these intiatives, the vast majority of governesses received no specialist instruction before they took up their posts, and most continued to offer only 'accomplishments'.

The 1851 Census of Population recorded 20,058 women and girls employed as governesses in England and Wales (of whom about 12 per cent were under the age of twenty). A decade later (and the last occasion when governesses were separately categorized in the census) numbers had risen to 24,770, of whom 13 per cent were under the age of twenty. It is, of course, impossible to estimate the proportion of these coming from a clerical background.

Without doubt, the most famous parsonage daughters to take up governessing were the Brontë sisters. Charlotte's first venture in that direction came in May 1839, when she went to instruct the children of John Benson Sidgwick, the owner of Stonegappe, a substantial property about a mile from Lothersdale in Yorkshire. Mr Sidgwick was the son of a wealthy cotton spinner and Charlotte was already slightly acquainted with his wife when she took up her post. However, she soon discovered that such connections had little meaning in their new relationship. On 8 June, she wrote to her sister Emily, complaining that her employer had made it painfully clear that she did not intend to 'know' her governess:

> she cares nothing about me, except to contrive how the greatest possible quantity of labour may be got out of me; and to that end she overwhelms me with oceans of needlework, yards of cambric to hem, muslin nightcaps to make, and, above all things, dolls to dress. . . . I see more clearly than I have ever done before that a private governess has no existence, is not considered as a living rational being, except as connected with the wearisome duties she has to fulfil.[95]

It was doubtless a relief both to herself and her employer when she left the post towards the end of July.

Charlotte's next appointment as governess came in March 1841, when she was engaged by Mr White, a Bradford merchant, and his family, who lived at Rawdon. Although she was happier with them than with the Sidgwicks, she disliked their snobbery and that of their 'nouveaux riches' acquaintances, and left the following Christmas.[96]

Meanwhile her youngest sister, Anne, had also embarked upon a career as a governess. In April 1839 she was engaged at £25 a year by the Inghams, an old landed family living at Blake Hall near Mirfield. She remained there for about nine months before being dismissed, to her great chagrin, because her charges had made so little progress.[97] Anne's second post as governess was taken up in March 1841, following an advertisement in the press. In this she suggested a salary of £50 a year and listed her qualifications as music, singing, drawing, French, Latin and German. Only two replies were received, and of these only one agreed to pay the sum she had requested. This was from the Robinson family of Thorpe Green Hall, near Little Ouseburn in north Yorkshire. They had three daughters and a son, ranging in age from fifteen to nine years, and it was to their household that Anne moved.

Although seemingly less prickly than her oldest sister, Anne, too, resented her employers' attitude. She soon discovered that not only was she ignored as a 'respectable, well-educated lady', but, like Charlotte, she was totally excluded from the inner life of the family and from that of their acquaintances.[98] Later she was to chronicle the humiliations and discomforts of the governess's life in her novel, *Agnes Grey*.

However, if most female members of clergy families who were forced to seek an independent career took up posts as companions or governesses, it must be remembered that for the vast majority there was no such necessity. Instead daughters continued to live at home until marriage, or else went to keep house for bachelor brothers who were also clergymen.[99] Once there, they assisted in parish affairs or busied themselves with charity. Perhaps, like Mrs Fenwick in Anthony Trollope's *The Vicar of Bullhampton*, they became 'knowing in blankets and corduroys, and coals and tea' and made themselves acquainted with every man and woman in the parish.[100] But always they had to remember that their role was a secondary and supportive one to that of the clergyman himself; they must in no way seek to usurp the authority which was properly his.[101]

5

Farming Families

Experience had long ago shown that cheese and butter were made of the best quality, and with the greatest economy, where the delicate processes of their manufacture, requiring above all the utmost cleanliness, were superintended early and late by a skilful mistress, who had the whole dairy, so to speak, under her own eye. It is notorious that very few wives of wealthy farmers are now either trained or disposed to undertake the incessant toil of dairy-management. . . . The same may be said of poultry-keeping and the production of eggs. Seeing that fowls now sell (1880) for above double what they fetched thirty or forty years ago, while the expense of breeding and fattening them has in no respect increased, it may well be asked why every farmer, with a capable wife, and a proper soil for the purpose, should not bestow far more care than he usually does on this most profitable accessory of agricultural industry. The reply must be that poultry-rearing, like cheese-making and butter-making, requires infinite pains and a study of details.

George C. Brodrick, *English Land and English Landlords* (Cassell, Petter, Galpin & Co., London, 1881).

Most accounts of nineteenth-century agriculture pay little attention to the contributions made by wives and daughters to the prosperity of farming. Nowhere is this clearer than in the reports of the royal commissions on agricultural depression which were published in the 1880s and 1890s.[1] Women were neglected as expert witnesses and their views were rarely canvassed by the assistant commissioners who toured the country to make the special district reports. Yet, in practice, the female role could be vital to the successful running of a holding. Not only did women manage the household and the domestic staff but, especially in pastoral counties, their work as butter- and cheesemakers and in caring for calves and poultry could be decisive in ensuring the profitability of the entire undertaking.

There were, of course, sharp regional differences in this female role. As the eastern counties turned increasingly to tillage, there was a decline in those aspects of farm work which had been, by tradition, female dominated. In such areas, especially on larger farms, wives and daughters became less partners in the family business than 'dependants'. Cornelius Stovin, a substantial tenant farmer in the Lincolnshire wolds during the mid-Victorian era, reflected this approach when he wrote approvingly in August 1871 of the 'loving meekness' of his wife's character:

> What discriminating guardian care she exercises over her family and household. . . . In society she professes all the elements of a true lady. Amongst the poor no haughtiness is shown but kindness and generosity. Amongst her friends unlimited hospitality. In the church no bitter prejudices or bigoted exclusiveness. The happiness of her home, neighbourhood and world at large is the main object of her life.[2]

In this catalogue of virtues no mention is made of her participation in the running of Mr Stovin's business, and his diary entries make clear that she played no such role.

In villages where there was no resident landowner and where the clergyman was unmarried or impoverished, the larger farmers' wives often took on some of the attributes of a 'Lady Bountiful'. This was true of Bowerchalke, Wiltshire, where Ellen Coombs, whose husband ran a major holding, assisted the bachelor vicar with fundraising for the church. She also organized collections in aid of Salisbury infirmary and ran a clothing club for poorer villagers.[3] A similar part was played at Crawley in Sussex by Mrs Robinson, whose husband farmed at the Manor House. Although herself the mother of ten children, she found time to set up schools in the village for the offspring of labouring families and to establish a training home for girls to fit them for domestic service.[4]

By contrast, on smaller farms, such as those in Wales and the dairying areas of Lancashire, Cheshire and Dorset, the time and

PLATE 14 *Outdoor milking at Felin Newydd, Cardiganshire, c.1900. This was one of the many tasks undertaken by farmers' wives and daughters on the small Welsh holdings.*

(National Museum of Wales [Welsh Folk Museum])

energy of wives and daughters were primarily devoted to the holding itself. 'The farm is a business in which a wife is of material service', wrote Richard Jefferies in the 1870s. 'The lower class of farmers usually marry quite as much or more for that reason than any others.'[5] George Eliot recognized this in her novel *Adam Bede*, when she wrote, regarding the redoubtable Mrs Poyser, that the 'woman who manages a dairy has a large share in making the rent, so she may well be allowed to have her opinion on stock and their "keep" – an exercise which strengthens her understanding so much that she finds herself able to give her husband advice on most other subjects'.[6] In the book it is Mrs Poyser rather than her husband who asks the squire's heir for new farm gates, and who boldly pronounces on the uncertainties of farming life:

> it's more than flesh and blood 'ull bear sometimes, to be toiling and striving, and up early and down late, and hardly sleeping a wink when you lie down for thinking as the cheese may swell, or

the cows may slip their calf, or the wheat may grow green again i'
the sheaf – and after all, at th' end o' the year, it's like as if you'd
been cooking a feast and had got the smell of it for your pains.[7]

An equally assertive fictional farmer's wife was Mrs Peggy Turnbull
in R. S. Surtees's *Ask Mama*. She attended the rent audit on Sir
Moses Mainchance's estate in place of her meek husband, whom she
considered not fit to be allowed away from home by himself. She
quickly rounded on her landlord, beating the table with her fist and
exclaiming at the top of her voice their need for a new barn. Sir
Moses fled, leaving the negotiations to his agent.[8] Yet it is clear that
Surtees disapproved of such determined action by a female. He
unflatteringly described Mrs Turnbull as 'a great masculine knock-
me-down woman, round as a sugar-barrel' and as a 'monster'.

Although Ethel Cramp, the wife of a grazier from Tur Langton,
Leicestershire, at the beginning of the twentieth century, was not
expected to negotiate with a landlord, since the family farm belonged
to her husband, she, too, displayed some of Mrs Turnbull's strength
and energy. According to her son, from the moment she rose in the
morning she issued orders far and wide:

> Domestic daily helpers and the family must be thrust into orbits
> that fitted her master plan for the day. From the kitchen
> command centre, messages would flow to the limits of house
> and farmyard. . . . Even salesmen whose call broke into morning
> routine were likely to receive sharp reproof. But knowing Mother
> and keen to take orders for cattle food, they suffered in silence.
> . . . Whenever we boys fell foul of Mother, the quickest way back
> to grace was to find a windfall of eggs. So in winter we scoured
> the barns and hay stacks, in summer the ditches, nettlebeds and
> woodpiles. Failing eggs, a rabbit would do.[9]

Even at the close of the Victorian era, when there was a growing
rejection of the idea of women engaging in manual labour of any
kind, wives and daughters continued to help on the smaller holdings.
Of Cardigan, it was said in the early twentieth century that no other
county in England and Wales used female labour so extensively on
the land: 'Girls in this county are trained to do farm-work from early
childhood . . . and by the time they have attained the age of fifteen
many of them are competent to perform all the lighter tasks that

generally fall to the lot of women on farms in this county.'[10] These included milking, butter- and cheesemaking, feeding calves, pigs and poultry, and cleaning the pens. 'On many farms . . . the women have entire charge of the cattle, including the cleaning of the cow-houses', the report declared. 'They also help, when required, in the field, and always assist in haymaking and corn harvesting.' Some Cardigan properties were run by the womenfolk, whilst the men went off to the South Wales coalfields, or to sea, or spent their time at markets and fairs buying and selling.[11]

At an individual level a similarly central role was played by Mrs Clifford, whose husband ran a small farm in north Oxfordshire. He had injured his hand severely in an accident, and until her son was old enough to help, it was she who carried out the milking. She also went into the fields to assist with drilling, binding, mowing and all the other tasks around the farm except ploughing. She could lift up sacks of corn weighing over two hundredweights, and her son remembered that sometimes 'she hadn't come in from milking at midnight.' Each week she took butter and eggs for sale to Banbury in two large baskets, walking to a point where she could get transport to take her into town. With her dairying skills, she was essential to the running of the farm. Prior to her marriage, she had also helped on her father's 200-acre holding, beginning to work with horses when she was only fifteen years of age, and learning to make butter and to cure bacon from the home-killed pigs which were slaughtered twice a year for the family table. She was one of thirteen children and had consequently to look after younger brothers and sisters as well.[12]

In pastoral areas, a woman's dairying skills were of major importance because of the higher price which well-prepared butter and cheese could command compared to those of less competent competitors. One such skilled producer was Alice Hawkins, whose husband farmed at Frampton, Dorset. In the late nineteenth century she built up a successful connection with Bournemouth, then a growing seaside resort, selling high quality Blue Vinney cheese, butter, eggs and pork. It was to his wife's abilities that Robert Hawkins owed his success, for Blue Vinney produced by lesser dairies secured a much lower price.[13] Even in Essex, a county not renowned for its dairying, Robert Bretnall, a farmer from Witham, revealed in his diary the contribution made by his wife's 'Cow Box' to the enterprise. Thus on 6 November 1847, he noted that during the previous year

PLATE 15   *Buttermaking at Brechfa, Carmarthenshire, c.1900.*
(National Museum of Wales [Welsh Folk Museum])

their two Alderney cows had yielded £50 6s. 6d., including the milk
and butter they had consumed at home. 'My wife took for her hard
labour in managing the two cows £5. 0. 0 and I received £45. 6. 6.
like all other lazy persons for doing nothing.'[14]

But the duties attached to dairying exacted a heavy physical toll.
One contemporary wrote of workers in Wiltshire, Dorset, Devon and
Somerset in the middle of the nineteenth century: 'Looking after,
cleaning or wiping cheeses weighing frequently a quarter of a cwt.,
and which have to be turned and moved from place to place, is work
that is occasionally followed by consequences to the health of women
employed in it which show that it is too severe.'[15] This view was
confirmed by a doctor from Calne, Wiltshire, who claimed that he
was often consulted by dairyworkers suffering from pains in the back
and limbs, 'overpowering sense of fatigue most painful in the
morning, want of appetite, feverishness, &c'.[16] Yet because cheese
sales were so important to a farm's success, the tasks could not be left
to underlings.

Half a century later, Arthur Wilson Fox was making similar
comments about the drudging toil carried out by the wives and
daughters of Scottish farmers who had migrated to low-rented

properties in the eastern counties when their English predecessors were bankrupted by agricultural depression. The Scotsmen sent their milk by train to London and relied almost exclusively on family labour to care for their livestock. According to Wilson Fox, the 'Scotch women' undertook work which no local girls would do. One man noted that his sister-in-law looked after the house, did the cooking, cared for his three children, and milked seven cows night and morning. 'I could not pay to have this work done', he admitted. Another pointed out that the daughters of Scottish farmers in north Suffolk not only milked the cows but sold the milk in the village, as well as feeding the cattle, cleaning roots, and doing 'any work however hard or rough'.[17]

'Wives and daughters', concluded Wilson Fox, 'prompted by affection or sheer necessity, may undertake labourers' work, but I believe that few women, who were free from either of these considerations, would deliberately choose it.' To another contemporary, the main fact was that the Scottish families came 'as strangers', and so their womenfolk had 'no social position to lose', unlike their East Anglian counterparts.[18] Many of the Scottish farmers were also extremely clannish, clinging together for purposes of marriage and friendship, and retaining their ties with their native land. Commercial travellers, known as Scottish 'Cuddies', came down from Scotland to sell clothing, blankets, oatmeal, cheese and even tea to the migrants, while a number of Scottish social customs survived. These included 'shows of presents' prior to a wedding, when a bride's family would entertain friends, serving shortbread and scones with the afternoon cup of tea.[19]

However, it was not only in farm work that wives contributed to the running of the family business. On many holdings they played an important part in marketing dairy produce and poultry to the end of the Victorian era, despite the emergence of specialist dealers. In the late 1860s, for example, farmers' wives in Westmorland, taking loads of poultry, butter and eggs to sell in nearby markets, were often intercepted by dealers from Manchester and other manufacturing towns in the area, and would dispose of the entire contents of their cart in roadside negotiations.[20] And a farmer's daughter from Wem, Shropshire, recalled women driving to Whitchurch market with baskets of farm butter and eggs as late as 1910. Some of these were sold direct to shops or private customers, but in other cases the wives took a stand in the market hall. Many travelled in from as far as twelve miles away and, in season, they also brought fruit, dressed poultry, vegetables and nuts.[21]

Another device, adopted by George Sturt's aunt, Susanna Smith, was for the wife or daughter to open a village shop to retail farm produce. Susanna sold butter, lard, bread, sides of bacon and milk from the parental farm, alongside other items, and thereby helped her father, and later her mother, to pay the rent.[22] Her mother, meanwhile, kept the accounts of both the farm and the shop.

Yet, despite female participation in these marketing activities, it is significant that when sales of livestock or grain were arranged, the farmer undertook those himself. Women were not considered capable of managing such important and prestigious transactions!

Elsewhere, particularly in the difficult years of agricultural depression from the mid-1870s to the late 1890s, when grain prices were slumping, some wives used their ingenuity to promote profitable sidelines to supplement family income. In south Lincolnshire in the 1890s the wife of one large farmer, who occupied several holdings, made a profit by arranging for the foremen's wives to rear chickens for her. In return, she paid them 6d. per bird and provided all the feeding stuff required. Another enterprising farmer's wife in the same area purchased about three thousand eggs a week from neighbouring farmers and cottagers. These she then sent away to market, gaining a profit of about £150 to £200 a year thereby.[23] In a further variation, farmers' wives at Wimboldsley, Cheshire, combined business with pleasure by organizing a special party to help prepare their geese for sale at Michaelmas and Christmas. Friends and neighbours were invited to the farm kitchen to lend a hand with plucking the forty or fifty birds laid out in advance. Then, as the work proceeded, the maids prepared a 'grand hot supper'.[24]

Mrs Flinton from Burgh-on-Bain, Lincolnshire, also remembered her mother selling eggs, butter, chickens and geese at Louth market early in the twentieth century. The geese were plucked in the wash-house, with the help of the waggoner, his boy and one of the village women. She also sold wild pigeons, which she enticed into the dovecote by keeping a large mirror inside. The birds stood in front of the mirror and began cooing; they would then settle down and soon started breeding.[25]

During the depression years it was usually the smaller farmers' wives who became involved in these commercial activities, in a desperate attempt to stave off financial disaster. In the mid-1890s Arthur Wilson Fox described the struggles of a woman from Badwell Ash to make ends meet by selling produce to private customers in London. This she despatched by train and post, but such hand-to-mouth arrangements precluded her building up any worthwhile connections. She also sold produce through a co-operative society until this, too, failed, and when Wilson Fox visited the family, they were about to vacate their semi-derelict 115-acre holding for a forty-acre farm.

> The wife seemed to think that it was a social disgrace to have to go to a farm of such a size. She had seen much better days, poor woman, and appeared to feel her position acutely. And it is no doubt hard for a man and woman possessed of some pride to be chiefly dependent on their relations for their food and clothes, notwithstanding they were leading a life of slavery.[26]

During the last quarter of the nineteenth century their plight was shared by many others. Richard Jefferies, whose own father was forced to give up farming because of financial difficulties, described in sympathetic terms the bitter fate of the farmer driven into bankruptcy: 'the descent is so slow . . . So far as his neighbours are concerned he is in public view for years previously . . . As he goes by they look after him, and perhaps audibly wonder how long he will last.' His humiliation was shared by his wife:

> She is conspicuously omitted from the social gatherings that occur from time to time. The neighbours' wives do not call; their well-dressed daughters, as they rattle by to the town in basket-carriage or dog-cart, look askance at the shabby figure walking slowly on the path beside the road. They criticize the shabby shawl; they sneer at the slow step which is the inevitable result of hard work, the cares of maternity, and of age. So they flaunt past with an odour of perfume, and leave the 'old lady' to plod unrecognized.[27]

Small wonder that in the face of these social sanctions Fanny Fieldsend, a farmer's daughter from Orford, Lincolnshire, should note anxiously in her diary on 31 October 1887 the speed with which local farms were being given up: 'we don't know who to hear of leaving next. How long will this agricultural depression last?'[28]

But most women were fortunate enough to avoid financial disaster. Instead they gained satisfaction and a degree of independence as a result of their hard work. In Wales, throughout the Victorian period, it was the custom for the proceeds of egg, milk and retail butter sales to be assigned to the wife. She arranged for their marketing and then used the cash to pay household bills. So widely accepted was the mistress's right to this income that husbands who surreptitiously raided the hen roost for their own benefit were accused of 'stealing eggs'.[29] In the border counties between England and Wales, where fruit growing was widespread, farm wives also took the proceeds of sales from the orchards for household use.[30] In such cases, wives were seen as having 'an equal share of work and management with husbands'.[31]

Women also contributed to farming through their savings before marriage or through the dowry they brought with them. In the Garstang area of Lancashire, during the 1890s many small dairy farms were occupied by ex-agricultural labourers who had been able to set up in business partly as a result of the savings – and the skills – of their wives, who were former dairymaids. One occupier of a 250-acre holding recalled that as a young man he had worked for his parents on their small farm. During this time he had received no wages and when, eventually, he announced his intention of marrying a servant from a neighbouring farmhouse, they told him bluntly that they had no money to set him up on his own. But, fortunately for him, when he told his prospective wife of this she announced that she had saved £200 out of her wages.[32]

The sense of partnership such events induced was underlined by another Lancashire couple, the Dobsons, who farmed fifty-seven and a half acres at Upper Rawcliffe. They had been tenants for twenty-two years, but prior to that Mr Dobson had worked as a labourer and his wife had been a maid on the same farm. 'I worked very hard', he declared, 'and so did my wife . . . We married while in service 40 years ago. We had not a sixpence when we married, but we then began to save a bit.' Their first step was to take a seven-acre farm on which they kept four cows, and from which they sold milk and butter, as well as bringing up the calves. Four years later they moved

SHE WAS "SORRY SHE SPOKE"!

Young Farmer (surveying the Stock). "A PRETTY TIDY LOT, MARIA."
Wife (considerably the senior). "AYE, BUT THEY WOULD NA BE THERE MAYBE WERN'T NO FOR MY BRASS!"
Husband (nettled.) "WHOY, LASS, GIN IT BE COOM TO THAT WI' YE, IF IT HAD NO' BEEN FOR YOUR MONEY, MAYHAP YE WID NA BEEN HERE
YERSEL'!"

PLATE 16   *The importance of a wife's contribution to the financing of a farm
is made very clear in this* Punch *cartoon.*

(1882)

to a fifteen-acre holding nearby, where they kept ten cows. 'We were
there nine years, and then took this farm . . . I and my wife and two
daughters work the farm and we employ extra labour at haytime.'
Their stock had increased to fifteen cows, nine heifers in calf, seven
calves, a bull and a horse. 'We make cheese, which we sell in Preston,
and butter, which we sell in Blackpool. I also keep hens. I believe last
year I cleared 30£ by them.'[33]

Mrs Dobson confirmed that they were now working harder than
when they were in service. 'I have sometimes gone out to shear sheep
all day, and then come in and do the housework and baking in the
evening.' Yet their pride in their precarious independence was
sufficient to keep them on their own farm. Much the same situation
applied in Cumbria, where daughters of even relatively affluent
parents were expected to join in the work of the farm, milking cows,
feeding calves and carrying out domestic chores. Small wonder that
one prosperous farmer attributed much of his success to his wife: 'she
has been a gold mine to me, and if she hadn't been with me I don't

think that I could have done at all.'[34] His view was confirmed by another large farmer, who, whilst looking for a servant at Ulverston hiring market in June 1895, ruefully commented: 'If I could only get a lass to work half as hard as my missus I should do.'[35]

In the light of such testimony it is ironic that from 1881 the population censuses ceased to include farmers' wives in the 'occupational' sector of the returns. The scale of the omission occasioned by this neglect is underlined by figures published in both the 1871 census and in the first Census of Production of 1908. In the former, 187,029 wives and 92,187 female relatives were recorded as working on farms, compared to 225,569 male farmers and graziers and 76,466 male relatives at work on the land. In 1908 the Production Census suggested that 144,000 female members of farming families were engaged in agriculture, three-quarters of them being over the age of eighteen. By contrast, the 1911 Population Census showed a mere 56,856 daughters and other female relatives of all ages helping on farms.[36] (The position of women farmers is examined later in the chapter.)

Within the farmhouse itself, especially on the smaller holdings, the contribution of wives and daughters was also of major importance. They cooked, washed, cleaned, cured bacon, made jams and preserves, supervised the domestic staff and, often enough, waited at table. In the North Riding of Yorkshire, the parson at Danby recalled the strong sense of community which developed when farmers, their wives, and their servants all ate together in the farm kitchen.[37] One woman who was born on a Swaledale farm in North Yorkshire in 1899 remembered that during the winter her mother knitted stockings and gloves for the servants as well as for the family. In a spirit of economy, she also saved the feathers from the geese she reared for Christmas to use for stuffing mattresses. All the feathers were roasted in the oven to purify them, 'and then we had to clean 'em . . . We used to do it in the outhouse . . . They were lovely beds, but, oh, they took *ages* to stuff.'[38]

Nevertheless, despite such examples of self-sufficiency, on many farms the living standards – and the social aspirations – of families were rising. This was especially true during the third quarter of the nineteenth century, before the onset of agricultural depression. At Danby the parson recalled how when he first came to the parish in the 1840s there had been only one piano among the farm households; by the early 1890s fifty or sixty pianos and harmoniums were to be found:

> one of our old inhabitants, on my noticing this great increase in musical instruments, gravely shook his head, and misdoubted how it would work; whether or no the farm-daughters and others who were learning to play, or had already learnt, would not become too fine-fingered, and too much given to other new-fangled ways, to attend as they ought to the dairy, with its cheese-press and butter-runner; and the household work; . . . and the 'mak'ing the meat' and its thrifty hospitality. But our butter is as delicate and sweet as it used to be, and our cheeses still take the best premiums at the shows of agricultural produce; and I am sure that no one who has partaken of the hospitality of one of our . . . farms, and . . . has sat down to a real 'Yorkshire tea' as provided . . . by our Dales housewives, can do so without being forced . . . to admit that the cunning has not left the hands of those who provided such pastry, such cakes, and . . . other delicacies.[39]

The culinary skills of a wife were obviously of major importance in ensuring the comfort of both her family and the resident staff. When male farm servants attended the annual hiring fairs to obtain a new place 'living in' they carefully enquired after a 'good meat house'. The generosity of the farmer's wife and the quality of the meals she served were an essential part of this. But, among the wives themselves, the extra cooking involved in catering for male servants, and the need to keep an eye on the maids when both men and women lived in, made the recruitment of male residents increasingly unattractive. By the mid-Victorian years only those holdings, usually in the north and west, which needed resident workers to look after livestock were still engaging male servants on any scale. One such district was Cumbria. Here a farmer's daughter noted that in the 1890s workers expected to have three meals a day, plus light refreshments at 10 a.m. and 4 p.m.: 'Formerly the "10 o'clocks and 4 o'clocks" were confined to harvest time, but of late years they have become general at other periods; and it is doubtful whether farm servants would now accept employment in a farmhouse where they were not provided.'[40]

Another farmer's daughter remembered the hard work involved

VERJUICE!

Farmer's Wife (whose Beer is of the smallest). "WHY, YOU HEVN'T DRUNK HALF
OF IT, MAS'R GEARGE!"

Peasant (politely). "THANKY', MU'M—ALL THE SAME, MU'M. BUT I BEAN'T SO
THUSTY AS I THOUGHT I WOR, MU'M!!"

PLATE 17　*This farmer's wife clearly did not belong to the category of those
offering workers a 'good meathouse'.*

(*Punch*, 1882)

in preparing hot boiled beef dinners and, at harvest, special cakes and home-brewed beer. She was not surprised that farm wives wished the men to be paid wholly in cash, so that they could make arrangements for board and lodgings themselves. Nevertheless, she admitted that it 'snapped some of the ties which bound the servant and master as fellow creatures'.[41]

The pressures under which wives worked caused a few to degenerate into bullies of the young maids they employed to help around house and dairy. One girl who worked on a small Devon farm early in the nineteenth century recalled that if her mistress were in a bad temper she would beat her or throw her on the ground and kick her. Three decades later she still had marks from the ill-treatment she had received.[42]

Happily such cases of gross physical abuse were relatively rare, but it was common to expect the maids to perform much heavy manual labour. Florence Stowe, who was born at Whichford, Warwickshire, in 1892, subsequently listed the jobs she carried out at a farmhouse on the Warwickshire/Oxfordshire border where she worked at the age of fourteen. Her first tasks each day were to clean and blacklead the kitchen range, polish the copper kettles and light the fire. Water had to be heated and coal scuttles filled before she cleaned the dining room, stairs and hall. It was then time to take hot water to the various members of her employer's family so that they could wash. All their boots and shoes had to be cleaned before she prepared breakfast, and milk had to be heated so that the cowman could feed the calves. After breakfast, there was the washing up, including cleaning and scalding dairy utensils and preparing vegetables for luncheon. If the hay harvest were delayed by bad weather, she had to help in the fields, too. One afternoon a week was devoted to churning and making the butter, 'a 2-hour work and about 30 to 40 lb. to pot up, weigh, mark, ready for market'. She also brought in the wood and coal needed for the fires and helped with the washing and ironing. For this, she was paid the princely sum of £5 a year, and was allowed one day off each month from 10 a.m. until 8 p.m.[43]

Alison Uttley's fictionalized account of her childhood on a Derbyshire farm gave a more attractive picture of mistress–servant relationships. Although Becky, the maid, helped in buttermaking, as well as in washing, baking, brewing herb beer, harnessing the horses, milking the cows and working in the fields, she got on well with

Alison's mother. When the pedlar came on his regular two-monthly visits to the remote farm, mistress and maid inspected his wares together:

> Becky fetched her worn leather purse and counted the pennies. She had no days off to go spending money in the villages, and here was her shop. She bargained for a new comb and a little looking-glass, a red ribbon – she was partial to red – and a bordered cotton handkerchief, which she intended to keep by her for her master's birthday.[44]

She was also an important member of the farm labour force. According to Alison, she was 'as strong as a man, and could carry a young calf in her arms, or two brimming cans of milk with anybody'.[45] Girls such as she seem to have accepted the hard labour put upon them without resentment; perhaps the fact that their mistress usually worked alongside them reconciled them to the exploitation which many undoubtedly experienced.

It was, of course, only on the small or medium-sized farms that wives and daughters were directly engaged in heavy manual labour around house and stockyard. On the larger properties they normally confined themselves to supervisory duties, and during the 'golden years' of agricultural prosperity in the 1850s and 1860s there were comments that many were getting ideas 'above their station'. Daughters were accused of paying more attention to piano playing and social functions than to their domestic and dairying duties, whilst their mothers were said to be too much involved in visiting neighbours or engaging in other frivolities to run their home economically and efficiently. Yet the fact that in the eastern counties, where holdings were larger, dairying was already of comparatively little importance robbed these reproaches of some of their point, for that area at least. Furthermore, the attitude of the critics had already been made clear as early as 1843 in John Robey's satirical rhyme; it was to be repeated, in amended form, for the rest of the nineteenth century:

1743
Man, to the Plough,
Wife, to the Cow,
Girl, to the Yarn,

Boy, to the Barn,
And your Rent will be netted.

1843
Man, Tally Ho,
Miss, Piano,
Wife, Silk and Satin,
Boy, Greek and Latin,
And you'll all be Gazetted.[46]

A 1900 version of the final lines ran:

Father gone to see the show,
Daughter at the pian-o,
Madame gaily dressed in satin,
All the boys learning Latin,
With a mortgage on the farm.[47]

George Eliot, herself the daughter of a Warwickshire land agent and thus with wide experience of farmhouse life, added to the condemnatory chorus in the mid-1850s when she sourly contrasted current practice with the position half a century before. Then, she claimed, daughters rose at 1 a.m. to brew, and instead of 'carrying on sentimental correspondence, they were spinning their future table-linen, and looking after every saving in butter and eggs that might enable them to add to the little stock of plate and china which they were laying in against their marriage'. But by the 1850s, it was virtually impossible to enter

the least imposing farmhouse without finding a bad piano in the 'drawing-room,' and some old annuals, disposed with a symmetrical imitation of negligence, on the table; though the daughters may still drop their *h*'s, their vowels are studiously narrow; and it is only in very primitive regions that they will consent to sit in a covered vehicle without springs.[48]

Her condemnation of these social aspirations rings hollow, however, when it is remembered that during a spell as her father's housekeeper in the late 1830s and early 1840s, she spent her spare time in reading and studying – as her correspondence makes clear – and had little enthusiasm for farming activities. 'Remember Michaelmas is coming', she wrote to a friend in September 1839, 'and I shall be engaged in matters so nauseating to me that it will be a charity to console me.' The 'nauseating' matters referred to were the farm's harvest home festivities.[49] On another occasion she referred disparagingly to making 'damson cheese' and the 'stupid drowsy sensation' it produced; she even claimed later that one of her hands was broader across than the other because she had made so much butter and cheese during these years.[50]

It is also an indication of the equivocal attitude adopted towards farmers' wives and daughters seeking to enter the ranks of the 'respectable' middle classes that one Oxfordshire country clergyman who married a farmer's daughter in the 1830s was subsequently condemned by a fellow cleric for his 'most foolish and imprudent' action.[51] Even the financial difficulties which farmers experienced during the depression years were attributed by some critics to the idleness and false gentility of their womenfolk. At the Northampton agricultural show in 1879, Lord Burghley declared that wives and daughters should 'give up the piano and French lessons and "put their shoulders to the wheel".'[52] Doubtless such commentators would have been gratified by the admission of a leading Staffordshire farmer in the late 1890s that whereas agriculturists in his area had previously employed domestic servants to help around the house and dairy, they could no longer afford that luxury. Instead they had to rely upon members of their family.[53]

But these short-term economic problems apart, it is clear that for most farming households the nature of social life was influenced primarily by the scale of the agricultural activities in which they were engaged. As Davidoff and Hall have recently pointed out,

> the 26 per cent of Suffolk farms where only family labour was employed would be a vastly different setting for the farmer's wife and female relatives than for a woman like Jane Ransome Biddell whose husband farmed over 1000 acres, and where numerous servants including a housekeeper were employed, releasing her to take part in the cultural and intellectual life of nearby Ipswich.[54]

Similarly, Elizabeth Stovin, whose husband cultivated 600 acres in the Lincolnshire wolds, spent little time in the kitchen, although she did keep a careful eye on the household accounts, and quickly informed her husband if she thought the maids were being too extravagant with the bread and meat. When, in December 1874, she made a batch of loaves, the event was sufficiently unusual for her husband to mention it in his diary.[55] Yet Elizabeth, who eventually had a family of seven children born between 1864 and 1883 (to say nothing of three miscarriages during the first ten years of married life), clearly found the daily round in a remote farmhouse a frustrating experience. Even occasional visits to family and friends, and charitable forays into the village were no consolation. She was also anxious about her husband's financial affairs. He was a convinced Methodist, and made loans to village chapels and to pay off circuit debts which he could ill afford. Her problems, as her granddaughter perceptively commented, were those of 'an active and intelligent woman shut up for most of her married life in an isolated and uncomfortable farm house, sick and weary with miscarriages and child-bearing and the worry of cheap and untrained young servants whom she had not the strength to cope with'. Even drinking water had to be brought in by a special cart from the village three miles away, and when snow made the roads impassable, stocks could run low.[56] In many respects her position resembled that of a traditional mid-Victorian middle-class wife, expected to concentrate on family, household and charitable concerns, rather than a busy farm wife, sharing in the work and responsibilities of the holding.

Martha Randall, the teenage daughter of a widowed woman farmer from Orsett, Essex, likewise played little part in agricultural activities, despite the fact that Mr Randall had died in 1844, when Martha, the third and youngest child, was only one. Martha and her sister, Fannie, were educated by a governess, and in a diary written in the late 1850s she described meetings with young friends, mostly the sons and daughters of neighbouring farmers, rather than life on the land. Her social round included musical evenings, private theatricals, picnics, visits to London and riding to hounds. She also taught at Sunday school and spent much time practising the piano; her mother employed an itinerant music teacher from Gravesend to give her two daughters singing and music lessons. In December 1859, shortly after her seventeenth birthday, Martha attended a tenants' ball to celebrate the coming of age of the heir to the Orsett estate. Dancing began at 7 p.m. and continued until dawn the following morning, although, as she rather pointedly noted, the heir himself did not attend.[57] In June

1858 she described a typical day: 'In the morning worked &c. [that is, did her needlework] in the afternoon went to W. Pollett's haymaking party . . . we had tea out in the hayfield, then we played rounders, we got quite beaten . . . Then we danced – Herbert had a regular flirt with Miss Clark. We came home about 12 o'clock.'[58]

Martha married William Sackett, a farmer's son about three years her senior, in the autumn of 1867. He came from the village and was a member of her regular social circle. He took over the tenancy of the Randall farm and by the early 1870s, he, Martha and their two young children were in residence, together with Mrs Randall, who had now retired from business. There were also two maids, and William employed six labourers on his 166-acre holding. During the next few years, however, as farming entered a downward spiral, William abandoned agriculture for a career as a rate collector and insurance agent – an occupation he continued to follow at Orsett until the early twentieth century. For his once frivolous and light-hearted wife this must have involved considerable readjustment. By 1881, she was the mother of five young children, and had only a 15-year-old maid to assist her. The status she had once enjoyed as a comfortably placed farmer's daughter and wife had now been lost. Martha died in February 1919 at Gravesend, where she and William had moved in their retirement; her estate was valued at under £800.[59]

The Frenchman, Hippolyte Taine, visited a far 'superior' farming household to this when he came to England in the 1860s. The 600-acre holding was rented for the substantial sum of £600 a year and when Taine and his companion arrived, they were ushered into a cool, lofty drawing-room:

> Long curtains held back by gilt loops; two elegantly framed looking-glasses; chairs in good taste. In the middle a table with a number of handsomely bound books. In short, the country drawing-room of a Parisian with a private income of twenty-five thousand *livres*. Adjoining the room was a conservatory full of flowers, giving on to a pretty countryside of sloping meadows and distant woods.

The farmer's wife matched the elegance of her surroundings. She wore a dress of narrow striped grey silk and had rings on her fingers. Her hands were white – an indication that she performed none of the rougher household chores – and her figure was admirable, tall and slender as a Diana, extremely beautiful, full of cheerfulness and high spirits, without a trace of awkwardness, and conversing very well. I heard later that she rides and plays the piano, but is nevertheless an excellent housekeeper. She goes to the kitchen every morning, gives her orders, supervises what is done and sometimes makes a little pastry herself.[60]

Women such as she had little in common with the countless 'working' farmers' wives, who were engaged in cooking, dairying and a thousand and one other tasks about holding and house.

Three decades later Alice Holtby, mother of the novelist Winifred Holtby, enjoyed much the same comfortable standard of life. Alice, a farmer's daughter, had worked for a time as a governess before marrying David Holtby, who ran a 940-acre farm in the wolds. In their spare time she and her daughter visited the newly-born babies and bedridden sufferers from asthma and bronchitis in the village. Later she was to become the first woman member and subsequently the first woman alderman on the East Riding County Council.[61] She served as the model for Mary Robson, the heroine of her daughter's first novel, *Anderby Wold*. Of Mary, Winifred Holtby wrote: 'she had no stronger interest left in life than her care for the village.'[62]

The social circle in which the Holtbys moved was in most respects highly conservative and inbred. Winifred herself wryly admitted that, but for a sympathetic schoolmistress at her boarding school, she would not have been allowed to attend university but would have remained in an environment of 'animals, . . . shooting-parties, the visits of foremen and pig-dealers, the calls of millers and their wives'. 'Even now', she added, 'quite half my life is there, and all my "roots."'[63] Winifred's subsequent literary fame was given scant recognition by her relatives, who, to the end of her life, referred to her simply as 'Alice's girl'.[64]

Wives without the status and resources of a Mrs Holtby would often provide charitable help to the needy, and particularly to the families of their husband's employees. It was to the farmer's wife or daughter that cottagers turned when in difficulty in rural Wales. At harvest time she presided over the meals prepared for the workers and doled out measures of flour to those who preferred this to having supper at the farm. To her came those women who set out their own potatoes on the farm and, in return, gave their labour at harvest time, for it was she who granted them small favours and occasional assistance in kind.[65] 'This sort of relationship between farm and cottage must go back deep into Welsh history', commented one Carmarthen farmer's son, 'perhaps back to the time of co-operation, when the community shared a plough and other implements, and provided each an ox to make up the team.'[66] Even the agricultural trade union leader, Joseph Arch, who was a bitter critic of most farmers, had a good word to say for their womenfolk. He particularly recognized their kindness to labourers' wives with young babies.[67]

So far attention has been focused on the *wives* and *daughters* of the farmhouse, since it was comparatively rare for women to be engaged as farmers or farm managers in their own right. In 1911, out of almost 229,000 farmers and graziers recorded in the population census in England and Wales a mere 20,027 were female. Of these almost 15,000 were widows who were presumably carrying on after their husbands' death, often with the help of other family members. Significantly, as table 5.1 shows, their relative position compared to that of their male counterparts (and their overall total) had changed little over the preceding sixty years.[68]

TABLE 5.1   *Farmers and graziers in England and Wales: 1851−1911*

Census year	Males	Females
1851	226,515	22,916
1861	226,957	22,778
1871	225,569	24,338
1881	203,329	20,614
1891	201,918	21,692
1901	202,751	21,548
1911	208,761	20,027

NB For the 1851-71 censuses the figure also included those who had retired.
Source: Census reports in Parliamentary Papers.

Part of the reason for this relative female scarcity lay in the fact that in a society increasingly concerned with female domesticity, the laborious tasks associated with farm supervision were considered inappropriate for women. Coupled with this was the need to control a largely male workforce, whose companionship was deemed unsuitable for any female with pretensions to gentility, and who might prove difficult to discipline. Allied to this was the fact that women were unfamiliar with the habit of command, and that they rarely took an active role in, for example, the administration of parish affairs.

By law they were excluded from exercising the parliamentary franchise, too, although this was something which a few, like Mrs Harriet McIlquham, who ran a farm in Gloucestershire, considered grossly inequitable: 'Fancy a woman farming 500 acres of land, and paying the usual contributions to the taxes of the country, having no voice in the representation of the country, while her own labourers have.'[69] Although she became active in local government, her pleas for the parliamentary franchise fell on deaf ears.

Meanwhile, apart from women's lack of administrative experience, another problem they faced in running a farm was in the matter of corn and livestock marketing. This was especially the case as the use of corn exchanges became more widespread, since the appearance of a woman in one of these created something of a stir. Furthermore, when business was completed, it was to the public house or market day 'ordinaries' that most farmers repaired to dine and to exchange local gossip. This, too, was deemed an unsuitable environment for women. Davidoff and Hall have drawn attention to a female cattle dealer in Suffolk who was notorious for sitting with male colleagues in the public house, 'drinking and smoking a pipe and locally known as "The Duchess".'[70] And at Dean Row in Cheshire, the road to the Homestead Farm became known as 'Pig Nellie's Lane' because of a widow who lived there and dealt in pigs. She was so strong that she could pick up a pig and hoist it into the float in which she travelled on business 'as far abroad as Wales'.[71] But few women would have relished either the physical effort or the notoriety which went with such activities.

A further difficulty was that, at a time when much emphasis was placed on the need for agricultural improvement and the payment of high rentals during the 'golden age' of agriculture in the 1850s and 1860s, landlords were reluctant to offer tenancies to women. Even widows were looked at askance when they sought to follow their husband on to a holding, unless they had a grown-up son or other male relative to help with its day-to-day running. George Eliot in *Mr. Gilfil's Love-story* recounted the typical view when she described how the fictional widow Hartopp pleaded with her landlord, Sir Christopher Cheverel, to be allowed to remain on the farm her late husband had rented. This had been his dying wish, but Sir Christopher was unmoved, declaring that if she and her children stayed on they would lose everything:

> You are about as able to manage the farm as your best milch cow. You'll be obliged to have some managing man, who will either cheat you out of your money, or wheedle you into marrying him. . . . A woman's always silly enough, but she's never quite as great a fool as she can be until she puts on a widow's cap.[72]

Mrs Hartopp vigorously argued that she knew a good deal about farming, having been 'brought up i' the thick on it . . . An' there was my husband's great-aunt managed a farm for twenty years, an' left legacies to all her nephys an' nieces.' But Sir Christopher was unimpressed. In the end he agreed to put her and the family into a cottage which he owned, and to provide 'a bit of land . . . as she will want to keep a cow and some pigs'.[73]

Outside the pages of fiction, the lot of widows seeking to continue a tenancy faced similar gender discrimination. In Essex during the mid-1860s the land agent John Oxley Parker listed the problems faced by a Mrs Orpen, who had gained the tenancy of a farm rented for £280 a year by her late husband. Not only was she in arrears with the rent but the condition of some of the fields and fences was described as 'melancholy', and her younger son, who was helping her, was considered 'quite unequal to the management'. Farming neighbours and the agent pressed her to give up the property, but at first she resisted, preferring, as she said, to 'struggle on'. Her brother-in-law then joined in the campaign and after a visit by Oxley Parker, she reluctantly agreed to leave – forced out by the pressure of local opinion.[74]

Other women were, however, more successful or more tenacious. In the 1860s and 1870s, two widows ran farms at Sutton Courtenay, then in Berkshire. Both had been left at an early age with a family of young children, and both continued in business until their sons were old enough to take over. Mary Ann Pullen was about thirty-four when her husband died in January 1854. During the 1860s, by judicious purchases, she extended the property from 340 acres, as it was in her husband's day, to 450 acres. In 1871 she employed six men, five boys and four women, and was aided by her sons, the youngest of whom was now seventeen. A decade later she had retired, and was living next door to the farm, with a young maid, whilst her eldest son and his young family had the farm.[75] Mrs Pullen died in 1882 and was able to leave two of her sons a farm apiece; her estate was valued at the comfortable sum of almost £5,000.[76]

The second widow was Mary Bobart. In 1871, at the age of fifty-two, she was running a farm of 250 acres and employing eight men and five boys. Two daughters and a son were also living at home. A few years later, the son took over the farm, following his marriage, but he, too, died very young in January 1881, leaving a young widow and two small children. Unfortunately, the son died heavily in debt and shortly afterwards the Bobarts left the farm.[77]

Despite the determination of women like Mrs Pullen and Mrs Bobart, however, the prejudice against female farmers persisted. It was reinforced by the fact that at a time when increasing stress was laid upon the application of science to agriculture, women's education – usually in small private schools or from governesses – ill-fitted them to take advantage of this. Their sex also debarred them from participating in the deliberations of the growing number of agricultural societies and farmers' clubs which were being established.[78] Many had libraries which included works on elementary agricultural science, and their meetings were normally held at the principal hotel in the town in which the club was based, or at one of the public houses. After official business had been concluded, the evening would be spent in friendly discussion, with a free circulation of alcohol.[79] Such an atmosphere was deemed improper for women with pretensions to middle-class gentility, and the menfolk, in any case, would have resented female interlopers. Admittedly, women attended the agricultural shows put on by these societies and inspected the equipment there displayed, but they could not take an active part in the organization, or in the spread of new ideas on husbandry and stockbreeding which such events were designed to promote. Only in the case of dairying were females able to show their mettle and, as we shall see, at the end of the century some of the societies began to organize special classes to improve butter- and cheesemaking skills on farms. In these, females were prominent both as instructors and as pupils.[80]

Yet, despite the handicaps, a number of women were able to run farms, as we have discovered. In 1911, the census recorded 4,043 unmarried women farmers in England and Wales, while not all of the widows, especially in the early days of widowhood, were able to call upon masculine assistance, as the Sutton Courtenay examples demonstrate. Another similar case was that of Mrs Watson of Market Deeping, Lincolnshire, who ran not only a 100-acre farm but a pork butchery as well. There she sold meat, pies and fruit, and other produce from the farm. 'I certainly could not have brought up my four children without the aid of the business', she declared in the mid-1890s.[81]

Likewise Mrs Eliza Marfleet of Wainfleet St Mary, Lincolnshire, ran her thirty-acre holding for over forty years. In the early 1890s she worked the land with the help of a male labourer, a lad and her niece. She admitted that living standards were spartan; for example, they never ate butcher's meat, only bacon. But despite the agricultural depression, she had always managed to pay her way and had 'lost no money since 1882', which was more than many of her male counterparts could have said. When she died in December 1907, she left her entire estate, valued at almost £1,700, to her niece, Ada Carden.[82]

Still more ambitious was Miss Kate Jenkins, who farmed in Llangadock, Wales. She combined her agricultural work with a land agency, and with voluntary service as vice-chairman of the local school board.[83] In another case, Mary Fairhead, who was left a widow in her late thirties with nine children, decided to move the family from her husband's farm to a new property in another Essex parish. There she carried on business from 1832 until her death in November 1871. At that stage the farm was taken over by her daughter, Louisa, who also farmed successfully for more than thirty years.[84]

But often women in business on their own account were regarded as freaks. An unmarried farmer's daughter who successfully ran a brick and tile kiln on a commercial scale was considered an oddity, devoid of feminine characteristics, even by her family.[85] Women who farmed on their own also had to be physically strong. Fred Kitchen, who began work on a South Yorkshire farm in 1904 at the age of thirteen, remembered the widow who ran it as a 'tall, raw-boned woman . . . , with skirts permanently tucked up aft, and wearing a black hat of no particular shape. She was as hefty as a young navvy, and as strong as a young horse. She tackled any kind of work that turned up, such as slicing turnips for the beasts, teaming loads of hay, or even assisting at calving a cow.'[86] When she and Fred picked apples and pears in the farm orchard he was astonished as she climbed up a long ladder resting against the tree, with a basket in one hand and a hooked stick in the other:

> She could get about like a two-year-old, and I had always thought I could scrim up a tree with the next, but she beat me hollow at reaching for apples and pears. She never let one fall to the ground, a thing I was always doing . . . Then she would call out, 'Butter fingers, ye'll demmock all the apples i' the orchard!'[87]

Those women farmers who lacked the physical strength and energy of this Yorkshire widow might employ bailiffs to carry out the more arduous tasks and to supervise the daily routine. Others concentrated on dairying and poultry-keeping, which had traditionally been female responsibilities. And at a time when a growing minority of middle-class women were anxious to follow careers of their own, a few began to consider these lighter branches of agriculture as a means of earning a livelihood. It was to cater for them that in August 1898 the Countess of Warwick rented a house at Reading and began to offer training courses for students in dairy work, horticulture, poultry-farming, beekeeping, fruit-growing and the marketing of produce. At first instruction was given largely by staff from Reading College (later to be Reading University), but in 1902 these links were severed, partly because Reading College considered the training offered at the Lady Warwick hostel to be inadequate. The following year staff and students moved to a new location, Studley Castle in Warwickshire.

During the first six years of its existence, Lady Warwick's organization trained 146 full-time students, of whom twenty-four were reported in 1904 to have smallholdings of their own (either farms or market gardens), while twelve more were working on home farms or gardens, perhaps attached to parental properties. Initially the Countess of Warwick had envisaged the training scheme as part of an ambitious plan to establish 'unmarrying women' on agricultural settlements in different parts of this country and in the colonies. The settlements were to comprise six to twenty holdings, each worked by two women, who would share a cottage and run the venture as a partnership. Alongside this she aimed to combine the advantages of personal management with co-operation in buying and selling, 'with a co-operative dairy, a "lady warden" to transact the business of each settlement, and with a central office in London'.[88] Although this broader plan failed to materialize, the training scheme was modestly successful, and Studley College remained in existence until 1969.

Other bodies followed along similar lines, such as the Women's Agricultural and Horticultural International Union, founded in 1899, to benefit women working their own land and in salaried horticultural and agricultural posts; and the National Political League, set up in 1911, both to find employment for women on the land and 'to further other social reforms on a non-party basis'. As a first step, this latter organization began establishing settlements where women could carry on poultry-farming and 'kindred industries', including fruit-farming and market gardening.[89]

Significantly, however, even those who applauded these initiatives were anxious that the women should not become so absorbed in agriculture that they 'unsexed' themselves. 'All ladies should devote a portion of their time to literature or music, or the practice of some other feminine accomplishments calculated to bring relaxation if not pecuniary gain', declared one well-wisher.[90] Much the same attitude was adopted by *Country Life* in an article on 'Ladies in Agriculture', although in this case the writer apparently regarded horticulture as a more suitable sphere for females than farming proper.[91]

In such circumstances, attempts to train professional women for careers as commercial farmers were doomed to failure. Far more useful were the efforts to raise dairying standards among existing practitioners. It was here that the agricultural societies, in particular, were able to play a pioneering role.

In the 1880s there was growing concern about the variable quality of much of the dairy produce from British farms, and about the poor standards of hygiene associated with its manufacture. In the Garstang area in Lancashire, for example, the medical officer of health commented disapprovingly upon cheese being kept in a bedroom 'which is generally slept in'. Another doctor in the same area likewise reported of the dairy producers: 'They make their butter in the kitchen, and keep it and also cheese in the sleeping-rooms. . . . I have seen butter-making going on downstairs in a farm where there was a case of infectious disease being attended to upstairs.'[92] The only solution was to improve dairying facilities and educate producers on the need for cleanliness.

Arthur Wilson Fox echoed these views when he visited Lancashire in the early 1890s. He noted that one well-known farmer, who was a tenant of the Earl of Derby, had no dairy, although he was a substantial cheese producer. 'This man's daughters turn out four tons of cheese in the year, and they were making it in the kitchen on the occasion of my visit.'[93] It was against this background that in 1880 the Bath and West of England Society held a ten-day dairying course at Swindon. It was followed by similar courses at Shepton Mallet, Chippenham, Exeter and Oxford, and soon there were enthusiastic reports of the improved skills which resulted.[94]

All the early schools concentrated on buttermaking. Not until 1890 was a cheese school established, at Palace Farm, Wells. The course lasted four weeks and the number of students was limited to four. Instruction was given by Miss Cannon, a farmer's daughter, who worked in her father's dairy, and Mr Cannon acted as supervisor of the school. Its success soon led to the establishment of another school at Frome by the Bath and West, with Miss Cannon again acting as instructor. Within a short time the Society had set up nearly 170 buttermaking schools and fifteen for cheesemaking – the former operating on a migratory basis in different districts, and the latter remaining fixed in one place for the whole of a cheesemaking season, and then moving on the following year.[95]

By this date other societies were following the Bath and West's example, aided in some cases by government grants paid under the Local Taxation Act of 1890. In the spring of 1890, the Essex Agricultural Society, for example, arranged courses in association with the Eastern Counties Dairy Institute, with a Miss Blackshaw, principal teacher at the Dairy School in Ipswich, as instructor. In Lincolnshire, the Eastern Counties Dairy Institute also arranged lecture courses on creaming and buttermaking.[96] One important aspect of the courses was the guidance they gave in the use of the most modern appliances. According to a Welsh witness, prior to buttermaking classes being held in her area, dairymaids had refused to use cream separators, but that was now changing.[97] Dairying skills were particularly valued by maids in Wales as an aid to matrimony, since it was recognized that farmers in the principality wanted wives who were familiar with dairy work.[98]

In order to stimulate interest still further, buttermaking contests were organized at the agricultural shows, thereby allowing women to demonstrate their skills and emerge as prize-winners in an environment which was normally male dominated. One buttermaker, who had won the Queen's Gold Medal and Champion Prize at the Royal Agricultural Society Show at Windsor in 1889, even had the satisfaction of seeing her name used to advertise a churn made by one of the major manufacturers, G. Llewellin & Son of Haverfordwest.

But these dairying initiatives apart, most women on farms at the end of the Victorian era – as at the beginning – were seen in an essentially subordinate role. It was the male members of the family who held the positions of prestige and power. That even applied on small dairy farms where the skills of the womenfolk were important in the overall prosperity of the holding. It was an example of the way in which the female contribution to Victorian and Edwardian farming became 'hidden from history', and the responsibilities they undertook ignored or undervalued.

6

Domestic Service and
Work on the Land

All females should go to service. Those employed in the fields remain in ignorance; they learn nothing, they know nothing; when they are married they are poor managers in every respect; the children feel the effects, the husband escapes to the public house, and so it gets worse and worse.

Rev. J. Macdougall of Blewbury, Berkshire, in *Second Report of the Royal Commission on the Employment of Children, Young Persons, and Women in Agriculture*, PP 1868–9, vol. XIII.

Throughout the Victorian years it was domestic service rather than agriculture which was the major employer of working women in country districts, as in the nation at large.[1] Many village parents regarded the occupation as acceptable in a way that factory work was not. Mrs Libby Low, born near Knighton in Radnor around 1900, recalled that girls who worked at Knighton's single factory were regarded as social inferiors: 'it was so *low* to come down to that. You see, most of the men were farmers . . . and I suppose they wouldn't let their girls go to the factory. Service, they didn't mind . . . though there was less money.'[2]

Among householders, meanwhile, the employment of a maid was a status symbol – a mark of respectability – which appealed to the skilled tradesman and his family as well as to the white-collar and professional classes. In 1871, in small country towns like Wantage, then in Berkshire, and Fakenham in Norfolk, where approximately one household in six kept a resident servant, two-fifths of the employers were small tradesmen.[3] They included drapers, grocers, plumbers, coal merchants, bakers, shoemakers and the like, and in the main they relied upon the services of the maid-of-all-work, who was the most common English domestic. At the 1871 census not far short of two-thirds of the nation's 1.2 million female servants fell into the 'general' category, and almost half of them were under the age of twenty.[4] Mrs Beeton considered the general servant 'perhaps the only one of her class deserving commiseration':

> she starts in life, probably a girl of thirteen, with some small tradesman's wife as her mistress, just a step above her in the social scale; and although the class contains among them many excellent, kind-hearted women, it also contains some very rough specimens of the feminine gender, and to some of these it occasionally falls to give our maid-of-all-work her first lessons in her multifarious occupations: the mistress's commands are the measure of the maid-of-all-work's duties.[5]

The pressures experienced by the girls were likely to be greatest when employers were themselves short of cash. One Surrey woman remembered going to work in a carpenter's family when she was twelve: 'there was eleven children. . . . I didn't get no wages, only my food, one frock and one bonnet, and a shillin' to take home.'[6] She stayed for a year before moving into farm service. Similarly, William and Mary Ann Loosley of High Wycombe recruited a general servant when they set up home in 1863, even though their building business was so small that Mary Ann had to help glaze the windows of many of the houses built by the firm.[7]

Except on farms, or in the large households of the landed classes, the daily routine of country servants differed little from that of their urban counterparts. In the mansions of the aristocracy and gentry, however, where an extensive staff was kept, there was a clearly established hierarchy of power. Each department was controlled by the head servant belonging to it, with the housekeeper or cook supervising the females as the house steward or butler did the males. Locally born servants were rarely recruited for these senior posts, although for junior positions the 'big house' became a legitimate target for village girls. At Waterperry, Oxfordshire, Mrs Henley, wife

PLATE 18   *Servants employed by the Wade-Gery family at Bushmead Priory,*
Eaton Socon, c.1900. Left to right: coachman; cook; gardener's son; Madge
Wade-Gery, aged 6; parlourmaid; housemaid and dairymaid; and gardener.
The maids are each carrying some article to denote their occupation. Domestic
service was the principal occupation for working-class country girls.

(Mrs Wade-Gery and Bedfordshire Record Office)

of the squire, often found a place for local youngsters in her own
household or, failing that, she would seek openings in the homes of
her friends. 'It is such a good thing for them to get out into nice places
and I hope they will all do well', she wrote to a friend in 1851.[8]

Life in these large houses in many respects represented a microcosm
of rural society in general. In both there were strict class gradations,
with the employer and his steward or agent very firmly at the head of
affairs, and the scullery maids, nursemaids, under-housemaids and
temporary charwomen and helpers—the humblest group of domestics
—at the bottom. 'We were never allowed to visit each other's
departments', recalled a girl who worked as a housemaid for Lord
and Lady Brownlow at Ashridge, Hertfordshire, in the late nineteenth
century.[9] Often the senior staff were waited on by junior members.

The stillroom maids, for example, attended to the housekeeper as well as helping her make preserves, cordials and intricate items of confectionery. Kitchenmaids waited on the cook, and the most junior housemaid frequently worked entirely for the staff.

Early rising was an essential part of the routine. A former still-room maid at Delamere House in Cheshire recalled getting up at 4 a.m. every morning to bake fresh bread and churn butter for the breakfast of her mistress, Lady Wilbraham.[10] And at Toft Hall in the same county, housemaids had to rise at 4 a.m. in order to finish their work before the family came down.[11] This was common practice, and in some households a maid seen by her employer with a duster in her hand would be dismissed on the spot. At Toft, all the staff had to attend family prayers, which lasted for about half an hour each day. And on Sundays they attended the village church, with the female staff dressed in black bonnets and capes.

In these large households domestic duties were clearly defined. At Englefield House in Berkshire, Mr Benyon firmly informed his housekeeper what was involved in supervising 'the Family of 16 to 20 Servants'. She had control of the day-to-day distribution of the stores, but her employer retained responsibility for the storeroom itself. The care of the household linen fell within her province, and she had to ensure that it was 'mended every Monday'. She must 'look after the rooms when there was company and keep a careful account of everything'.[12]

Cooks were cross-questioned by the Benyons as to their professional skills as well as being informed that they would be allowed no perquisites. 'Have you been used to sending up Soups, Entrées, Pastry, Spinning Sugar, Confectionery?', they were asked. 'Have you been used to trussing Poultry, to Game and Venison? . . . Broth & Gruel for the Poor and Sick'. In this household all successful applicants had to be of the Protestant religion, and to attend prayers each morning. Most were told that if they were ill their employer would not be responsible for the apothecary's bills.[13]

Senior staff rarely ate with the juniors in such houses. Usually only the main course of the dinner was consumed in the servants' hall by the seniors, who then repaired to the housekeeper's room or the steward's room to eat their pudding. The housekeeper's or steward's room where these privileged servants took most of their meals was nicknamed the 'Pugs' Parlour' by irreverent juniors.

Often the servants were expected to consume leftovers from the dining-room meals, although some mistresses provided separate menus for them. In the mid-1820s, shortly after her marriage, the future Lady Dashwood of West Wycombe Park carefully drew up detailed dinner menus for the family and for the servants. Thus on 6 January 1827, while the servants consumed boiled neck and breast of mutton, the Dashwoods themselves dined on roast leg of pork, oysters and mince pie.[14] Nevertheless, despite the distinctions, such meals were far more lavish and varied than labouring families would have eaten in their own homes at that time, and there were frequent opportunities for the staff to add to their rations surreptitiously. In this respect a letter written by a late Victorian maid working for the Garths at Haines Hill, Twyford, Berkshire, would have aroused the alarm of many householders. 'I can swim in beer if I wish to, plenty kicking about', she told a friend:

> I wish you were here. Mrs. Wilton [her previous employer's housekeeper] would have a fit if she had a fire going like we do. I put three scuttles of coal [on] at once . . . You must come and see me. I will then give you some dripping to give Mrs. Wilton. It is better than her old cooking. I never let on about the grub we had there to these servants. I would not let them know I was in such a show. Our cook-housekeeper is a better Lady than Mrs. Wilton. You can tell Mrs. Wilton I don't need to drink on the sly here as I get more than enough. I shall get as fat as a pig.[15]

Nursery staff lived very much apart from the rest of the household, and often formed bonds of affection with their young charges which lasted for the rest of their lives. Mary Carbery and her sister felt that 'nothing really [mattered]' as long as they had 'Nanny'.[16] The girls were heartbroken when she was forced to leave to look after a sick mother.

Sarah Sedgwick, a gardener's daughter, who took a post as nursemaid in a large house in Yorkshire, recalled the routine she had to follow. Each morning she lit the nursery fires at 6 a.m. and then cleaned the fireguards. At 7.30 a.m. she called the head nurse with a cup of tea, and at 8 the children had their breakfast:

> Everything had to happen to the minute. At ten sharp we were out with the prams, and pushed them until half-past twelve.

Luncheon was one o'clock. Then from two until half-past three another walk with the prams. This was followed by tea at four o'clock. Then there was dressing up the children before they went downstairs, and they were taken into the drawing-room to the minute, and brought up again to the minute.

This might be their only encounter with their parents during the day. Afterwards, there were baths to prepare and then bed. In this house the nursery servants were excused from morning prayers, but they had to attend church on alternate Sundays. There they and their fellows sat in a special pew, in strict order of precedence. 'We left the church before the family, and stood outside until they came out, and as they passed we women gave little bob-curtseys.'[17] Sarah had grown up on a large estate, and so was well used to the conventions of country house life. In her first place she was one of a domestic indoor staff of twenty-two.

Contacts between employers and junior servants in these large households were minimal. It was the senior servants who were the juniors' real employers, and often they 'treated beginners as a sergeant treated recruits, drilling them well in their duties by dint of much scolding'.[18] At Englefield the housekeeper was expected to keep 'order & quiet' among the servants and not to let the maids go out without leave, or unless they were 'dressed quietly'. If the senior servants were bullies, they could make the lives of their juniors a misery.[19]

'Below stairs' quarrels provided a further source of anxiety for the younger women servants. The diary of the Rev. W. C. Risley, a north Oxfordshire landowner and former vicar of Deddington in that county, shows he not only had to dismiss his cook for drunkenness, but had to settle a dispute between the housemaid and footman. The latter had insulted the maid 'by using obscene Language to her in swearing at her'. After bringing the two together and satisfying himself of the truthfulness of her claim, he dismissed the footman.[20]

In carrying out their duties in the larger properties, the servants had to perform much physical labour as well as display skills in cleaning and handling valuable objects. Hot water for washing had to be carried upstairs by the housemaids, and ashes from bedroom fires brought down. Some employers insisted on fining servants who broke china or glass objects in order to teach them to be more careful in the future. At Waddesdon, the housekeeper and the still-room maid were responsible for washing up the delicate Sèvres and Dresden china used in the dining-room.[21]

Despite the discipline and the high standard of service demanded, however, life in these establishments had many compensations. Not only was food usually more plentiful and varied than in humbler households, but they were able to enjoy some of the reflected glory of their employers' superior status. At Ashridge, one of the housemaids recalled that when shooting parties were held at the weekend she and some of the other maids would 'hide behind the pillars to watch' the arrival of the guests. These included, on occasion, the Prince and Princess of Wales: 'Lovely to see all the ladies in their beautiful dresses and jewellery.'[22]

Senior staff often had an opportunity to travel with the family, too, or to spend the season in London. And in all the larger houses provisions were made for servants' leisure hours. At Longleat, the Marchioness of Bath remembered the weekly staff dances held in the servants' hall.[23] A pianist was engaged and a buffet supper organized. The outdoor servants also attended, as well as the unmarried grooms and gardeners who lived in a bothy close to the house. 'I like to think of those still room maids and housemaids discarding their printed chinz dresses and muslin caps for their evening finery', wrote Lady Bath, years later.

Nevertheless, large establishments like Longleat were untypical of the households in which most servants worked, even in country districts.[24] Far more typical was the experience of a 14-year-old girl who went as a 'tweeny' in the household of a Norfolk doctor early in the twentieth century. For several weeks before taking up the post she helped her mother make her uniform. This consisted of two print dresses, six morning aprons, four caps, four afternoon aprons, two blue check aprons, a hessian apron for scrubbing and a black afternoon dress. 'My wages were to be one pound a month which had to be taken home to help pay for my outfit.' Each morning she rose at 6 a.m. to light the kitchen range, and to blacklead and polish it until it shone. Then there was the surgery to scrub, three large door-steps to hearthstone, and morning tea to take upstairs at 7.45 a.m. 'After breakfast I had to help the house maid until noon, then help cook prepare lunch and afterwards wash up and clean the kitchen floor. The rest of the afternoon was taken up helping the parlourmaid clean brass and silver.'[25] She also had her honesty tested when her mistress put pennies under the edges of the carpets. She told her father, who in turn informed the mistress that if his daughter found any more coins, she was to pocket them. Wryly she added: 'I never found another one.'

Some employers were distinctly eccentric. A girl who was employed by a spinster at Milton-under-Wychwood, Oxfordshire, at the turn of the century recalled being accused of stealing 'the breadcrusts, the wood and coal and candles. Each night . . . [the mistress] looked for a man under her bed.' She also accused her maid of 'having followers in the kitchen, then of hiding them in the attics to steal after [the mistress] had retired for the night'.[26] Not surprisingly, the girl decided to move to another place – this time in a farmhouse. Here, as well as her domestic tasks, she was expected to put her master to bed when he came home drunk from market! She also escorted the daughter of the house to chapel and to wood-carving classes, and waited for her whilst she drank tea with her friends.[27]

But if the economic and social circumstances of an employer affected the working conditions of the servant, another factor was the widespread regional difference in the number of domestics employed. In counties like Lancashire and the West Riding of Yorkshire, where employment in the textile mills was widely accepted by labouring families, servant numbers were lower. The same was true of counties like Bedfordshire, Buckinghamshire and Hertfordshire, where alternative job outlets were available in cottage industries, especially up to the 1870s. In 1871 about a third of all females living in Bedfordshire worked as cottage lacemakers or straw plaiters, compared to little more than a twentieth working as servants, and in both Buckinghamshire and Bedfordshire it was claimed that 'a native female domestic servant was rarely to be found.'[28] Girls preferred the relative freedom of the cottage industries to the close personal surveillance and regulation of behaviour which were the accompaniments of domestic service.[29]

Towards the end of the nineteenth century, as educational opportunities widened following the passage of the 1870 Education Act, there was a still greater reluctance to take up the drudging daily routine of domestic work. Farm service was particularly unpopular, since hours were long and the work arduous, with many girls expected to help with dairying and livestock feeding alongside their normal household chores. In parts of Wales, maids rose at 5 a.m. and did not retire to bed until about 10 p.m., after the family had gone upstairs. But farmers' wives in the principality denied that the servant scarcity was due to the hard work expected of them. They blamed it on 'too much education'.[30]

So it was that domestic service reached a peak of the proportion of the female population of England and Wales which it employed in 1871. At that date around one in eight of all women and girls in the country was engaged in service or in allied occupations like laundry work and charing. Most – probably around two-thirds – had been born in rural districts, and many, both then and later, were very young. In the early 1870s over a tenth of all general servants were under fifteen.[31] 'Domestic service is . . . distinguished from most other occupations by the very early age at which it is undertaken', commented the 1891 census report.[32]

Many village girls going to their first 'place' at the age of thirteen or fourteen (and some even younger) experienced a bitter wrench as they parted from home and family. One woman who went into service on a farm at the age of eleven, after being recruited by a farmer's wife at Witney hiring fair, in about 1890, recalled walking the seven miles from home to her place of employment 'crying her eyes out'.[33] And in 1875, 12-year-old Kate Faggetter from Lower Heyford, Oxfordshire, wrote to her former headmistress to tell of her daily round as a nursemaid. She sadly admitted that she 'did not like Woodstock near so much as Heyford and I long to come home again to see some of my friends and playmates. . . . Dear Teacher we are having a new kitchen built and it does make me such a lot of work that I scarcely know how to do it.'[34]

In *Lark Rise to Candleford*, Flora Thompson described several servant departures from her own north Oxfordshire hamlet. Usually the tin trunk containing the girl's uniform and other possessions would be sent in advance to the railway station by carrier's cart, and then mother and daughter would set off on foot to follow its three-mile journey. They left perhaps before it was light on a winter's morning, and neighbours came to the garden gate to see them off and to wish the girl well, or, more comfortingly, to call 'You'll be back for y'r holidays before you knows where you are and then there won't be no holdin' you.' 'What the girl, bound for a strange and distant part of the country to live a new, strange life among strangers, felt when the train moved off with her can only be imagined', wrote Mrs Thompson.[35]

To obtain these posts, some of the girls applied to the servants' registry offices which were established in most country towns; others answered advertisements in the press. Such appeals as 'Wanted – Strong active Girl for House-Work, about 15 or 16, from country preferred', or 'Wanted – At an Inn at Chipping Norton a good General Servant, about 18 years of age; must have been out before, an early riser, and capable of undertaking plain cooking', which appeared in the *Oxfordshire Weekly News* in 1888, give a flavour of what was expected.

Despite the loneliness which the girls experienced when they left home and family, a number forged warm relationships with their employers. One youngster mentioned by Flora Thompson was eventually adopted by the elderly employers to whom she had gone as a maid at the age of eleven.[36] Higher up the social scale, Loelia, Duchess of Westminster, claimed that 'nannies were loved as much as any mother, . . . cooks and housemaids considerably preferred to some aunts.'[37] And at Erddig near Wrexham, the Yorke family not only had numerous portraits and photographs of their servants hanging on the walls, but even composed verses about their favourite maids.[38]

Yet it is also true that there was a very clear social gulf between master and servant and that this widened during the Victorian years, as the number of servants and the kinds of household in which they worked both expanded sharply. Edward Salmon, writing on 'Domestic Service and Democracy' in 1888, claimed that beyond the paying of wages or the performance of duties 'the barrier between the drawing-room and the servants' hall is never passed. Life above stairs is as entirely severed from life below stairs as is the life of one house from another.'[39] This attitude was epitomized by the requirement in one Suffolk country house that maids should flatten themselves, face to the wall, when members of the family or guests approached.

Yet, records show that not all servants accepted their lot as meekly as these comments suggest. Many showed their independence by moving frequently, and in 1899 a government survey estimated that about a third of all servants in England and Wales had held their current post for less than a year. Around a further one-fifth had served for between one and two years, and under a fifth had worked in the same household for more than five years.[40] Even in large households, moves among the junior staff were frequent, although housekeepers, cooks and lady's maids might stay for many years.

The household records of an anonymous north Oxfordshire housewife in the second half of the nineteenth century show that she, too, had difficulty in retaining staff. Many apparently gave as their excuse for moving that they had a sick relative at home whom they must nurse – a device which would inhibit the mistress from giving an unfavourable testimonial.[41] It was to counter this high mobility that agricultural societies and similar bodies offered awards to long-serving maids. The Thame Agricultural and Horticultural Societies, for example, offered annual prizes of £1 5s. for this purpose. Among the winners in 1885 was Emma Allen, who had worked for a farmer in the nearby village of Haddenham for nine years.[42]

The wages earned by these girls inevitably differed according to the position they held and the size of household in which they worked. Whilst young servants in their first post might receive as little as £2 10s. or £5 a year, the most senior could obtain many times that amount, exclusive of board and lodging. At Nuneham Courtenay, Oxfordshire, in 1894 the Harcourts paid £75 a year to their housekeeper-cook, £25 a year to the first kitchenmaid and first housemaid, but only £14 to the third housemaid.[43] Often the maids sent most of their earnings home to help with the family budget. 'In addition to presents', wrote Flora Thompson, 'some of the older girls undertook to pay their parents' rent; others to give them a ton of coal for the winter; and all sent Christmas and birthday presents and parcels of left-off clothing.'[44]

Finally, there is little doubt that some mistresses welcomed the chance to dominate the life of another human being – the maid – at a time when their own existence in a patriarchal society was controlled by husband, father or brother. The real or imagined faults of the maid could be used as a way of relieving frustration built up in other areas of family life.[45] Perhaps fittingly, books of advice for servants also reiterated the need for discipline and subordination: 'never allow pleasure to take the place of duty in your *heart*', is a typical comment from one of them.[46]

As for the maids, for much of the nineteenth century girls living in the rural areas of England and Wales had little choice but service if they needed to earn their own living. In this sense domestic service could be seen as a form of 'disguised under-employment', at any rate in the non-industrial areas of England and Wales.[47] Such work offered a roof over their head, a small wage and meals, as well as a protected environment for the youngest girls who were leaving home for the first time. Many maids also enjoyed reasonably cordial relations with their employers – although a few experienced unwelcome sexual advances from its adult male members, which were difficult to repulse. Joseph Ashby's mother, Elizabeth, was one such victim. Late in 1858, at the age of twenty-one, she returned to her native village of Tysoe in south Warwickshire, pregnant with her employer's child. He was a major local landowner. Joseph was born the following June and Elizabeth never returned to service.[48]

However, whilst the majority of women and girls who had a job in the Victorian countryside worked as maids, many also helped on the land, particularly at the busiest seasons of the farming year. Permanent women labourers were still employed in a few areas, including Northumberland, Durham and north Yorkshire; while in pastoral counties like Cheshire, Lancashire and Gloucestershire, or Cardigan in Wales, girls engaged ostensibly as domestic servants in practice spent a large part of their day in the dairy or in feeding livestock. They assisted in the fields at haymaking time, too.

Female labour was also important in those arable and mixed farming districts where male wage rates were low and there was a need for wives and daughters to contribute to family income. Some farmers made it a condition of employment for a male worker that his wife would lend a hand when required. Newspaper advertisements for labourers in Dorset often referred to the need for the successful candidate to have a 'working family'. And in the late 1860s there were reports of wives in that county having to send a daughter or another substitute because they were unable to work themselves. The typical view was expressed by a Dorset farmer who openly admitted that if he wished to use his steam engine for threshing he would 'go to [his] carter's wife and tell her I want her for a day or two. We consider that they are liable for that sort of work.'[49]

A similar policy applied in Wiltshire, especially where families lived in tied cottages. One mother of six children from Durnford complained that in her village females who worked on their landlord's holding were often paid a mere 6d. a day, well below the 8d. or 10d. a day paid where there were no such link. 'It is not a good plan to let the farmers have cottages', she declared: 'those who live in the farmer's cottages have to put up with a great deal, because if out of occupation you are out of your house. If the farmer wants the women to work for him they are obliged to go whether they like it or not.'[50]

Mrs Grout, a labourer's wife from Martley, Worcestershire, who also had six children, strongly disliked these arrangements, too: 'It answers well for women to work when they have no children, but it does not answer for me because I have to take my children out with me and therefore to provide them with good shoes; but I am tied to go out, that is part of the agreement under which we hold the house.'[51] She began her working year with stone-picking and dressing the ground ready for sowing in the spring:

> Then in May and June hop-tying; last year me and another took 10 acres at 4s. an acre, two poles to the stock; we usually only get 3s. or 3s. 6d. an acre. It takes all a woman's time to tie five acres; children cannot help at that. Then from June to August haymaking and harvest; . . . In September hopping, at which I can earn 1s. 2d. a day; . . . then comes fruit-picking at 8d. a day and cider; and last, topping and tailing turnips at 7s. an acre.

Work of this kind was still being performed by women in Worcestershire and Herefordshire up to the First World War.[52]

In parts of south-west Wales, where labourers were allowed to set potatoes in their employer's field for their own benefit, it was customary for payment to be made for this in the form of free labour from the womenfolk. The rate was one day's work by a wife at harvest for each load of manure supplied by the farmer. If the cottager provided his own dung, then the female work debt was limited to helping set the farmer's potatoes, with each farm having its own potato setting group.[53] From the employer's point of view, women workers were attractive because of their relative cheapness – they were normally paid only about half the male rate – and because of the flexibility with which they could be deployed.

But whilst many females continued to work on the land in this fashion, by the 1850s and 1860s, as chapter 1 showed, their role was increasingly coming under question. In particular, it was felt that the

PLATE 19   *Stone-picking at Bangor Teifi, near Llandysul, Cardiganshire, c.1900. This was an unattractive and laborious female occupation.*
(National Museum of Wales [Welsh Folk Museum])

freedom they enjoyed as field hands led to a coarsening of their language and behaviour. It was also alleged that where they had young children, these were neglected whilst the mothers were at work. Either they were left in the care of a neighbour, who perhaps dosed them with opiates like Godfrey's cordial to quieten them (sometimes with fatal results); or they were locked in the house whilst the mother was out. She then returned in the evening to find 'crockery smashed, clothes torn, and furniture broken'.[54] Occasionally the youngsters accidentally set fire to the house or themselves. In the late 1860s a Warwick GP claimed to have attended eight such cases, four of them fatal, while a Monmouth mother, compelled to work by family poverty, nonetheless confessed her anxieties about her children: 'one is only a few months old, and none are old enough to take any real care of the others. I lock them into the kitchen, and they play about. Must leave a bit of fire because of the supper, but it is dangerous, and I am always afraid they may come to some harm.[55]

The heavy labour expected of the women, especially during the heat of harvest or the cold and damp of winter, adversely affected the health of some. Pregnant workers suffered especially as a result of the

A MERE PREJUDICE.

Tourist. "I SEE YOU EMPLOY A GOOD MANY WOMEN ABOUT HERE, FARMER."
Farmer. "HAVE TO DO HARVEST-TIME, SIR. BUT FOR MYSELF I MUCH PREFER MANUAL LABOUR!"

PLATE 20   *The growing prejudice towards women's work on the land is indicated in this* Punch *cartoon.*

(1892)

exertions of harvest, with doctors commenting on the increase in miscarriages and premature births which occurred during that period.[56] Wages books confirm that women continued to work both whilst they were expecting a baby and soon after the birth. Thus at Ireley Farm near Winchcomb, Gloucestershire, Susan Randall, wife of one of the farm's regular male workers, was hoeing wheat until early May 1870, about three months before the birth of her third child. She resumed work the following April, when the baby was aged eight months and her eldest child was four.[57]

Not all contemporaries, however, joined in the general condemnation of women's field labour. Arthur Munby, the barrister and diarist, was a particular advocate of their right to choose their own employment, as we saw in an earlier chapter. And in his accounts of meetings with some of them he stressed the pride they felt in their skills. A young Yorkshire woman, who could plough and harrow, as well as carry out more usual female tasks around the field and dairy, boasted to Munby that she had won a shilling by beating a male fellow worker in an impromptu ploughing match. 'Ah can shear as well as a man', she added; by that she meant that she could reap as efficiently as a male labourer, using a sickle.[58]

But such robust views on women's role were already waning in the 1860s and by the end of the century there were many comments on their reluctance to take up field work.[59] These changing attitudes on the 'supply' side of the female labour equation were reinforced by alterations on the 'demand' side, too, especially in regard to developments in harvesting techniques. By the late eighteenth century the scythe (which women rarely used) was superseding the sickle, which they had deployed, as the principal tool for the harvesting of corn. That trend continued in the nineteenth century until, by the 1830s, over nearly the whole of England the scythe and the fagging hook, primarily used by men, had become the main harvesting tools. Later in the century reaping machines, especially the self-binders of the 1880s and 1890s, further undermined the female role at harvest. Consequently, farmers no longer needed large numbers of women to help with the gathering of the grain. Instead on many farms the peak demand for their labour came in the spring and early summer, when they were engaged on weeding, turnip singling, stone-picking, haymaking and the like. After that they became 'increasingly vulnerable to unemployment'.[60] In the final quarter of the nineteenth century that situation was further aggravated by the effects of agricultural depression, as farmers moved away from labour-intensive arable cultivation to pastoral production, or merely decided to prune wages bills by dispensing with the weeding, stone-picking and similar 'female' tasks they had once regarded as essential.

So it was that the number of women recorded as agricultural labourers and farm servants in the population censuses dropped sharply. In 1851, 143,475 females were so reported; by 1871 that had fallen to 58,112, and to 11,951 by 1901. Although such figures seriously underestimate the true position, in that many part-time or casual workers did not declare their occupation to the census enumerator, the overall trend is clear. Even the 1908 census of production, based on returns submitted by farmers, showed only 68,000 females permanently employed in agriculture (other than family members), plus another 32,000 temporary workers at the busy

PLATE 21 *Sharpening sickles in a Cardiganshire corn harvest, 1903.*
(National Museum of Wales [Welsh Folk Museum])

seasons. Admittedly that combined total of 100,000 was nearly nine times the 1901 population census equivalent, but it still fell far short of the level noted in the census half a century earlier.[61]

Farm wages books, especially in arable and mixed farming areas, do suggest that in the mid-Victorian years many more women were engaged in land work than declared that occupation in the census. Celia Miller, in a survey of female field workers in Gloucestershire between 1870 and 1901, has shown, for example, that of seven women working at Park Farm, Fairford, in 1870–1 only one – a widow – is so recorded in the census return. The remainder were given no occupation, even though three of them worked for about two-thirds of the year at day- and piecework.[62] At that date they were performing almost a third of the total day labour carried out on the farm. Again at Ireley Farm, Hailes, where four women were at work in 1870–1, none declared an occupation to the census enumerator, although three of them worked between 100 and 150 days in the year. Among the tasks they carried out were threshing, stone-picking, dung spreading, weeding, hoeing, sorting and planting potatoes, fruit picking, haymaking and harvesting, work in the garden, household chores and mending sacks. One of the most active of them, 51-year-old Emma Seabright, who had three children living at home, earned £5 10s. 3¼d. for the year. This compared with her labourer husband's annual income of £26 5s. 9d. Clearly her earnings were an important part of total family resources, and in each of the years 1868–71 inclusive she worked 130 days or more at this farm or its associated holding, Postlip Farm.[63]

Similar results can be obtained in other counties. Thus at Wick Farm, Radley, Berkshire, the farmer, John Badcock, made no mention in 1861 of employing women labourers at all. Twelve men and five boys only were recorded in the census as working on the 400-acre holding. Yet wages books show that as many as seven females were employed on the farm during certain weeks in that year. In addition, from Michaelmas, Mrs East, the carter's wife, earned 1s. a week 'for looking after the fowls'– a sum which exactly equalled the family's weekly cottage rent.[64]

At Tarrant Monkton, Dorset, too, neither of the women who worked regularly for John Butler on his 220-acre farm in the early and mid-1860s is shown as having an occupation in the 1861 census. Apart from farm work they earned small sums carrying out such additional tasks as mending sacks at 1d. each. In return they pledged part of their earnings to purchase butter, bacon, cheese and firing.[65] A similar practice was followed at Snowshill and Parks Farms, Stanway, Gloucestershire, as late as the 1890s, with women workers regularly spending part of their harvest earnings on fuel, mutton, cheese, hops and rabbits; some of the men on this farm adopted the same policy.[66]

The wages books also confirm the changes which took place in the size of the female labour force over time and in the rates of pay they received. Thus at Wick Farm, Radley, where women were employed for forty-three weeks during 1861, their daily wage varied between 8d. or 9d. and 1s. In the week ending 18 January one woman only was employed for one day at 8d.; by 12 April, five women were at work, three of them earning 4s. a week, one 3s. 8d. and the fifth 2s. 8d. With the beginning of haymaking in mid-June, the female total rose to seven and remained at that level until the first week of July. By 26 July, with hoeing in full operation, five of the six women then at work earned 5s. a week, while the sixth secured 2s. 6d. On 30

PLATE 22   *Fruit pickers at Paxton Farm, near Sevenoaks in Kent, 1907.*
(Institute of Agricultural History and Museum of English Rural Life,
University of Reading)

August, as the corn harvest got under way, the number of women individually employed by Mr Badcock dropped to three, with one earning 6s. a week (1s. a day), one 4s. and the third 2s. Others may have assisted their husbands as part of a family team, but they are not mentioned in the wages books. By 6 September, the labour force had diminished to two, earning respectively 4s. 3d. and 2s. 6d. a week, and about a month later, except for two forays by three women during December, and one week in which a wife was helping her husband, female employment on this farm dried up completely. It did not fully resume until the first week of January 1862.[67]

Twenty years later, on another Berkshire farm – that of John Cozens at Little Wittenham – just two women were at work on the 195-acre holding. Neither was mentioned in the census as so occupied, and Cozens claimed to employ six men and two boys only. One of them, a Mrs Wheeler, worked for sixty-three and a quarter days (spread over twenty-seven separate weeks) during 1881, and earned £4 10s. 11d. Not only did she carry out work in the fields and the barn, but she helped with the threshing, assisted in the house, mended sacks and washed and repaired clothes. Her colleague, Mrs Belcher, worked for sixty-seven days, as well as earning 12s. 'reaping' at harvest on piecework rates. She did not perform the non-agricultural tasks carried out by Mrs Wheeler, and so although she worked more days than her companion they were spread over just nineteen weeks, and her total earnings were only £3 4s. 5½d.[68] In both cases, the women were wives of male employees on the farm, and their daily rates of pay varied from 9d. for 'field work' to 1s. 6d. for threshing. Both were aged forty-four and had four children.

By the end of the nineteenth century most wages books reveal a decline in women's employment compared to the 1850s and 1860s. Thus on the Butler farm in Dorset, where five women had helped at harvest in August 1864, only two women were recruited a decade later, and by the 1880s all mention of female labourers had disappeared from this farm's wages books.[69] Likewise at Ireley Farm, Hailes, where five women had been at work in May 1865, by 1871 there was no week during which more than three females were employed.[70]

The principal exception to this general downward trend which has so far been identified relates to Snowshill Farm and Parks Farm in Gloucestershire, a two-farm unit of around 700 acres. Here eleven women were at work as late as 1890–1, six of them for around 200 days in the year. They performed about a third of the total day-work carried out.[71] However, even here by the mid-1890s numbers were falling a little.[72]

The reminiscences of some of these part-time women workers confirm the informality of their hiring. Thus Mrs Daisy Record of Harrietsham in Kent recalled that when spring arrived she would go to the farmer to ask if there were work available. He would reply, '"I'll be lookin' for you"', and she then started work, labouring from 8 a.m. until 4 p.m. each day. In the summer she picked fruit, but at other times she carried out a variety of tasks, including helping the men to make fencing pales in the winter and spreading dung in the early spring.

> Then it'd be hoein' strawberries all up, and puttin' the straw underneath the fruit. Then we'd git the potaters in, and the swedes and wurzels. An arter that come hayin'– we 'ad five or six weeks o' that . . . Then, between haytime and harvest, there

was the 'wild white' clover to git in: and arter that was harvest . . .
Then you're pickin' up your mangels and swedes . . . Arter *that*,
you come round to winter again, and that was threshin' time.[73]

She then added ruefully, 'I could do everything a man could do, jest
about; but they never give me no man's money!'

The toil was particularly arduous for those women who went
reaping, as Richard Jefferies described in the 1870s, at a time when
the use of the sickle was already in sharp decline:

> From earliest dawn to latest night they swing the sickles, staying
> with their husbands, and brothers, and friends, till the moon
> silvers the yellow corn. The reason is because reaping is piece-
> work, and . . . the longer and harder they work the more money
> is earned. . . . Grasping the straw continuously cuts and wounds
> the hand, and even gloves will hardly give perfect protection.
> The woman's bare neck is turned to the colour of tan; her thin
> muscular arms bronze right up to the shoulder. Short time is
> allowed for refreshment; right through the hottest part of the
> day they labour. It is remarkable that . . . very few cases of
> sunstroke occur. Cases of vertigo and vomiting are frequent, but
> pass off in a few hours. Large quantities of liquor are taken to
> sustain the frame weakened by perspiration.[74]

Bodies became caked with a mud-like mixture of sweat and dust, and
occasionally the exertion proved too much for some older workers.[75]
When women were suckling babies, these, too, had to be carried to
the field. Often they would be placed on a heap of coats or shawls in
the shade of a hedge where they would be watched over by one of
the older children.[76]

When the women's services were no longer needed for reaping,
many were still recruited to bind the corn into sheaves. Arthur
Randell, who lived in the Norfolk fens, recalled that even in the early
twentieth century, his mother went off every summer to the fields
with her children. There she tied and shocked the sheaves 'as fast as
any man. About four o'clock she would take some of us back home,
and when my father and the others came in about half past seven the
tea would be on the table and the youngest children all in bed.'[77]

Later, a mother and her children would go out gleaning, to collect
the scattered grain left behind by the harvesters. This would help to

PLATE 23   *Gleaning in readiness for the winter.*

(*Country Life*, 1903)

feed the family pig or else be taken to the miller to be ground into flour to make bread for the household during the difficult winter months. Gleaning had its special rituals and regulations, too. In some villages the church bell was rung as a sign that it could begin; in other cases, farmers left a single sheaf in the field, which the women nicknamed the policeman. This indicated that all was not yet ready, and any who disobeyed the prohibition could have their grain confiscated or even be charged with theft, for this meant the farmer was still carrying his crops. However, especially in the early Victorian years, women defended their *right* to glean tenaciously, and, often enough, were upheld in this by the local courts.[78]

Women's land work was, then, heavily dependent on seasonal demand. It also covered a wide range of tasks, so that around Porlock in Somerset there were five different 'harvests' in which they were involved between June and November each year. These were haymaking, whortleberry picking, corn harvest, acorn gathering and apple picking. The acorns were either sold direct to farmers for feeding to the pigs, or disposed of to an acorn buyer who came round the villages.[79]

Much the same situation existed in other areas. 'I have found special employments exist for women in almost every county I have visited', wrote Mr F. H. Norman, an assistant commissioner with the 1867-9 Royal Commission on the Employment of Children, Young Persons and Women in Agriculture:

> In Herefordshire, Worcestershire, and Surrey they are employed in tying hops to the hop poles in May and June, and in hop-picking in September. Wherever there is much wood, as in the south of Surrey, in Worcestershire, and in Herefordshire, they are occasionally employed in stripping bark at the end of April and the beginning of May. In Surrey they are also employed in washing carrots in winter, in the neighbourhoods of Guildford and Chertsey; and in the medical herb gardens of Carshalton and Mitcham, they are employed in transplanting the plants in spring, and in assisting to harvest them in autumn. In the neighbourhood of Evesham they are largely employed in the fruit and vegetable gardens during the spring and summer.[80]

Hop-picking was always a major user of temporary female labour. Around Farnham, Surrey, one important centre, a network of agencies was established by local farmers, with each agent paid commission on every collecting 'bin' for which he supplied pickers. At Dippenhall Farm, Mrs Paine, the farmer, had 200 acres of hops and in 1868 she recruited about 2,660 pickers to work at 760 bins. Migrant pickers were housed in large sheds, sleeping on beds of straw. Mrs Paine supplied a pair of sheets and a counterpane for each bed, but there were no proper washing or sanitary facilities, and no means of drying wet clothes, other than the camp fires on which the pickers cooked their meals. Bread, tea and herrings were the most popular items of food among the Dippenhall workers, and each day carts of bread came out from Farnham and the surrounding villages to the hop gardens.[81]

However, it was in Kent that hopping reached its peak of importance. According to one major landowner, it was 'looked forward to to pay off old debts and rents, and the woman here is the chief contributor'. A girl who picked in West Kent early in the twentieth century remembered leaving home at 6 a.m. in order to arrive ready to start work at 7 a.m. At 12.30 came the luncheon break:

Our favourite meal was a large plate of meat and potatoes, followed by a stiff rice pudding, all made the evening before by Mother. . . . All work stopped at 6.30 p.m., and, tired and weary, we would set off to walk across country back home. . . . With the money we had earned, mother fitted us out with new clothes for the winter.[82]

Another worker remembered that in the month or so before picking began, the women were busy in the oasthouses, mending bin cloths and pokes (that is, the 10-bushel sacks used for measuring the hops when they were collected from the picking bins). In the cottages, wives also made coarse aprons to protect the pickers' clothing, and husbands produced besoms to place by the back door, ready to clean the family's shoes when they returned from a day's 'hopping'.[83]

Vast numbers of pickers came from outside the county, particularly from the East End of London, where special agencies were set up to recruit them. Some cottage wives, anxious to earn extra cash, secured a few pence by cooking Sunday joints or cakes for the 'migrants'. Their husbands likewise sold potatoes and other vegetables, as well as poultry, when the pickers returned home to London. Overall, one mid-century writer considered the hop gardens provided more employment than any other agricultural pursuit, except for market gardening.[84]

This latter had its migrant labour, too, with women coming long distances to help plant and harvest crops in the market gardens of Middlesex and Surrey. Many were from Ireland; others travelled from north and west Wales and Shropshire. The journey from one collecting point, Tregaron in Cardiganshire, took about a week, and in the middle of the nineteenth century small parties of about half a dozen girls would set off on foot to make the trek of nearly 200 miles.[85]

Some stayed in inns, some in barns . . . During the journey they were reported to pass the time telling stories, singing, laughing and exchanging remarks with young men they passed on their way. . . . Some . . . [carried] bags of bilberries and cranberries with them, selling the fruit to people on the route. Others were reported to be knitting stockings as they walked, the proceeds going towards the cost of their lodgings in London until they received their first pay.

The first migrants arrived in early April and remained until September. Many then returned home, but some, anxious to earn extra cash, joined the exodus of Londoners to work in the Kentish hop gardens. Although migration from Wales diminished in the second half of the nineteenth century – perhaps because the women now worked on farms in the principality or had moved into domestic service – migrants continued to come from Shropshire and Ireland until the eve of the First World War.[86]

Elsewhere, there were accounts of women moving from Berkshire and Wiltshire during the 1860s to take temporary employment in Monmouthshire, while the superfluity of female labour in south Cardiganshire during that decade led some to migrate to the north of the county or into Montgomeryshire at harvest time. There they offered 'their temporary services to any farmer who may happen to be short of hands', and in return earned 1s. 6d. a day and their keep.[87]

However, whilst women's labour on the land remained important, at least on a seasonal basis, until the last quarter of the nineteenth century, it reached its highest degree of organization in Northumbria. For much of the Victorian era the 'bondager' system prevailed, whereby male workers, or hinds, were expected to supply and house an extra female labourer to work as required. She might be a wife, daughter or sister, but if there were no suitable relative, an outsider would be recruited. This led to charges of immorality and to complaints from the workers of the inconvenience of the practice. By the late 1880s the system had largely died out, save where the girl concerned was a family member. But annually hired males were still expected to find a woman helper when needed – in a county where it was easy for young fit *men* to obtain remunerative employment in the expanding coal industry.[88]

Females were considered essential for the efficient running of the county's farms, especially as their rates of pay were only about half those of the men, and yet they could carry out much the same tasks. 'Our women working at the turnips would kill all the men we have got', was the tribute of one estate steward.[89] In 1911 (as in 1851) more than one in five of all Northumberland's farm workers were female, according to the population census, and in Durham, where women's labour was also important, it was over one in ten. This compares with a proportion of less than one female employed to every fifty males in most English counties on the eve of the First World War.[90]

The majority of the bondagers were under thirty and were expected to perform a wide range of tasks; indeed, according to Arthur Munby, who met some of them in the summer of 1863, once afield they might be called upon to carry out any task 'except ploughing and ditching'. He then added significantly that the farmer liked 'to have his wenches under bondage', because then he could 'send them afield to hoe or dig in all weathers, and they can't shirk it'. When at work the bondager wore 'a rough straw bonnet tilted over her eyes, with sometimes a kerchief underneath; a short cotton frock; a big apron of sackcloth, or a smock; and stout hobnailed boots and woollen stockings'.[91]

Munby met other full-time women labourers in north Yorkshire, including a group of potato pickers near Brotherton. They were a 'gang of twelve stout women and girls, all in white smocks and rustic bonnets and kerchiefs: . . . moving slowly over the rough plough-lands, stooping or kneeling on the ground, & digging up the potatoes with their hands.' One of the younger women ran up to him, saying they would like to drink his health – a clear hint that they wanted a cash gift. He seized the opportunity to question her about her employment and discovered that she and the others were paid 1s. a day to work from 7 or 8 a.m. until dark at hay and harvest; in May they helped at osier peeling, in June they went peapicking, and in October, potato gathering; then came turnip pulling, but 'in the winter, alack! we have to stop at home idle . . . and do our bits of household work & sewing.'[92]

Many of the unmarried women workers in the north were still recruited through hiring fairs, and in 1862 Munby, on a visit to York, saw a 'double row of farm lasses' standing for hire on the pavement: 'They were homely wenches, . . . plainly drest, some wearing cotton gloves . . . Here and there a farmer or a farmer's wife was bargaining with one of them.'[93] In view of the criticisms often levelled at hiring fairs as places of immorality and drunkenness, it is interesting to note that Munby considered all the girls to be 'honest and stolid looking creatures; . . . I did not see or hear an ill word or look, much less an insult of any kind, offered to them either by the male labourers or by the public who gazed at them in passing.'[94]

PLATE 24   *Osier peeling, another subsidiary rural occupation taken up by women.*

(From P. H. Emerson, *Pictures of East Anglian Life* [1888])

Women's employment on the land on a full-time basis thus persisted longest in the arable districts of the north of England. The only other area of permanent farm employment where they remained important in the late nineteenth century was dairying – a role we considered in the last chapter.

However, in the middle of the nineteenth century the situation had been very different. Then it was the public gang system of East Anglia which provided the most dramatic and controversial employment of full-time female land labour. The gangs were first reported at Castle Acre in Norfolk during the mid-1820s, in a village surrounded by large arable farms but with a scanty population. They increased sharply after the passage of the 1834 Poor Law Amendment Act restricted the distribution of out-relief to needy families, and encouraged wives and daughters to seek to supplement inadequate male earnings. By the mid-1860s the gangs were found in Lincolnshire, Huntingdonshire, Cambridgeshire, Norfolk, Suffolk and Nottinghamshire, as well as to a minor extent in the neighbouring districts of Northamptonshire, Bedfordshire and Rutland.[95] Children, youths and women were all recruited by a gangmaster to carry out weeding, stone-picking and other tasks, first on one farm and then on another. About half the workers were under eighteen, but older girls and women were also prominent, and overall females predominated in most gangs.

Interviews with individual labourers confirmed this pattern. Mary Ann Gallay, an 18-year-old from Wimbotsham, Norfolk, went out with a gang of thirty-seven people, of whom only eight were boys. They worked from 8 a.m. until 6 p.m. in summer, and to 3 p.m. in winter. Often they had to walk miles to reach their destination. In wet weather they were soaked through, and in winter their hands became sore and painful through handling icy roots. There were also the relentless cold winds to contend with, as well as the rigours of the work itself. On one occasion, Mary Ann hurt her back carrying an apron full of turnips 'to fling them up; for two or three days I could not move, and they had to turn me over'.[96]

Another gang member was Sarah Ann Roberts of Tilney-Fen-End, also in Norfolk. She became a permanent invalid as a result of long exposure to the damp, especially when weeding corn:

> I have been so wet that I have taken off my clothes and wrung them out and hung them up to dry on the top of the wheat . . . while we went in again to weed. . . . We have had to take off our shoes and pour the water out, and then the man would say, 'Now then, go in again.' . . . My knee is so bad, and nearly as big as that loaf, but I have to keep moving it about for ease. I can only go with a crutch and stick. . . . We started at 6.30 a.m. If it was too far they would send and fetch us, but we have started at 6 a.m. and not got on the ground till after 7 if we made ever so much haste. . . . The man knocked us about and ill-used us dreadfully with hoes, spuds, and everything.[97]

However, what most offended mid-Victorian sensibilities was not the physical hardship which the women endured but the moral hazards posed, with some of the girls seduced by gangmasters or fellow male workers. Their bad language and lack of what were considered appropriate feminine graces were also condemned. 'A mixed gang composed of women, boys and girls returning from their distant labour on a rainy evening, weary, wet and foot sore, but in spite of their wretchedness singing licentious or blasphemous songs, is a spectacle to excite at once pity, detestation and disgust', wrote one critic.[98] Modern commentators might marvel that they had the spirit to give voice in this way after a day of exhausting toil!

Another outspoken opponent of the gangs was the vicar of Chatteris, in the Cambridgeshire fens, where 180 females and 80 males worked in gangs in the mid-1860s. According to him, the girls were 'more immodest and impudent . . . than the boys'. Their language was 'low, debasing and disgusting' and after they had eaten their supper they would 'flauntily dress themselves . . . and prance about the streets'.[99] As a result fornication and bastardy were widespread. His criticisms had some validity in that nearly 14 per cent of all births in the Chatteris district were illegitimate, compared to 5.9 per cent for England as a whole.[100]

Spalding in Lincolnshire was another major ganging centre, with 280 women and children regularly employed and 100 more going out occasionally. A medical officer with the Spalding poor law union complained that girls as young as thirteen were brought into the workhouse infirmary to be confined; their 'ruin has taken place in going and returning from gang work'.[101] In 1867 around 22 per cent of all births in the Spalding sub-district were illegitimate.

Not all ganging communities, though, conformed to this depressing picture. At Binbrook, Lincolnshire, where 213 males and females went out with the gangs in the mid-1860s, and March, Cambridgeshire, where 388 did so, illegitimacy rates were actually below the national average in 1867, amounting to 5.0 per cent and 4.3 per cent of total births respectively. Critics also conveniently ignored the fact that, with few other jobs available and male wage rates notoriously low in many of these counties, wives and daughters had to work on the land to help support the family.[102]

Other opponents concentrated on the links between gang employment and high levels of infant mortality. In 1863, Dr Hunter, reporting on behalf of the Medical Officer of the Privy Council, pointed out that in ganging districts one-third of illegitimate children born to labouring mothers died before they reached the age of one, and among older women there was more than a suspicion of infanticide. Even more lethal than straightforward neglect of the infants was the practice of administering opiates. According to Dr Hunter, in the marshlands of East Anglia there was 'not a labourer's house in which the bottle of opiate was not to be seen, and not a child but who got it in some form'.[103]

Nevertheless, the statistics, whilst revealing some cause for concern, do not confirm the views of the most vociferous critics. In 1866, when infant deaths (that is, deaths of children under one year) accounted for 24 per cent of all deaths in England, in the North Witchford area of Cambridgeshire (which included Chatteris) they comprised 27.5 per cent of the total, and in Spalding, 29.3 per cent.[104] And although infant mortality rates in Norfolk, Lincolnshire and Cambridgeshire were higher than in some other rural counties, they were still below the average for the nation as a whole in the mid- to late 1860s.

It was against this background, however, that the 1867 Agricultural Gangs Act was passed, prohibiting the employment of children under the age of eight in public gangs and forbidding the licensing by magistrates of gangs of mixed sex. This went some way towards satisfying the *moral* concerns of opponents, but it did not lead to an ending of gang labour. More successful in this respect were changing farming methods during the agricultural depression years of the 1880s and 1890s, coupled with a greater use of machinery. Nevertheless, even at the end of the century, gangs continued to be deployed in Norfolk, Lincolnshire and Cambridgeshire to help with seasonal tasks in areas of scanty population. A report on the Swaffham district of Norfolk in the early 1890s sounded a familiar critical note, when it observed that although women gangmasters were now in charge of female gangs, 'I am told that a young girl will very soon deteriorate if she has to work in company with one or two bad girls, which is not an uncommon occurrence.'[105]

By that time, though, the controversies over gang labour had largely faded away, and so had the major participation of women in land work. Their diminishing role was neatly exemplified by successive editions of Henry Stephens's popular *The Book of the Farm*, based largely on agricultural practices in the north of England and Scotland. In the first edition, published in 1844, Stephens clearly distinguished between the role of male and female field-workers, and supported these with carefully executed drawings. By the fourth edition, published in 1891, not only had the womenfolk been reduced to fleeting references in the text, but some of the drawings depicting them at work had been omitted. As Eve Hostettler, who first noted this sleight of hand, has wryly pointed out, the 'conventional view' of the agricultural labourer was of a male. 'Never mind that women worked in fields, barns and dairies . . .: it is their obliteration which, knowingly or not, is the image perpetuated in our history-books.'[106]

7

Rural Crafts and Village Trades

[G]loving is a resource to the mass of the people, and 'keeps many above want who could not work in the fields'.

Evidence on the Somerset gloving trade, in appendix to the
Second Report of the Children's Employment Commission, PP 1844, vol. XIV.

We . . . employ lace makers in almost every village, and some of these in almost every house, within a circle of 10 miles from Bedford . . . In some of the villages we have also lace schools under our control, so far as regards the kind of lace made there, and the patterns used, which we supply.

Evidence of Thomas Lester, lace manufacturer, Bedford, to the
Children's Employment Commission, PP 1863, vol. XVIII.

Although domestic service and, to a lesser degree, agriculture employed the majority of women workers in the Victorian country-side, there were certain areas to which this did not apply. Sometimes the reason lay in competing job opportunities in factories and workshops, as happened in Lancashire or parts of the Black Country.[1] In other cases, especially up to the 1860s, the cause was the survival of a cottage industry, in which a mother and her children working together might earn 'as much or more than the husband who [was] at work on the neighbouring farm'.[2] These crafts were particularly important in the rural Midlands and south, where alternative female employment was limited and male wages were low.

The range of activities involved was wide: pillow lacemaking in the

PLATE 25 *Bedfordshire straw plaiter, c.1900, with her supply of split straws under her left arm.*

(Luton Museum and Art Gallery)

south Midlands and Devon; straw plaiting for the hat and bonnet trade around Luton and Dunstable and extending into Essex; glovemaking in Somerset, Devon, Dorset, Oxfordshire, Wiltshire, Worcestershire and Herefordshire; buttonmaking in east Dorset; hosiery work in the east Midlands; the production of straw ropes and thatching mats around Newborough in Anglesey; and netmaking or 'braiding' on the East Anglian, Dorset and Cornish coasts, were but a few of the tasks upon which women were engaged.

Many years ago it was suggested that cottage industries were most likely to flourish in pastoral districts, where there was little work for women and children on the farms, and their labour was thus available for alternative employment.[3] Hence in the early 1840s domestic knitting was widespread in the dales of north-west Yorkshire, in an area described as 'one large grazing and breeding farm'. Stockings, jackets, and sailors' caps were among the items produced.[4]

A similar situation existed in parts of Wales, with about a thousand women in south Wales classing themselves as 'knitters' or 'hose and stocking makers' in 1851, and much the same total employed in 'hosiery' two decades later. Around Tregaron in Cardiganshire even at the end of the nineteenth century it was said to be unusual to see a woman over forty without some knitting in her hands.[5] To obtain the wool they needed, many of the women searched hedgerows and hillsides for the wisps left behind by the flocks of grazing sheep. They often spent several days on their travels, each party of about six women carrying with them sufficient provisions to last for a week or a fortnight, together with sacks to carry home their booty. Whilst they were away they were given shelter in remote farmsteads, and sometimes a bundle of wool as well.[6] Later, groups of workers met together in cottages to knit their stockings and exchange gossip or recount traditional tales.

The development of the glove industry in south Somerset was likewise attributed to the pastoral character of the local agriculture. Here the women were engaged in sewing gloves at home for entrepreneurs in Yeovil, Milborne Port and similar centres.[7]

But whilst pastoral farming might be a decisive factor in the development of domestic industry in some areas, other influences could ensure its growth in arable districts, too. In Bedfordshire and parts of Buckinghamshire, cottage crafts were established in grain-growing areas where there was much poverty and male under-

PLATE 26 *Cottagers plaiting straw and sewing bonnets: a study by Carlton A Smith, RBA, 1891.*

(Luton Museum and Art Gallery)

employment. A supplementary income outside agriculture was thus necessary. Locally produced raw materials (like the fine quality straw used by the Bedfordshire and Buckinghamshire plait trade), and the existence of a ready market for the finished produce, were also important in deciding an industry's location. In both of these counties not only were there straw hatmaking centres close at hand in Luton and Dunstable (which created a further demand for female labour), but London, the prime outlet for all fashion goods, was within easy reach. The 1871 census of population showed that more than half the straw plaiters in the entire country were located in Bedfordshire and Buckinghamshire; at this date more than one in four of all females living in the former county was a plaiter. Hertfordshire, too, was heavily involved, with nearly one in eight of its female population employed in the trade in 1871.

In the cottage lace trade, likewise, proximity to London seems to have played an important part in its development. Of the five major domestic lacemaking counties (Northamptonshire, Devon, Oxfordshire, Bedfordshire and Buckinghamshire), the two last provided three-fifths of the total workers in 1871. At least a tenth of all Buckinghamshire females and around a thirteenth of those in Bedfordshire worked as lacemakers in that year; and since part-time workers often did not declare an occupation to the census enumerator, the true proportion was undoubtedly much higher.[8]

One major lace dealer, Thomas Gilbert of High Wycombe, claimed to employ about 3,000 workers in south Buckinghamshire and the adjoining area of Oxfordshire. 'They are not absolutely engaged by me as workpeople', he said,

> but I sell them the materials, i.e. patterns, and silk or thread; and there is a mutual understanding, though no legal obligation, that I should take all lace for which I have sold the patterns . . . From some I buy in their own villages, travelling round for the purpose . . . In some places I do not deal directly with the lace-makers themselves but through the agency of small buyers, to whom I supply the materials and patterns.[9]

Many of the smaller dealers also kept a general shop and encouraged workers to have goods on credit before the lace was completed. In this way makers became tied to one particular buyer, irrespective of whether he or she offered the best terms. And on the rare occasions when cash payments were made it was common for the dealers to deduct a penny in the shilling from the payments as a penalty. A number of these smaller traders were women, with a quarter of Bedfordshire's twenty lace dealers and a fifth of its 125 straw plait dealers at the beginning of the 1840s female; nearly a third of Buckinghamshire's twenty-three lace dealers were also female.[10] They included entrepreneurs like Mrs Allen of High Wycombe, Buckinghamshire, who recalled that in earlier years she had visited weekly the six or seven villages in which her makers resided: 'When buying on my own account I had to buy the cards and silk from the wholesale buyers, to whom I sold the lace, and I sold these materials in turn to the lace makers, taking the value out of the price of their lace, which is the usual custom still.'[11]

Residing as they often did in isolated rural communities and with little education, these craft workers were poorly placed to bargain effectively with the middle-men (or women) with whom they dealt. If they did not accept the dealers' terms, they found difficulty in getting employment. As Mrs Gardner, a glovemaker from Stonesfield, Oxfordshire, bluntly declared, two of the manufacturers for whom she worked made her take part of her earnings in tea, or candles, or sugar. But if she did not co-operate, 'they would "sack" me.'[12] It is significant that this practice of paying workers wholly or partly in kind persisted in the domestic industries despite the fact that it had been outlawed by the Truck Act of 1831.

However, whilst the nature of local agriculture, the availability of alternative female employment, the supply of raw materials and proximity to a market for the disposal of the finished goods all played a part in deciding the location of a cottage industry, its survival depended upon the severity of the competition it faced. So it was that the growth of textile factories in the north of England destroyed the domestic cloth trade of East Anglia and the west of England in the early nineteenth century. A similar fate overtook the button-makers of East Dorset, where in the early Victorian years the making of thread buttons on a ring of brass wire had been a major source of income for cottage families.[13] But then came the development of a buttonmaking machine in the mid-nineteenth century, and shortly afterwards the industry collapsed. Subsequently some of the women then turned to gloving and to knitting as a way of earning extra cash.

The problems of the English straw plait trade came not from mechanization but as a result of the importation of cheap foreign plaits from China, Japan and Italy from the 1870s. In 1893, it was estimated that less than 5 per cent of the plait sold in the major centre of Luton was English. There were complaints that much of the English plait was made in lengths too short for the sewing machines which were increasingly used in the bonnet trade, while its quality was inferior to that imported from Switzerland and Italy.[14] By 1901 Bedfordshire had only 485 female plaiters recorded in the census and Buckinghamshire a mere 173, compared to the 20,701 and 3,412, respectively, registered thirty years before. Rates of pay also slumped, while in 1912 there was an all-time peak import of plait.[15] Consequently, whereas once the wives of village tradesmen had been involved in making plait, as well as the families of agricultural labourers, by the end of the century it had become a low status occupation taken up by the poorest women only. In the early 1890s a woman from Shillington, about eleven miles from Luton, admitted that she was only earning about 6d. a score (that is, a length of twenty yards) for plait which fifteen or twenty years before would have realized 1s. 2d.[16]

A mixture of adverse factors also accounted for the collapse of the domestic lace industry. In the early nineteenth century, during the French war period, the craft had prospered, as imports of foreign lace were curtailed by the hostilities and by protective duties. But with the coming of peace, imports were resumed, despite the retention of some protective duties up to 1860. At the same time, the development of cheaper machine-made lace in Britain, especially from the 1840s, and changes in fashion also affected demand for the home-made fabric, thereby further undermining its profitability. By the 1820s, cottage producers were already under serious competitive pressure, and that remained the case despite a brief upturn in demand around the middle of the century. This was associated with the manufacture of cheaper and more showy Maltese-style lace, which was adopted by Bedfordshire makers in particular. It was quicker and easier to make than the fine quality traditional patterns and for some years could not be imitated by machine. But in the long run it served only to blunt the workers' technique and to reduce the overall standard and quality of their lace.[17] In parts of Buckinghamshire, meanwhile, there was an increased output of black lace in the 1850s which provided work for some domestic producers. Then came further improvements in the machine-made product during the 1860s and a reduction in overall demand for lace from the fashion trade. Caught in this economic pincer, domestic lacemaking had collapsed by the 1870s.

In the interim, some former lacemakers switched to the still lucrative plait trade until this, too, as we have seen, experienced difficulties in the 1870s. By 1881 Buckinghamshire had only 4,442 female lacemakers declaring an occupation to the census enumerator, compared to 10,487 recorded in 1851, and that total had fallen to a mere 789 by 1901. In Bedfordshire, numbers fell from a peak of 6,714 in 1861 to 1,144 at the end of the century.[18]

The Devon trade was similarly affected. A visitor to the Honiton area in 1888 described the distress which had arisen. At Woodbury, for example, the women's anxiety was 'great. People had not been trained to any other industry but lace-making and they beg the dealers and anyone to take their work and keep them out of the

PLATE 27 *Mrs Jane Mayes of Sharnbrook, Bedfordshire, making lace. She was left a young widow with several children to support. Beside her stands her daughter.*

(Mrs I. Horn)

union [workhouse].'[19] Of 150 lacemakers in Honiton itself there was now none 'under thirty years of age'.

It was against this depressing background that middle-class sympathizers sought to revive the domestic trade by setting up special lace associations to win orders for the workers and secure marketing outlets, particularly in London. It was also a response to general concern in the second half of the nineteenth century about the maintenance of overall standards of craftsmanship, as exemplified in the writings and work of William Morris and John Ruskin. Fears of rural depopulation played a part, too. It was argued that if women had work in the villages they would remain there instead of adding to the overall urban drift.

One of the first of the charitable organizations was the Winslow (Bucks) Lace Industry, established by a Miss Rose Hubbard in 1874 and claiming to employ seventy to eighty women thirty years later. In 1880 the wife of the vicar of Paulerspury in Northamptonshire set up a similar body called the Paulerspury Lace Industry, through which she sold the output of local makers to the Ladies' Work Society in Sloane Street, London. Her initiative aroused sufficient interest for orders to be received from two of Queen Victoria's daughters.

A third organization was the North Bucks Lace Association, formed in 1897, which sought to raise standards by discouraging the production of 'vulgar and degenerate forms of lace'.[20] By 1905 it claimed to employ 300 workers and to be arranging classes to teach children the essential skills of the craft. A fourth body was the Midland Lace Association, formed in 1891 to recruit workers in Northamptonshire, Bedfordshire and Buckinghamshire. By December 1910, after fluctuating fortunes, it had just over a hundred women on its books. At its peak it had employed about 400 workers in sixty villages.

Yet, despite the good intentions of the promoters and their elevated social status – Princess Beatrice, youngest daughter of Queen Victoria became president of the Midland Lace Association and Queen Alexandra was a patron of its North Bucks rival – overall achievement was modest in the extreme. The returns to the makers were often paltry, with even diligent workers hard pressed to earn more than 1d. or 1½d. an hour. In 1911, for example, an elderly Northamptonshire worker employed by the Association secured a gross income of £2 6s. 3d. for making ninety-seven yards of lace. On one occasion she apologized for the delay in fulfilling her order: 'if you pleas . . . I am been so hidl, I have don 4 yards of the cream Lace and will you kindly take that as I wanted the money . . . I will do the other in a week or to if better.'[21] Another woman, who had net earnings of £8 17s. in 1911, also seems to have found the work a struggle. A month before she died, she wrote to the Association, admitting sadly: 'i Carnt do any more this Winter as i carnt see to do it and it upsets

me . . . i have Been in bed again very ill but a little better . . . when i
can do a little i will try to do you [a] bit more.'[22]

In supplying orders to elderly makers like these the associations
were doing little to save the industry, for young workers were reluctant
to take up a craft which was so badly paid. A further problem was the
shortage of teachers even for those youngsters willing to learn.
Consequently, although these organizations survived into the inter-
war years, their contribution was negligible.[23]

Many of the other domestic trades faced similar problems.[24] Of
Wiltshire glovemaking it was noted on the eve of the First World War
that it had become 'a purely parasitic industry. No woman has been
met with who attempts to support herself by it; those who work at it
are married women, or elderly women depending upon private
incomes or upon outdoor [poor] relief, and girls, who for some
reason are living at home instead of following the usual practice of
going away to service.'[25] The money helped to eke out a husband's
low wage or some other small income, or was used for pin money. It
was also virtually impossible for a woman to combine agricultural
work with gloving (or lacemaking), since the softness of hand and
delicacy of touch required for the craft soon disappeared if she
engaged in heavy manual labour.[26]

Not all domestic industries, of course, fared as badly as these
examples suggest. Even at the end of the nineteenth century, there
was a flourishing mass tailoring trade in some Essex, Suffolk and
Berkshire villages. In the first two counties it was concentrated around
Colchester and Ipswich respectively, with garments sent out either
from London or from factories in the towns themselves. A similar
situation developed around Abingdon, then in Berkshire, where at
the end of the nineteenth century the firm of Clarke's employed
almost two thousand female outworkers. Women from the surrounding villages collected bundles of garments, already cut out at the
factory, which they the carried home to sew on their machines.[27]
Wives welcomed the work because it enabled them to carry out
household chores as well as pursue a money-making sideline, and
caused less wear and tear to clothes than field labour.

Netmaking for the fishing trade likewise continued to occupy
women in parishes around Bridport in Dorset in the early twentieth
century. Before the First World War there was no machine capable of
making nets with square meshes, or those with variable meshes

within the same net, and it was in this circumstance that the cottage workers made their contribution. Individual villages specialized in a particular kind of net, and the twine was despatched from the Bridport mills by carrier's cart.[28] Despite complaints from mothers that school attendance regulations prevented the children from learning the craft at a sufficiently early age, the industry prospered until 1914, and sent its nets to fishing communities all over the country.

Elsewhere, as one industry declined another took its place. In late nineteenth-century Buckinghamshire and Bedfordshire, a few women took up tambour work, sewing glass beads on to silk to provide ornaments for ladies' dresses, mantles and other fashion goods.[29] In villages around the chairmaking centre of High Wycombe, as the lace trade faded away, chair caning was taken up by some women. This was a relatively simple process and the equipment needed for it was also inexpensive – always an important factor in deciding whether labouring households could pursue a craft. One woman from Beaconsfield Old Town recalled that as a child she and her sister walked each day to a local chair factory to collect the chair seats or frames and the canes and wood for pegging that her mother needed for the work. Whilst the girls were at school the mother completed the task, ready for the finished products to be returned to the factory and fresh materials collected. In fine weather the women sat at their front door, 'with a bundle of canes hanging from a nail' as they caned the chairs.[30]

But however important these surviving domestic industries were to particular communities, their overall contribution was insignificant compared to the part played by domestic employment in earlier decades. Mechanization and the concentration of production in factories ensured that the domestic industries' contribution to the income of most labouring families was of peripheral importance only. Inevitably this limited village women's money-making prospects and increased their financial dependence on the male members of the family.

In the middle of the nineteenth century, however, when most of the cottage trades were still major employers of labour, the female role was very different. Then workers began to learn their craft at a very early age. In the case of lace, experts considered a start must be made at five or six years if the maker were to acquire the dexterity needed to produce the best work in later life. Economic pressures reinforced this attitude. As Thomas Gilbert pointed out, until the children could work 'a family is only expense, but a mother with some of her little girls at lace may make nearly as much as the father'.[31] Significantly, at the 1851 population census around a fifth of all the lacemakers in Buckinghamshire and Bedfordshire were under fifteen. For straw plaiting, a still earlier start might be made. Youngsters of two or three years were occupied in clipping off the loose ends of straw from the plait, 'with their scissors tied to their bodies'. At four or five they began to make plait on their own account.

Mothers encouraged this early employment of their children, and many started to teach their offspring the rudiments of the trade at home. However, in the case of lacemaking, plaiting, and glovemaking in the west of England, youngsters were frequently sent to special craft 'schools'. These also offered busy mothers a child-minding service for the youngest pupils, thereby enabling them to get on with their own work free from the care of their offspring.

The schools were normally held in cottages and were usually conducted by women whose prime recommendations were their trade skills and perhaps their iron discipline in extracting the maximum output (and thus income) from their young charges. Mary Driver of Beer, Devon, who kept a lace school in the early 1840s, deplored parents' insistence that she keep the youngest children working long hours in order to maximize their earnings:

> When they are 'out of their time,' which is about a year or a year and a half after they are 'put to it,' they can earn 3d. a-day if they are kept seven or eight hours in the school. 'They are sent by parents to work under the mistress . . . and . . . their parents take out in goods the value of their work.' . . . She thinks that 'sitting so long as some do hurts their constitution,' and 'she regrets that their parents order her to keep them so long'.[32]

Nevertheless, she considered that lacemaking was of benefit to the women of Beer since the men were mostly fishermen, and when they were out of work in winter, it was the women and children who had to 'support the town'.

Youngsters had few opportunities to learn basic academic skills in the craft schools, although a few teachers made half-hearted attempts to teach their pupils to read.[33] To while away the time and speed up the work, special rhymes or lace 'tells' were recited, and competitions were held to see which youngster could work the fastest. Those who failed to complete their assignment might be kept in 'from morning to night without food' as a punishment, instead of going home for a mid-day break. But it was not only the teachers who treated the children harshly. 'I have known mothers as severe as a mistress in keeping their children without food when they will not work', declared a Northamptonshire maker, Mary Ann Sumter of Broughton, in the 1860s.[34]

Given the bulkiness of the pillow on which the lace was made, workers had to adopt an awkward bent posture whilst occupied upon it, thereby causing neck and shoulders to ache. The intricate nature of the work led to eye strain, especially when it was carried out in a poor light or when black lace was being made. At Mrs Harris's lace school at Newport Pagnell, Buckinghamshire, in the early 1860s a visitor discovered girls working in a hot and overcrowded room 'without candle after it was so dark that I could hardly see to write'.[35] But the shared light of a candle, which was customary in the evening, was no great improvement. Perhaps most harmful of all was the practice adopted by some girls of wearing a 'strong wooden busk in their stays to support them when stooping over their . . . lace; this being worn when young [acted] very injuriously . . . causing great contraction of the chest'.

Much the same conditions applied in the other crafts. In 1871, one of HM Inspectors of Factories complained that young plaiters were working in poorly ventilated cottage rooms

> in any numbers, from 5 or 10 to 50 of them, sitting on little benches or stools, or anywhere where they can find a seat, in rows generally one behind the other; the master or mistress presides over them often with cane in hand to remind the idler of its duty . . . I . . . have been told that one of the reasons why parents send their children to the plaiting school instead of allowing them to plait at home is because the master or mistress 'gets more work out of them' than they could venture to attempt themselves.[36]

His views were confirmed by William Horley, postmaster and registrar of births, deaths and marriages at Toddington, Bedfordshire.

According to him, the mistresses who got the most work out of the youngsters were those best patronized:

> the children are packed as close as herrings . . . In some places they have to sit so close into the fireplace that the fire cannot be lighted, so they have coal or wood in earthen or even tin pots, which they call 'dicky pots.' . . . Great girls and women put them under their clothes, and children may be seen with them in their laps. These make a disagreeable smell.[37]

In fact the 'dicky pots' were also used by both plaiters and lacemakers to avoid ashes from an open fire soiling their work; an open fire would, in addition, have made the straws too dry for easy plaiting. Where they were widely used, not only did they add to the generally foetid atmosphere, but they caused chilblains and swollen ankles among the workers.[38]

As in the case of lace, the output and consequently the earnings of plaiters of all ages depended on the achievement of a high level of dexterity through constant practice – as well as on the kind of plait produced. 'There is no place drove like this for plait', declared Mrs Turry, a plait schoolmistress from Edlesborough, one of the major Buckinghamshire centres.[39]

Plaiting was essentially seasonal, with lower prices normally paid for plait made during the winter than in the spring and summer. The records of Henry Horn, a Dunstable plait dealer, show that his total outgoings (and the number of workers employed) were lowest in August, September and October, immediately after the harvest. They then picked up around November and December, presumably as the hat trade laid in stocks ready for the spring. Horn's records also show the wide variety of plaits which were produced. In the mid-1880s he had 137 different kinds in stock, including some made from dyed straws.[40]

In the major centres, the workers purchased their raw materials from specialist dealers, though in less important areas they might be obtained from the farmers direct. There are accounts of Essex plaiters carrying large bundles of straw home, tied round in their check aprons.[41] When completed, the finished plait was normally sold in lengths of twenty yards (or 'scores') either at one of the special weekly markets, the largest of which was held at Luton, or to local dealers. Some women obtained their straws from the village shop, and then sold the plait to the shopkeeper. At Bowling Alley near Harpenden, Hertfordshire, one shopkeeper, Jackie Saunders, always paid for these small quantities in kind.[42]

Henry Horn and his partner, Walter Gray of Edlesborough, were in a much larger way of business than this. They travelled around the villages with traps piled high with plait, dealing direct with the makers or with small sub-agents. Horn had himself been a child plaiter in the Buckinghamshire hamlet of Ivinghoe Aston, and he remained in business as a dealer, with brief intermissions, until his death in 1897, at the age of sixty-two.[43] During his early business career, his wife had worked as a bonnet sewer in Dunstable.

Plaiting had the advantage of not confining the workers indoors so much as did lacemaking, with its bulky pillow, but it had the drawback that they could be kept almost continuously employed upon it, carrying the bristling roll of finished plait under one arm and a bunch of split straws under the other as they walked around. A selection of these splints was also held in the mouth whilst they were working, and by the feel of the tongue and the movement of the lips, the plaiters twisted and moved the splints about so that a pair was always ready to be 'set in' to the plait, when needed. This practice made the lips of workers rough and sore. Some of the young men were reluctant to court girls who had permanently chapped lips. 'It's like kissing a cow's backside', was the ungallant comment of one Edlesborough lad,[44] while a plaiter ruefully admitted that she had 'almost worn a hole in the edge of [her] teeth. But I have to be working constantly at it if I want to do a score yards a day.'[45] Even in the 1890s a visitor to the Bedfordshire plait area was struck by the 'groups of women . . . standing at the garden gates or cottage doors talking and plaiting, rarely looking at their work; little girls just out of school were walking along the road with a similar inattention to the work of their fingers'.[46] In the winter, when they worked indoors, they would often sing together.[47]

Given the preoccupation of plaiting families with the trade (and in a few households, especially in the 1850s and 1860s, even the father would be permanently employed upon it) it is small wonder that home life was often uncomfortable, and that tensions built up as domestic activities were carried on in what was, in essence, a workshop.[48] The women were condemned as poor housewives, utterly ignorant of such common things as 'keeping their houses clean, mending their own or their children's clothes, and cooking their husbands' dinners'. The fact that they had to be constantly occupied if they were to earn even a modest livelihood inevitably contributed to this, as did the fact that their stocks of raw materials had to be stored in the cramped living accommodation.[49] The need for the finished plait to be trimmed before it was taken to market also meant that floors became covered with pieces of discarded straw which were difficult to sweep up.

A woman from Hawridge, Buckinghamshire, described the routine followed in her family early in the twentieth century. Her first recollections of her mother were of her plaiting

> with one foot rocking the cradle where there was always a baby
> . . . When I was quite a small girl I used to go to the other end of
> the village to buy the bundles of straws from an old lady called
> Dinah. They were 2½d. a bundle and I would carry 3 bundles in
> my pinafore. This was usually in my dinner hour from school
> and on the way back I had to collect from my granny the
> machine for splitting them. This my mother would do in the
> afternoon, then when I came out of school at tea time I had to
> take back the machine and the straws my mother had split to be
> put through the straw miller; this was a small polished wood mill
> like a small wringer fixed on the back of my granny's door. She
> would slightly damp the straws, a handful at a time and put
> them through the mill. This was to make the straw pliable.
> When she had done them all I took them back to my mother
> and she was ready to start plaiting. She worked at it every spare
> minute she had . . . It . . . had to be clipped, quite a long job,
> then wound from thumb to elbow and made quite smooth, then
> piled up in a clean cloth ready to take to the Friday market, piled
> up one end of the pram and walked into Tring where the
> dealers from Luton were waiting to buy. Sometimes these men
> would come up the hill to meet the women and offer to buy on
> the way, but prices varied and they liked to see what was being
> offered in the market.[50]

In the heyday of the cottage industries, family ties were often weakened by the early financial independence of many young workers, and this provided a regular cause for comment among clergymen in the parishes where they flourished. In 1854, the vicar of

Ivinghoe, a major plait centre, sadly observed: 'I think straw plaiting –
without which the people would starve – is a bad thing. It makes
children independent. It makes parents afraid of offending their
children, who thus become hardened and intractable. How to remedy
it, I know not.'[51] Lacemaking was the target of similar criticisms, with
the incumbent of Gawcot, near Buckingham, blaming it for
'destroying improvement & begetting bad habits' among the women
and girls.[52] Young workers in both industries were condemned for
their over-fondness for dress and their lax moral standards.[53] One
commentator also deplored the tendency for 'male and female plaiters
to go about the lanes together in summer engaged in work which has
not even the wholesome corrective of more or less physical
exhaustion'.[54] A similar theme was expressed in a popular ballad
which circulated in the area:

> In Buckinghamshire and Hertfordshire
> Amind maidens what you're at,
> And shun the naughty married men,
> Who deal in ladies' plait.[55]

Yet statistics show that between 1860 and 1900 a smaller proportion
of children were born out of wedlock in Buckinghamshire and
Bedfordshire than in predominantly agricultural counties like Norfolk,
Westmorland, Cumberland and Shropshire (see chapter 2). More
significant was the fact that plaiting and lacemaking discouraged girls
from leaving home to go into service and this led to overcrowded
cottages, where privacy between family members of the opposite sex
was difficult to arrange. Sometimes young workers went as lodgers to
neighbouring households, to escape the overcrowding and other
family pressures. Occasionally, this led to unfortunate liaisons
between the girls and adult males in the host family. That was the
case with Deborah Rawlings of Ivinghoe. In 1861, she was living as a
lodger with the Short family in their small cottage. A decade later,
one of the Short sons had become head of the household, although
his mother was also living there. Deborah, now aged thirty, was still
in residence and was euphemistically classed as a household servant,
although she had a number of Rawlings (or Rollings) children living
with her, who were recorded as the offspring of the head of
household! But such blatant cases were relatively rare, and it was
sheer pressure of numbers which was the main problem.[56]

To modern eyes it seems that what critics most disliked about these cottage craftswomen, however, was not their moral failings but the opportunity they enjoyed to secure an independent income within the usually male-dominated family circle. In the early Victorian years the more skilful might even accumulate modest savings, perhaps in readiness for their marriage. In 1850, a reporter from the *Morning Chronicle* interviewed a Bedfordshire worker who was engaged in making a fine quality plait. The girl had learnt to plait at the age of three and in the succeeding sixteen years had never had the work 'out of hand for a month together in any year . . . I've got a savings-bank book, but I'm goin' to draw it out in the spring.' She was 'a goin' to be married on the plait money'.[57] At the end of the nineteenth century, with the collapse of plait prices, such savings would have been impossible.

In all of the areas where the cottage industries were strong, however, the children's schooling was sadly neglected. To remedy this and to protect them from exploitation by parents and employers, in 1867 the Workshops Regulation Act was passed. Under it no child below the age of eight could be employed in any handicraft. Between eight and thirteen he or she must attend an approved elementary school for at least ten hours per week, on a half-time system, and must obtain a certificate from the teacher stating that this had been done. Unfortunately, despite being boosted by the general education legislation of the 1870s, the regulations were hard to enforce. Many mothers resented this interference with their freedom to dispose of their children's labour as they thought fit, and they evaded it where they could. 'I know how much judgment, temper, and patience are necessary in dealing with the people in these districts', declared an inspector in 1874. They look 'upon the law as heartlessly interfering with their earnings and their privileges, [and] . . . the weekly earnings of their children, small though they may be, are of vastly greater importance than prolonging, or even making regular, attendance at school'.[58]

Another inspector complained of the difficulty of catching children at work because 'the arrival of a stranger is telegraphed about', and the youngsters consequently at once ceased operations.[59] Furthermore, even when prosecutions were initiated, magistrates were often reluctant to convict, or else they imposed relatively small penalties.[60] Only with the collapse of the domestic trades themselves was the difficulty at last resolved, as children ceased to work on a half-time basis.

Even at the end of the century, some mothers continued to teach their children at home. Mrs Turney, born at Great Horwood, Buckinghamshire, in 1900, began to make lace at the end of her mother's pillow when she was five. Later she took her pillow to school, as did five or six other girls in the village, 'and I used to teach them the right way to work it'. When she returned home in the late afternoon, her tea was ready on the table and 'then the chair was put down [before the pillow] and I had to make [lace]. Mother would always stand guard. She was a good lace worker herself.'[61]

In glovemaking areas, too, mothers taught their daughters the relevant skills in the early twentieth century. 'I used to help mother with oversewing for lambskin gloves', recalled Mrs Wright, who was born in 1905 and now lives in the west Oxfordshire gloving village of Leafield. 'From helping mother you gradually advanced into making a glove. If you wanted to work for one of the manufacturers you had to make a pair of gloves. And if they were satisfactory you got work.'[62] Another present-day Leafield maker began by helping her mother sew the lining of the gloves, when she was eleven. 'If mother got behind and had to finish it, daughter helped out', was how she put it. She also had to cycle to the nearby village of Charlbury two or three times a week during her lunch break from school to return gloves to the factory when her mother had completed them.[63]

By the end of the century, machine sewing had become general among a growing number of glovers, particularly around Witney. Some had the machines in their own homes, purchasing them on an instalment plan, or hiring them from the manufacturers for a small charge. Others went to the glove factories to work. And one Woodstock firm took the club room at a public house in Leafield to hold short courses to teach young workers how to use the treadle-operated Singer machines in their own homes. Many of the younger Oxfordshire glovemakers in the early twentieth century preferred factory work to the cottage industry because of the greater companionship it offered. Then, when they married, they took up domestic making again.

The gloves were sent to the cottage workers in bundles, together with the requisite sewing thread and any money owing from previous work. If makers did not arrange collection and delivery themselves, this would be undertaken by the local carrier, or by special village 'bag women', who carried the gloves in carts and perambulators, or simply in a sack on their back. Mrs Wright's mother acted as 'bag woman' at Leafield for a time. According to her daughter, the makers brought their gloves to her cottage in specially marked bags, and she then wheeled them in a perambulator to a nearby village, where she met the glove manufacturer's representative. He took them from her, handed over a new consignment and paid her the cash due. Gloves which failed to reach the required standard would also be returned for rectification, and makers complained bitterly that if trade were bad, the manufacturers would try to find fault, in order to avoid paying them.

The position of 'bag woman' was a responsible one, but it was not always enviable, especially if orders were in short supply, for there was jealousy among the makers if all did not receive work. Similar arrangements applied in Somerset, where as late as 1901 over 2,000 women were still engaged in the trade, producing mainly heavyweight gloves, such as those for driving or those with a lining.[64] Glovemaking suffered from the effects of mechanization and foreign imports at the end of the Victorian era, but the process of change was more gradual than in lacemaking and plait. Even in 1896 Messrs Dent of Worcester employed several thousand outworkers.[65]

The disappearance of the cottage crafts was, however, important in other respects than mere finance and employment. One of the most significant of these was in regard to female literacy. This was usually low in craft communities, as a result of the neglect of elementary education, and only improved when the domestic crafts waned. Thus Bedfordshire and Hertfordshire in 1851 had among the lowest female literacy rates in the country. By 1900, the position had been transformed. In that year only 2.4 per cent of those marrying in Bedfordshire and 2.2 per cent in Hertfordshire were unable to sign, well below the average of 3.2 per cent female illiterates for England and Wales as a whole.[66] Analysis of individual craft communities has confirmed this trend.[67]

Finally, while *male* craft workers, such as blacksmiths, wheelwrights, carpenters and, in the glove trade, leather cutters, enjoyed a high status, the skills of the *women* engaged in domestic handicrafts were held in little esteem. That applied even to lacemaking, in which much skill was involved and the best work could only be produced after years of practice. The women themselves, nonetheless, took pride in their abilities – 'I loves a bit o' gloving', declared an Oxfordshire maker in the 1970s, after more than forty years in the trade.[68] But it seems that the prejudices and values of a male-dominated society prevented their gaining the wider recognition and larger financial rewards that their craft skills should have merited.

Much the same was true of trades involving female apprenticeship. In the eighteenth century there are occasional examples of women being formally apprenticed to such 'masculine' occupations as those of blacksmith, carpenter, ironmonger and cordwainer.[69] But in the new century male hostility and changing social values made the acceptance of girl trainees in such crafts unthinkable. By Victorian times, those females who were apprenticed were normally restricted to appropriately 'feminine' trades such as millinery and the dress trades. When women were involved in craft jobs elsewhere, as in woollen textiles and printing, they were restricted to tasks which guaranteed the more skilled employment and higher earnings to their male colleagues.[70]

Against such gender stereotyping only the most determined countrywomen and girls could gain entry to occupations which allowed them to compete equally with men and to develop their talents and skills to the full. It is this small group of rural businesswomen that we must now consider.

Although cottage industries provided the main opportunities for females to pursue a craft or trade of their own in Victorian villages, a few, despite limited access to capital and lack of commercial training, were able to run various other small businesses. Trade directories confirm the range of undertakings they took on, even in apparently 'masculine' spheres. Thus in the mid-1890s, at least nine Oxfordshire women were running blacksmith's businesses and six, carrier's businesses. Among the former was Mrs Kezia Whitton of Fringford, who combined control of a smithy with running the village post office. It was she who taught the young Flora Thompson the rudiments of post office work. Mrs Whitton had continued the business after the death of her blacksmith husband in August 1891, shortly before Flora went to live with her. At this time she was aged about fifty-six, and a surviving photograph shows her to have been a stoutly built woman of formidable appearance. Flora claimed, indeed, that had she lived a century earlier, she would probably have been at the forge herself with a sledge-hammer in her hand, for she possessed indomitable energy and a passion for doing and making things:

> But hers was an age when any work outside the four walls of a home was taboo for any woman who had any pretensions to refinement, and she had to content herself with keeping the books and attending to the correspondence of the old family business she had inherited. She had found one other outlet for her energy in her post office work, which also provided her with entertainment.[71]

Elsewhere she described Mrs Whitton as having the 'most observant eye and the keenest brain of anyone I have known'.[72] When she died in February 1898 her estate was valued at over £1,700 – more than three times the amount left by her husband less than seven years before.[73]

Another widowed Oxfordshire blacksmith who took over her late husband's forge, and ran it for some years in the 1870s and 1880s, was Ellen Morley of Woodstock. She boldly advertised herself in the *Woodstock Herald* as a 'farrier and jobbing smith', adding reassuringly: 'A competent foreman kept on the Premises'.

In the case of carrier's businesses, it was common for the women to take a more active personal role in them than was possible with smithing. Many drove the cart and its load of passengers and small items of freight on its weekly journeys to local market towns. One such entrepreneur was Mrs Venables of Marbury, Cheshire. She owned a donkey and cart and did a good deal of shopping for the villagers. 'She could neither read nor write but was never a halfpenny wrong in her change', it was remembered.[74] In a larger way of business was Mrs Blade, Arthur Randell's great-aunt, who continued to drive her old-fashioned carrier's cart three times a week into King's Lynn when she was well into her eighties.

> Passengers sat on three planks placed across the cart, with their feet in deep straw; . . . It took us three hours to do the seven-mile journey so we usually reached Lynn just before mid-day and, after delivering orders, we pulled up at the Three Tuns where the mare was taken out of the shafts and given a feed and

water while we went inside . . . to have our dinner. . . . [W]e started off on the return journey about three o'clock, calling at the same places on the way home that we had stopped at in the morning.[75]

Mrs Knight of Milton, Dorset, who ran a carrier's business in the 1880s, also collected eggs, chickens, butter and other farm produce to take into Weymouth market for sale.[76]

Trade directories suggest the variety of businesses that women owned. Thus at Potterspury and its hamlet of Yardley Gobion, in Northamptonshire, nearly a fifth of the businesses advertised in 1877 were female run. Entrepreneurs included a boot and shoe manufacturer; a beer retailer; the landlady of a public house; two shopkeepers; a wheelwright and sub-postmistress; a rope and twine manufacturer; and a farmer and grazier.[77] Likewise at the small Berkshire market town of Lambourn at that date about one in ten businesses had women proprietors. They included a druggist; a milliner and draper; a stationer and fancy goods repository keeper; a postmistress and assistant overseer of the poor; a baker; the owner of a girls' private school; two sisters who ran a grocery and drapery business; a shopkeeper; a beer retailer and draper; and three farmers. These are but two examples of many that could be quoted, and, of course, there were always a few women who ran businesses too small to be included in the trade directories. Among these, dressmaking was one of the commonest.

The occupation of dressmaker employed thousands of workers, with more than one in ten of all rural females recorded as in employment in 1901 engaged as a tailoress, dressmaker, milliner or shirtmaker. Part of its appeal, especially in the late nineteenth century, was the more genteel image it offered compared to farm work or domestic service.

For girls engaged in higher class work, it was customary to serve an apprenticeship with a skilled practitioner. At Bere Regis in Dorset, where the number of dressmakers increased from four in 1841 to sixteen a decade later, the sixteen included Harriet Moore, who struggled to maintain a pauper grandfather, and Elizabeth Boswell, the daughter of a woodman. Elizabeth was a girl of determination and skill, and she succeeded in raising the status and scope of her business until by the 1880s an apprenticeship in her establishment was eagerly sought after by local girls. This was despite the fact that it involved working without pay from 9 a.m. to 8 p.m. each day, with short breaks for lunch and tea.[78]

In the larger firms, apprentices often boarded on the premises, and were subjected to strict rules and regulations. A woman who worked for a Bath dressmaker claimed that they sometimes had as many as eighteen young girls working as apprentices or improvers at any one time.[79] There were few holidays, but in the autumn, when trade was relatively slack, they were allowed to return home for a fortnight or a month. Provision for their intellectual and spiritual needs was confined to hearing a chapter of the Bible read each evening and attending church on Sunday with their master and mistress.[80]

Another important area of female commercial activity was shopkeeping. In 1901 about as many females as males ran general shops in country districts.[81] At their lowest level, these businesses were probably like that owned by Madam Lund of Thame, Oxfordshire. Early in the nineteenth century she combined teaching in a dame school with the sale of sweets. Her stock was replenished weekly when an old man called on her, carrying a good sized oblong tin box in which were the following week's supplies. Other women turned their culinary skills to advantage by making sweets for sale. At Headington Quarry near Oxford, early in the 1900s, there were three shops of this kind. In one case, the woman's husband also took supplies of her toffee to sell on the local recreation ground. Another Headington Quarry housewife, Nancy Kimber, had a profitable sideline in selling black puddings,[82] while other women again, as in parts of Wales, collected nettles, dandelion leaves and other ingredients to make herb beer.[83] Many of these small businesses had a fleeting existence only, and rarely survived the death of their proprietor.

On a more impressive scale was the shop at Winterbourne Bassett, Wiltshire, where, according to the rector's wife, the owner sold 'at *enormous* profit to herself'

> currants which might readily be mistaken for bullets, bread of massive weight, and sweets which savour of soap and hair oil. . . . I never saw such a motley collection in any single shop of its size: — onions, cheese, spirits of nitre, tobacco, tinned beef, hair-brushes, gloves, prayer-books, infants' comforters, boots,

oranges, bacon, candles, sardines, Owbridge's lung tonic, and half the pharmacopoeia are thrown together in magnificent confusion.[84]

Yet, despite the rectory's disapproval, by providing such a wide range of goods the shopkeeper was doubtless performing a valuable service for her humbler customers, especially in view of Winterbourne's isolated location.

At the end of the nineteenth century Martha and Henrietta Soffe conducted a similar kind of shop at Bowerchalke, also in Wiltshire. Their establishment, grandly known as West End Store, was also licensed to sell vinegar, snuff and tobacco.[85] A great deal more imposing was Mrs Chase's shop at Romsey in Hampshire. Her husband kept a high-class grocery business in the town and she ran a cake shop. Mrs Chase took an active part in the charitable life of the market town, arranging a concert each autumn for the benefit of a coal and clothing club which she ran to help the poor.[86]

For those women unable to amass sufficient funds to run even a small shop, charring for better-off members of village society, or laundry work, were other common alternatives. This latter usually meant they were employed as washerwomen in middle-class households on one or two days a week and were paid a shilling or so a day plus a meal for their pains. But in other cases, as at Pimperne in Dorset or Headington Quarry and Cowley near Oxford, washing could become an important commercial activity. At Pimperne, the rector attributed the village's comparative prosperity to the large amount of laundry which the women carried out for the nearby market town of Blandford. This more than compensated for their menfolk's low earnings.[87]

At Headington Quarry, laundry work was considered 'the greatest industry' in the village, apart from brick-making and stone-quarrying. The laundries were run from cottages, with a shed put up at the back where the scrubbing and ironing could be carried out. The clothes were dried in the long gardens – householders 'used to plant a willow tree for posts', it was recalled – or, in wet weather, on nails in the kitchen. It was laborious work, with water having to be brought from the wells before being heated. A Cowley woman whose mother ran a cottage laundry with four employees recalled the tiring routine:

When water was hot enough they put it in baths, and filled the copper up for the next lot of water . . . Women did all of it. . . . [Then they] started scrubbing and rubbing, using bars of yellow soap. . . . Clothes [were] hung in [the] garden [and the] next wash started. Hands got sore when it was very frosty . . . got terribly cold hanging out the clothes. . . . Ironing [was the] longest part – almost as hard as washing.[88]

This family had a contract to take in laundry from Magdalen College, and the most successful Cowley and Headington businesses were those which had regular contacts with the Oxford colleges or the main churches and major hotels. At Headington Quarry, Mrs Narroway, a builder's wife, received the washing from Balliol College, while that from the Anglican seminary at Cuddesdon Palace went to a widow, Charlotte Webb, who also took in laundry from the university lodging-houses.[89]

Mrs Webb's husband had died at the early age of thirty-seven, leaving her with a large family to bring up. It was this laundry work which largely kept the family out of the workhouse. She supplemented it by the sale of Aylesbury ducks, which she bred in the yard of her cottage.[90] The older boys were responsible for the collection and delivery of the laundry.

Alongside these more common female occupations were some less usual ones, like that of the elderly cottager from Steventon, Berkshire, who in the early twentieth century made a living preparing chickens and pheasants for the table.[91] Fred Kitchen's mother, left a widow with young children and living on a landed estate in south Yorkshire, combined work as a needlewoman with the sale of teas to visitors during the summer.[92]

A few women turned hobbies to commercial advantage. One such was Mary Anning, born at Lyme Regis, Dorset, in 1799, the daughter of a carpenter. She began collecting fossils, at first for interest and then for sale. She supplied various museums and private individuals, selling some specimens for more than £100. 'Mary Anning', asserts her biographer, 'developed into one of the principal sights of Lyme', and when she died in 1847 the district guidebook claimed that her death was 'in a pecuniary sense, a great loss to the town, as her presence attracted a large number of distinguished visitors'.[93] Shortly before she died, the Geological Society made her an honorary

PLATE 28 *Mrs Caroline Irons of Sutton Courtenay with her hand cart en route between Oxford and Sutton Courtenay, 1898. Each week she walked to Oxford and back to collect meat for sale around the village. Her plight was typical of that of many elderly widows in Victorian times.*

(Mr D. J. Steptoe)

member, and her name is included in the *Dictionary of National Biography* – a distinction which very few Victorian carpenter's daughters could expect to achieve.

Another unusual and determined businesswoman, although far less illustrious than Mary Anning, was Mrs Caroline Irons of Sutton Courtenay, then in Berkshire. She eked out a tiny living by walking to Oxford and back each week with a handcart to collect meat for sale among the villagers – a journey of over twenty miles. When her husband died in 1879 she took over his small butchery business, supplementing it with occasional needlework and washing. She lived with a twin sister, Sarah, and a younger sister, Angelina, both of them tailoresses, and they also took in lodgers. In 1898 a few charitable friends collected a fund to provide Mrs Irons with an income so that she need no longer make her exhausting weekly journeys. Her last trip was made in November 1898, when she was already in her early seventies.[94]

A number of women ran public houses, often inherited from a husband, although many wives also took on an inn or hotel in their own right.[95] Among the widows was Sarah Nunn, who in 1851 was still running the Spread Eagle in Witham, Essex, thirteen years after her husband's death.[96]

Nevertheless, despite these various ventures, social pressures during the Victorian era discouraged all but the most strong-minded and ambitious – or the most desperate – women from running their own businesses. In bringing this about, the industrial revolution itself had played a part. For in the reorganization of manufacturing which accompanied industrial change, women's former craft skills were often undermined or destroyed. As Clara Collet commented at the end of the century, over the previous fifty years there had been 'no real invasion of industry generally by women, but rather a withdrawal from it'.[97] Furthermore, with the exception of school teaching, midwifery and nursing, most of the professional and white-collar jobs open to women had little impact in country areas before 1914, largely because of the lack of suitable employment opportunities.

8

Professional Women: Teachers and Nurses

There are at this moment 1,300 village schools in this country, in each of which the little flock of learners who gather day by day numbers less than 40. In at least a thousand of those diminutive establishments there is a woman-teacher toiling at her lonely post unaided and unsupported.

> T. J. Macnamara, 'The Village Schoolmistress' in
> *Report of the National Union of Teachers for 1894.*

The 1861 Census found that 72.5 per cent of teachers were women. It was the only occupation to which the Census awarded professional status [to women] except midwifery.

Peter Gordon, *The Victorian School Manager* (Woburn Press, London, 1974).

At a time when the range of jobs open to women in the Victorian countryside was becoming increasingly restricted, as a result of technological change and growing social pressures, there were two occupations to which this did not apply – school teaching and nursing. Both were, in essence, extensions of women's traditional roles as rearers of the young and carers for the sick and elderly; as such, they conformed to the prevailing domestic ideology. Both also underwent major change and development in this period, as old, informal methods of recruitment gave way to new concepts of training, discipline, and professionalism. Yet in neither case had the elimination of the untrained practitioner been completed by the time of the outbreak of the First World War. Nursing was, indeed, rarely a specialist job in the villages before the 1890s, and even after that date improvement was often dependent on the growth of charitably financed district nursing associations and the training programmes they introduced. Significantly, it was in the 1891 census of population that nurses were for the first time included unequivocally among the 'professional' classes, although midwives had been so categorized in 1861.

The untrained practitioners who dominated teaching, nursing and midwifery at the beginning of Victoria's reign had a number of characteristics in common. All were normally well-established members of the communities they served rather than outsiders brought in to provide a specialist service, as often applied to the professionals. Unlike these latter, too, they had no underlying moral mission to perform, such as preaching the virtues of cleanliness, good order, social subordination and morality, in the way their trained counterparts were usually expected to do.

To be a teacher in a working-class 'private' or 'dame' school implied no more than a mastery of the basic skills of literacy and some ability to communicate them to others. Such private teachers neither sought nor were accorded inflated status or a recognition of their special position, in the way their professional successors frequently considered their due.[1]

Likewise the position of village nurse was often taken up by women whose only qualification was perhaps the large size of their own family, or the fact that their mother or another female relative had followed the calling before them. 'The woman who one day is the parturient mother surrounded by gossips and midwife', declares Lesley Hall, 'may on another support a neighbour through her confinement – or become through experience a trusted midwife. The wisdom gained through raising her own children and tending her family's health might lead to a role in the immediate community as a folk healer, or even to the sale of her remedies as a widely-distributed patent medicine.'[2] Although few village nurses could hope to achieve that level of commercial success, a substantial minority gained a wide reputation on account of their knowledge of herbal and folklore remedies, or their special powers as 'white witches', able to counter malign influences.[3]

Many dame school teachers or nurses also had another occupation, perhaps as a shopkeeper or charwoman, since their earnings from these callings rarely sufficed to support them. At Ufford cum Bainton in Northamptonshire, the redoubtable Mrs Sopps during the 1850s not only ran a dame school, but acted as a washerwoman and monthly nurse, caring for mothers and babies immediately after the birth of the child. According to the rector's daughter, Mrs Sopps was supposed to teach reading, writing and arithmetic to her young charges, as well as knitting. But her principal characteristics were a ready use of the birch rod and a stress on the need for her pupils to show proper deference to their social superiors.[4]

Another village nurse was Anna Williams, a smallholder's wife from Bowerchalke, Wiltshire, who played the dual role of midwife and layer-out of the dead. 'When we saw her with a white apron and bag she was delivering a baby', remembered a fellow villager, 'and when it was a black apron and bag she was laying out. We called her the bringer-in and the goer-outer.'[5]

A second farmer's wife who acted as midwife, nurse and layer-out was Mrs Scott of Muker in north Yorkshire. According to her granddaughter she attended at every birth in the parish, and 'when the children wasn't well, people used to send 'em to Granny's: "Mam's sent me to see what you think *this* spot is" . . . She was very clever with herbal remedies.'[6] Prior to her marriage, Mrs Scott had been a maid and, like Mrs Williams at Bowerchalke, she was entirely untrained.

But at a time when the status of most countrywomen depended on that of their menfolk, these teachers and nurse/midwives earned the trust and respect of villagers by their own efforts. In *Lark Rise to Candleford*, Flora Thompson stressed the value which the hamlet wives placed on the assistance given by an elderly woman who, as she said, saw the beginning and end of everybody. When she attended a confinement, she was no superior person entering the house, as some of the trained district nurses later in the century were thought to be. Instead she was welcomed as a neighbour, poor like her patient, 'who could make do with what there was, or, if not, knew where to send to borrow it'.[7] The importance of this concept of 'neighbourliness' was later recognized by some of the promoters of the trained nursing service. Thus in Hampshire a nursing inspector noted, in 1892, that where 'trained Nurses can be employed who actually belong to a village . . . it seems to work very well. The people

PLATE 29   *The village schoolmistress. Infants at Clifton Hampden School, Oxfordshire, in 1906, with their mistress, Mrs Creswell.*

(Oxfordshire County Council)

have great confidence in anyone they have known all their lives.'[8] Another inspector likewise pointed out that in Somerset, while qualified midwives only stayed in the home of a woman who had given birth long enough to attend to her medical needs, an untrained 'nurse' was prepared to 'do for' husband, children, and house for a few days for a very modest fee. Clearly a number of wives preferred this, even when skilled help was available.[9]

It is against this background that we have to examine the lives of women teachers and nurses in the Victorian countryside.

Females had always played an important role as instructors of the young. Already in 1841 the census of population recorded 29,840 schoolmistresses and governesses in England and Wales, compared to 17,620 males. By 1901, these figures had climbed to 171,670 and 58,675, respectively.

For many women, unable to earn a living in any other way, teaching offered the prospect of a modest income in a respectable occupation. This applied both to those involved in the instruction of middle-class girls and to those lower down the social scale, who were in the 'dame school' category. Even the Brontë sisters considered opening a boarding school for a few girls at Haworth parsonage, as an alternative to their much hated 'governessing'.[10]

Typical of many such establishments was that run by the Misses Hore at Lower Heyford, Oxfordshire, during the third quarter of the nineteenth century. They were the daughters of a grocer, tallow chandler and maltster in the village, and after his death they converted a tallow candle workshop into a schoolroom. There they taught the basic three Rs (reading, writing and arithmetic), plus religion, music and French. At the beginning of the 1870s they had seventeen resident pupils, and each Sunday they escorted the girls to a service held at the Methodist Chapel in Lower Heyford. Every summer they organized a bazaar to which they invited their friends and neighbours and at which articles of needlework made by the pupils were sold for the benefit of the Church Missionary Society. George James Dew, a tradesman's son, who lived next door to the school, recalled the two ladies as possessing 'unswerving firmness of character', while the younger of them had 'all the appearance, save of dress, of a nun'.[11]

Likewise, many Norfolk schools for middle-class girls in the mid-1890s were conducted by women whose father had found 'farming does not pay'. They had shown 'a praiseworthy desire to help their parents. And as tuition is the most respectable way of making a living, and at the same time the only trade for which training seems a positive disability, they take to the business.'[12] In Devon, too, there were small middle-class schools which operated on a variation of 'the private governess idea'.[13]

Far more numerous than these 'elite' schools, however, were those conducted by working-class women for the children of the lower orders. For a fee of 1d. or 2d. a week the youngsters learnt to read and sew, plus in some cases to write and do a little simple arithmetic. Often they were set up by women who were too sick or too old to do anything else, or who had failed at a previous occupation.[14]

The standards achieved in these dame schools were highly variable, though few made any ambitious claims. Some were little more than child-minding institutions where youngsters could be sent when their mothers were working or otherwise engaged, rather like the lace and plait schools discussed in the last chapter. A few offered efficient instruction in the basic elements of the three Rs, plus religious knowledge, and needlework and knitting for the girls. And all, if they hoped to survive, had to reflect the cultural milieu in which they operated, and the needs of their community. 'I likes 'em to read well', declared one teacher. 'It's a good thing for 'em at home. A little girl as reads clear and pleasant-like, can read to 'em at home, while they's all at work round their candle on a winter's night: . . . and all's cheerful and happy.'[15]

Outsiders shared this limited vision. 'A very pleasing specimen of a dame's school. Mistress quiet and sensible', reported the Rev. John Allen, one of the first HM Inspectors of Schools, of a class of seventeen girls and seven boys he had examined at Clanfield, Hampshire, in 1845. However, the results show that of the twenty-four pupils, nineteen were unable to read words of four letters at sight, and only eight could 'read a Verse in the Gospels without blundering'. Eight of the children were able to write, and no attempt had been made to teach them arithmetic.[16] For this instruction, parents paid a fee of 3d. a week.

Mary Smith, who was born in 1822, the daughter of a boot and shoemaker from Cropredy, Oxfordshire, attended dame schools of both the efficient and the ineffective kind. Her first, to which she went from the age of four, was kept by the aged Dame Garner, who instructed a few little children in the tiny living room of her cottage. Her young charges sat on two forms and from these she called them out, in turn, to stand by her knee to read. During the year or so Mary attended at Mrs Garner's, she learned virtually nothing. The dame's principal object was to keep the children quiet. 'No smile was ever seen to illuminate her stern countenance from the time of our arrival at school, to the time we made our curtsies and hurried out of it.'[17] Doubtless Mrs Garner was a reluctant recruit to the ranks of the teaching profession, but knew of no other way of earning a living.

When Mrs Garner died, Mary moved to a second school 'where I learned to knit and sew, the sole object for which I attended'. This was a parish school and was visited by ladies from the vicarage. According to Mary, it was kept

as most village schools were kept then, by a woman, who, by some disease or other was unable to move from her chair or lift her hand to her mouth. . . . Her knowledge was very small. The girls had a lesson once a day in the New Testament, and the little ones read out of the 'Reading Made Easy'. But knitting and sewing occupied nearly the whole time of the girls.[18]

From there, the little girl graduated, at the age of eight, to a more pretentious establishment kept by the two daughters of a Cropredy wharfinger. Here she began to read extracts from some of the major books in English literature and commenced a rudimentary study of history, although most of her time was still devoted to needlework. But at least this school laid the foundations which enabled her to become a teacher in her own right several years later.

None of the teachers so far considered had been trained for their task, and this was scarcely surprising, for apart from the fact that most had taken up the task as a result of economic pressure rather than choice, training facilities were minimal in the 1830s. Even the two major voluntary societies which were set up to promote public elementary schooling in the early nineteenth century – the Anglican National Society and the ostensibly unsectarian British and Foreign School Society (which, in practice, enjoyed nonconformist support) – did little more than instruct trainees in the methods of their organizations. Both used the monitorial system whereby unpaid child monitors taught fellow pupils under the overall supervision of an adult teacher. Much emphasis was placed on religion and morality, and upon the need for teachers to have high principles rather than advanced academic qualifications.[19]

In many respects those who taught in the National and British schools were seen as lay missionaries, or what one HM Inspector called in the 1860s the 'secular officers of the Church', working to dispel 'ignorance, and [elicit] the dormant powers of self-help and progress' among the lower orders.[20] As a result of support received by the National Society from clergy and gentry, Anglican schools rapidly outstripped both their British and Foreign rivals and those of other denominations, like the Roman Catholics and the Wesleyans. Even at the end of the Victorian era, when rate-aided, non-denominational board schools had been set up in some areas to meet gaps in the voluntary system, church schools continued to predominate, especially in rural areas.[21]

To provide teachers for these schools, a number of dioceses (and the British and Foreign Society) opened training colleges, some of which catered for women. However, many were very small. As late as 1858, Truro had only twenty-one students and Durham thirty-seven, while overall academic standards were highly variable. Thus the college of Sarum St Michael in Salisbury admitted thirteen students when it first opened in 1841, and a further eight in its second year, but they differed widely in both age and ability. The first-year entrants included girls as young as fifteen and sixteen, although one candidate, a former lady's maid, was thirty-seven.

The 15-year-old had taught in the National (that is, Anglican) school at Warminster before coming to the college, and she remained there for two and a half years. Then, aged barely eighteen, she became head of Lady Bath's infant school at Horningsham, Wiltshire. After holding the post for almost two years and seemingly giving satisfaction, she was abruptly dismissed when Lady Bath decided to close the school. At this point, still under twenty, she abandoned teaching and married a local stone mason.[22] Another young recruit was Elizabeth Dyke, a bricklayer's daughter, who entered Sarum St Michael in September 1841 at the age of seventeen. She left about two years later to take the headship of Nether Avon school. There she gave 'great satisfaction but died of a fever at the end of six months'.[23] These cases illustrate the early age at which mistresses took up headships and the uncertainties many faced both in their relations with their managers and in their personal health.[24]

At this date, in the early 1840s, a number of students were still leaving after a few weeks or months to take a teaching post in a school, and the courses they pursued whilst at college varied considerably. At the same time there was anxiety that they should gain no exaggerated view of their own importance in discharging the duties of what one HMI called 'their humble but important office'.[25] Training college attitudes reflected this concern. Typical was the claim of the National Society's Whitelands Training Institution for Schoolmistresses, opened in 1842, that it was 'a place of religious training . . . [T]he officers of Whitelands . . . believe that a young person, however clever, well informed, and free from . . . obvious faults . . . is not a fit person for a training-school, unless there be reason for believing her to be influenced by religious motives.'[26]

To the Rev. F. C. Cook, HMI, writing in 1850, elementary school-mistresses in country areas were 'the educators of the mothers of the peasantry, of our domestic servants, and, to no small extent, of the wives and sisters of the small shopkeepers and tenant farmers'. Hence it was essential that their training should be of 'a thoroughly practical character'. In the colleges, their academic work was to be combined with domestic duties, so that they would not only understand the work of servants but would be 'in sympathy with the girls whom they have to educate'. They would also be able 'to superintend whatever domestic work it may be found expedient to encourage in connection with elementary schools'.[27]

Later in the century, as teachers grew more professional in outlook, they came bitterly to resent this approach. It also hampered those reformers anxious to encourage women from the established middle classes to become elementary teachers. 'Why should a lady be less esteemed as a village schoolmistress than as a governess in a private family?' asked one reformer plaintively.[28] But the daughters of impoverished clergymen, doctors and army officers, to whom she was primarily appealing, were well aware that village teachers were traditionally recruited from the humbler ranks of society. They understood the covert dislike of their own class for the 'pretensions' of schoolmistresses, and few wished to place themselves in a position to be snubbed. So they preferred to take poorly paid posts as governesses and companions. 'There are better educated persons in the village', one country teacher wrote sadly in the 1890s, 'but they hold themselves far superior to the village schoolmistress.' That was a common experience.[29]

Meanwhile, despite opposition from the religious bodies and the voluntary school societies, the state was beginning to intervene on an increasing scale in elementary education. In 1833 it made its first annual grant for school buildings; six years later a supervisory Committee of the Privy Council was appointed, and in November of that year the first HM Inspectors of Schools were recruited. They soon pointed to the weaknesses of the existing monitorial system, with its constant repetition and rote learning, and much inaccurate information passed on to pupils by the child monitors entrusted with teaching duties.

To combat these deficiencies and to meet the shortage of trained staff, in 1846 the government introduced its pupil-teacher scheme. Under it, candidates aged thirteen and above who were approved by

HMI could be apprenticed for five years as trainees in a school. During that time they would be instructed by the head and would also act as assistant teachers. At the end of the apprenticeship, the youngsters could sit for a scholarship examination to give entrance to a training college, although, in practice, many continued to work in the schools as unqualified assistants. Government grants were paid to trainees during their apprenticeship, providing they passed annual examinations conducted by HM Inspector, and small payments were also made to the supervising teacher. In those rural schools where heads were unable to train apprentices because of their own poor academic qualifications or lack of suitable facilities, the post of stipendiary monitor was created, for youngsters between the ages of thirteen and seventeen.

By the mid-1840s the hallmark of professionalism for a teacher was the possession of a government teaching certificate, gained either by examination at the end of a training college course, or, from 1847, by passing the examination externally as a practising teacher. This meant that qualified status could be gained without attendance at a college, and for various reasons, including a shortage of college places, that was a path followed by many women candidates.[30]

Apprentices were to be drawn from the cream of elementary school pupils, and college records confirm their social background. Thus of the first hundred students recruited by the diocesan training institute of St Matthias at Bristol between October 1852 and January 1858, thirty-nine were the daughters of shopkeepers and artisans, ten of servants, nine of farmers, five of schoolmasters and twenty-one in the 'miscellaneous' category; in sixteen cases no information was provided.[31] Likewise at Sarum St Michael, Salisbury, nineteen of the thirty-seven students admitted early in 1861 were the daughters of artisans and craftsmen; three of shopkeepers; two each of farmers, white-collar workers and labourers; and nine were 'miscellaneous', including a milkman, a seedsman, and a coachman.[32]

Among the Salisbury students at this time was Mary Hardy, sister of the future novelist, Thomas Hardy, and daughter of a Dorset builder and stone mason. Neither her experiences there, nor those of her sister, Kate, who attended in the 1870s, were enjoyable, despite the friendships they made. 'I think they are having rather better times than we used to have', Kate wrote to her sister-in-law, Emma, in 1882, after meeting a current Sarum student, 'but I don't mind if Tom publishes how badly we were used.'[33] In *Jude the Obscure*, Tom did, indeed, do just that.

Fellow students confirmed the harsh domestic regime: 'Being in the pantry meant rising early enough to get the fires lighted and breakfast prepared before early lesson time', wrote one. This was followed by clearing away and washing up 'from all meals, with a goodly addition of sweeping and scrubbing . . . It was no matter of surprise that students so trained found that nothing in the way of work came amiss to them.'[34]

When they had completed their training, many of the girls took up headships, particularly in rural areas, where the fact that their salaries were lower than those of the men attracted hard-pressed school managers.[35] On average, male certificated teachers in such areas as East Anglia and parts of the north and east Midlands in 1858 secured between £80 and £90 a year, compared to about £50 a year earned by their female counterparts.[36] Even at the end of the nineteenth century there were nearly 1,300 headmistresses of country schools who earned less than £50 per annum.[37]

Once installed, these young teachers not only had to instruct a wide range of age groups and abilities within their small school, but they also had to overcome problems of truancy. Even when attendance regulations were tightened in the 1870s, children were kept away to help with seasonal land work or, in areas where cottage industries flourished, they would be employed upon these. 'The attendance has not been at all good this week on account of the haymaking', wrote Kate Hardy in August 1879, a few months after taking up the headship of the remote Sandford Orcas school in Dorset.[38] Much the same situation existed at Bramley, Hampshire, where the mistress recorded absences in the autumn of 1864 because youngsters had to 'mind cows' and sheep, and to gather acorns. Illness and bad weather were other causes of absence in this and most country schools. And at a time when punctuality was considered unimportant by many labouring families, there were repeated reprimands for poor time-keeping.[39]

These problems were, however, made more serious by changes in government grant policy from 1862. In an attempt to raise standards of literacy and numeracy in elementary schools, the Committee of

Council introduced its Revised Code. Under it, all state grants to elementary education, other than building grants, were linked to the children's attendance and their success in an annual examination in the three Rs conducted by HMI. The examinations were arranged in a series of six standards, with each child supposed to move up a standard every year. Only the infants were exempt from the ordeal of the examination.

Teachers now concentrated on winning the maximum grant for their school, since often their own salary, as well as their security of tenure, partly depended upon the sum awarded. Advertisements in the teaching press confirm the link between salaries and the amount of grant earned. At Flexbury, near Bude in Cornwall, an appeal inserted in the *Schoolmaster* of 15 June 1872 for a mistress at the village school mentioned a basic salary of only £20, plus furnished lodgings; but an incentive for good examination results was offered in that the teacher would receive all the grant earned by the school.

Apart from financial considerations, however, an unfavourable inspection could lead to a head teacher losing her job. At Drayton St Leonard, Oxfordshire, there were six different mistresses in the ten years 1867 to 1876 inclusive, before one was recruited who could satisfy the requirements of HMI. She was aided informally by the rector's wife and a daughter of the principal landowning family, while the rector, too, took occasional classes.[40]

The Revised Code also affected the position of pupil-teachers. They now had to make their own financial arrangements with school managers, instead of receiving a government grant, while supervising teachers were expected to instruct them for an hour a day, five days a week, without payment. Naturally many regarded such unpaid duties with scant enthusiasm, and arranged to instruct their apprentices at times to suit themselves rather than to benefit the trainee.[41]

The poor rates of pay which apprentices received under the new regime are confirmed by surviving pupil-teacher agreements. At Aldermaston, Berkshire, one girl was engaged for a five-year term in 1869 'entirely at her own charge', that is, without any salary at all. Another apprentice recruited by this school in January 1872 was paid 1s. a week during her first year, rising by steps of 1s. per week to 5s. in the final year. Overall, at the end of the 1860s about one in six of all female pupil-teachers in church schools had starting salaries of under £5 a year. Only about one in twenty-five started at over £10. Three decades later, complaints about the inadequacy of stipends persisted.[42]

These poor salaries discouraged male apprentices, who could gain better-paid employment in offices and shops – posts from which girls were largely excluded on gender grounds. For them, even under these conditions, teaching offered an assured position in village society which few other occupations open to women afforded at that time.[43] By 1870, therefore, there were 6,384 boys and 8,228 girls serving apprenticeships in the schools of England and Wales. In 1896 the respective figures were 7,737 and 28,137, with the latter figures also including probationers who were below the minimum age for apprenticeship, which had now been raised to fourteen. In rural areas, female recruits were particularly common because of their relative cheapness.

One girl who started pupil-teaching at the age of fourteen in an Essex infant school at the turn of the century remembered beginning her day by reading Bible stories to her small charges. Next came bead counting on a frame and singing: 'Then the children used to play with sand on slates. I was paid a shilling a week and received it once a month. I thought I was very rich with the first four shillings I earned.'[44]

But for older children and their teachers the 'payment by results' system introduced by the 1862 Revised Code meant that life in grant-aided schools deteriorated into a drudging routine of the three Rs, plus scripture and needlework, which was compulsory for the girls. Some benefits did accrue, in that more reading books had to be supplied to meet the demands of the annual inspection, while teachers had to give attention to all pupils, not merely the brightest, since all had to pass the examination. Over the years, the grant-earning subjects were widened to include, in 1867, English grammar, history and geography. These were converted into 'class' subjects in 1875, with the grant earned by the proficiency of the whole group rather than the individual. In the early 1870s, too, the *range* of grant-earning subjects was further widened to include modern languages, mathematics, science and the like, while singing became a grant-earning subject from 1872. But in the countryside, lack of equipment and teacher shortage inhibited the adoption of these extra subjects.[45] For village teachers, the three Rs combined with average attendance formed the basis of the education grant to their schools up to the 1890s.

Meanwhile, inspection day became feared by pupils and teachers alike, with mock tests held in some schools for weeks before the great day. At Cottisford, Flora Thompson remembered the mistress hovering anxiously around HMI, replying in low tones to his scathing comments or, with twitching lips, smiling at any child who caught her eye. As for the youngsters, the sound of the Inspector's voice scattered the wits of most of them.[46]

In Flora's early years the Cottisford head teacher was Miss Susannah Holmyard, who is disguised in *Lark Rise to Candleford* as Miss Holmes. She had moved to the village in 1867 after completing an apprenticeship at North Malvern Girls' School in Worcestershire. She was uncertified and untrained when she arrived, and her salary at the beginning of the 1870s was still a mere £27.10s. a year. In December 1872, however, she gained a teacher's certificate by external examination and her annual income then rose to £32 4s. She remained at Cottisford, living in the small school house, until her marriage to Henry Tebby, the squire's gardener, in April 1885.

According to Flora, Miss Holmyard was 'a small, neat little body with a pale, slightly pock-marked face, snaky black curls hanging down to her shoulders, and eyebrows arched into a perpetual inquiry'. She wore in school stiffly starched, holland aprons with bibs, one embroidered with red one week, and one with blue the next, 'and was seldom seen without a posy of flowers pinned to her breast, and another tucked into her hair'.[47] Such frivolity was a clear indication that she had never attended a training college, where these vanities would have been firmly stamped upon.

Miss Holmyard, like most village heads, taught all the classes simultaneously, aided by two young monitors, aged about twelve. She was a firm disciplinarian and, like other country teachers, also knew her place in society. When the squire's mother visited the school to examine the children's needlework, she sketched a slight curtsey as she held open the door for her. Doubtless she was much gratified when that lady acted as a witness at her wedding. But she was an efficient teacher, too. In a typical comment, the diocesan inspector of schools reported in 1882: 'The Condition of Religious Knowledge is satisfactory: and the answering generally was very creditable. The written work (in the lower Standards especially) was decidedly above the average.'[48]

A far less successful example of a village teacher was Ruth Alma Kelly, who came to Tadmarton, also in north Oxfordshire, in May 1876. She was born in 1853 and had taught for seven years before moving to her new school. Her previous career had included an apprenticeship at St Michael's School, Lichfield, and service at Bayford National School, Hertfordshire, where she gained her teacher's certificate by external examination. On arrival at Tadmarton she complained of the backwardness of her pupils: 'not one of the Infants know the Alphabet, and even Boys of 9 and 10 cannot make the letter "o" properly.' This was a defensive ploy adopted by many heads when taking over a school, since by blaming their predecessor they could hope to deflect blame if the pupils failed when HMI visited. One of the Tadmarton residents, in the meantime, agreed to help Miss Kelly with the needlework instruction, and the rector also taught regularly, as well as performing other duties – such as reproving children who had brought 'impudent messages to the Mistress'. Nevertheless, despite this assistance, Miss Kelly soon lost interest in her work. Perhaps her uneasy relations with some of the parents or problems of poor attendance contributed to this. In any event, early in November the rector gave her three months' notice to leave. For much of the ensuing period, she attended irregularly, finally leaving more than a week before her notice expired. For a few days the school had to be closed until a temporary substitute could be found. Her permanent successor, a certificated mistress from Strensham, near Tewkesbury, came on 19 February 1877.[49]

These examples show some of the problems encountered by a village school teacher expected to cover all subjects in the curriculum, without help save that of a child monitor or the casual assistance of a well-meaning but untrained adult. As late as 1893 the mistress of Hittisleigh school, Devon, complained bitterly of the anxieties experienced: 'One always feels that the fate of a whole year's work may hang on the humour or caprice, and absolutely on the stroke of a pen, of some Assistant Inspector, . . . and the Teachers are ruined professionally.'[50] Not until the late 1890s did attitudes become more relaxed. By then the curriculum included such subjects as cottage gardening, natural history, and cookery for the girls. And at a time when rural depopulation was causing concern in political circles, village teachers were seen as having an important role in countering this.[51] Much stress was laid on inculcating the virtues of patriotism and hard work, thereby fitting pupils for the burdens of empire. Military drill became more important in the curriculum, especially during the Boer War of 1899–1902, although it had first been introduced in the early 1870s.

Mistresses in remote rural schools sometimes found difficulty in complying with the new requirements. At Bulkworthy, Devon, Mrs Andrews, the head, wrote plaintively in 1901: 'I will at once send away and get the Model Course of Physical Training, and do my best to teach them what I can, but I do not know but little about it.'[52] At Lower Heyford, Oxfordshire, the headmistress attended a drill class in Oxford conducted by a drill sergeant from Cowley barracks. At school she used broom handles to enable her pupils to perform the requisite rifle exercises.[53] The motives underlying this approach were pinpointed by HMI Holmes in 1900. 'The village school', he wrote, '. . . has a high function to fulfil . . . Its work is national, not to say imperial . . . Its business is to turn out youthful citizens rather than hedgers and ditchers.'[54] It was the teacher's task to achieve that transformation.

As the examples of Susannah Holmyard and Ruth Kelly showed, many certificated 'professionals' who were teaching in country schools during the second half of the nineteenth century had gained their qualification externally, whilst at work. This was especially the case when the 1870 Education Act laid down that only schools with a certificated head teacher would be recognized as efficient by the Education Department. Training places failed to keep pace with the growing demand, despite an increase in their number. As late as 1901, little more than a quarter of those who passed the Queen's scholarship examination actually went to college, and country pupil-teachers were particularly handicapped in the competition for places, for they were rarely able to attend the specialist central classes which were set up in many urban areas during the 1880s to instruct apprentices.[55]

To these difficulties was added another unsatisfactory development, namely the growing reliance upon unqualified assistants, as village school managers sought to cut staffing bills. Often monitors were employed on grounds of cheapness instead of pupil-teachers, and since they were little older than their charges and frequently had minimal interest in their work, this created discipline problems.[56]

Furthermore, when adult assistants were recruited they tended to be merely 'supplementaries' or 'additional' teachers, rather than the uncertificated ex-pupil-teachers or young certificated teachers of earlier years. 'Supplementaries' were introduced in 1875 in an unsuccessful attempt to eliminate the monitors. Their only qualifications were that they were over eighteen, had been vaccinated against small-pox, and had been accepted by HMI as suitable to 'assist in the general instruction of the scholars and in teaching needlework'. Their numbers rose sharply in the last years of the nineteenth century, as impoverished church schools, in particular, sought to reduce expenditure on salaries.[57]

Elsewhere unqualified teachers continued to hold poorly paid headships into the last quarter of the nineteenth century. At Rydal Infant School near Kendal, Westmorland, the head in 1882 was paid £22 a year. She had started work there in 1870, when aged fourteen, and had remained ever since.[58] Similarly the uncertificated Rose Knowles moved to Thorpe Malsor school, Northamptonshire, in January 1882, and stayed for almost seven years before she was dismissed abruptly by the squire's wife. In a letter to her mother she described the uncomfortable final interview:

> I wished her good morning . . . [but] she never spoke so I knew there was something up. She layed [sic] my money down and then said there were going to be a great many changes here. She therefore wished to give me two months notice . . . I thanked her and asked her if she would please write me out a testimonial, she said yes and that ended it. She did look savage.[59]

Miss Knowles had great difficulty in obtaining another school for, as she despairingly noted, 'there are so few [schools] about that are not under government.' Eventually she secured a poorly paid appointment in a village she described as 'about Noah's time I should think. My days have been buried here, they will be worse there I expect . . . We shall have to live seven weeks on nothing if I get paid monthly.'[60] This last comment referred to the fact that in order to economize, her mother, a widowed dressmaker from London, was coming to live with her, and all Rose's spare cash had been set aside to finance the move to their new location.

These developments meant that whereas trained certificated teachers had represented 57 per cent of female staff in elementary schools in 1875, by 1914 that share had fallen to 32 per cent. By contrast, the proportion of uncertificated and untrained women had advanced rapidly from 13 per cent of the total at the earlier date to 41 per cent in 1914.[61]

Many young teachers living in villages were, like Rose Knowles, extremely lonely, cut off from virtually all outside contacts, 'with no shop windows to look at, and no eligible young men'.[62] As one HMI put it, through her job the school mistress became 'separated . . . from the class to which she had originally belonged, while it did not bring her socially into contact with a different class . . . She could not marry a labourer, nor an artisan who was not an educated man, and she was not very likely, generally speaking, to marry a person very much above herself.'[63] This was the case with Rose Knowles. To her mother's evident disapproval, she became engaged to the butler at Thorpe Malsor Hall, but when she lost her employment, the engagement was broken off.[64]

By contrast, Mary Banfield, headmistress at Lower Heyford, married the local poor law relieving officer, who was a former carpenter in the village. After a courtship of almost four years, they were married in March 1872, after Mary had obtained permission from the rector to continue as schoolmistress after her marriage.[65] This was a common requirement at a time when some school managers considered that a married teacher might offer a bad example of neglect of home and family, if she carried on with her career.

Yet, despite all the disadvantages, school teaching offered intelligent girls from a relatively humble background the chance to obtain a professional training and a qualification which enabled them to enjoy modest independence. Typical of many was Lucy Lampet, who took charge of Hursley school, Hampshire, in 1863, at the age of twenty-two. When she died it was noted that 'Clergy trusted and looked up to her as the truest of friends, leaders in the parish sought her help in all manner of details for the welfare of the community, while the women and girls of Hursley for half a century loved her . . . and regarded her as "a Mother in Israel".'[66]

Mary Dew, headmistress of Lower Heyford school for forty-six years, was likewise described (in an obituary written in 1936) as having provided 'a constant example of honesty and truthfulness . . .

and of devotion to the welfare of others'. Although it may be argued that such eulogies are customary in obituaries, evidence from elsewhere suggests that in Mrs Dew's case the praise was merited. Quietly and unostentatiously, such women as she were able to help along the feminist cause by demonstrating that females could exercise authority and initiative efficiently. Although outwardly conforming to the Victorian stereotype of the female carer and educator, they were able to use their position to carve for themselves a respected social niche.

But whilst the standing of village school teachers had become well established by the time of the First World War, for nurses and midwives the position was much less assured. Among midwives, in particular, the divisions within the profession between the trained workers and what were called 'bona fide' practitioners remained a point of friction, long after the passage of regulatory legislation in 1902. In Somerset, for example, there were in 1908 117 'bona fides' at work compared to 97 trained midwives. But, according to the county's inspector of midwives, around three-quarters of these 'bona fides' were illiterate and depended on relatives, the village clergyman or the inspector herself to complete the record books they were required to keep.[67]

Unlike France and Prussia, where midwives had long formed an officially regulated and respected profession, in England the occupation was shunned by most educated and genteel women because of its lower-class 'Sarah Gamp' image. Much the same was true of nursing, despite attempts from the 1840s to establish training institutions like St John's House in London. This was an Anglican foundation and opened in 1848. A year later its lady superintendent lamented that even relatively humble parents preferred to put their children 'to some already known or tried employment as dressmakers, schoolmistresses, &c. &c.' rather than nursing.[68] Nevertheless, St John's seems to have tried to recruit girls from agricultural areas. The daughters of small farmers, agricultural labourers and rural craftsmen featured largely among its entrants, doubtless because it was thought such girls would be used to hard physical work and would be reasonably healthy.[69] But, once trained, they rarely returned to work in the villages.

Even in the 1860s and beyond, when the formal training of nurses had increased in importance as a result of the work of Florence Nightingale and other reformers, and when the recruitment net had been widened to include educated middle-class girls as well as those of the 'domestic servant class', the number of trained specialists in country districts remained small.[70] This was especially true of the poor law infirmaries, where pauper inmates were used to assist the tiny permanent staff until the beginning of the twentieth century. Thus in one poor law district, covering Wiltshire, Worcestershire, Gloucestershire, Herefordshire, Somerset and Staffordshire, there were 3,117 pauper patients in January 1901 cared for by 210 paid nurses and 222 paupers.[71] At Banbury, Oxfordshire, where the superintendent nurse was paid only £35 a year, the woman who held the post in 1913 was described as 'hardly fitted' to be a parlour maid; 'like all her class she was not strictly truthful so that when inquiries were made it was difficult to fix the blame.'[72] Yet it was recognized that the salary was too low to attract a capable trained woman.

This unsatisfactory situation persisted despite the fact that in 1897 the Local Government Board had issued an order banning pauper nursing. But the restrictions were evaded by referring to the paupers as 'attendants'. Hence the minority report of the Royal Commission on the Poor Laws sadly admitted, in 1909: 'In spite of all the efforts of the Local Government Board . . . there are still many rural workhouses without even one trained nurse; . . . there are even some, so far as we can ascertain, in which there is no . . . salaried nurse at all.'[73] Not until 1913 were paupers finally barred from employment in sick wards unless 'supervised by paid staff'.[74]

However, outside the penny-pinching ranks of the rural poor law guardians, there was an increasing appreciation of the value of professional nursing care. In country districts that was given an impetus in the 1860s by the growth of the cottage hospital movement. By the mid-1890s there were about 300 such hospitals at work, financed largely by the subscriptions of the well-to-do, though with patients contributing when they could afford it. Each hospital was staffed by local doctors on a rota system, and there was at least one full-time nurse on the premises. Typical of many was the Faringdon Cottage Hospital in Berkshire. It had ten beds and was staffed by a matron and a probationer. The latter received two years' training and was paid £12 a year for the first year and £16 for the second. As the matron of this hospital also carried out a limited amount of outside nursing among the sick poor of the area, the probationer received instruction in the rudiments of district work as well.[75]

Initially it is clear that simple nursing only was attempted in these hospitals. 'I am of opinion that the most useful person to act as nurse in a cottage hospital, will be found to be a homely, motherly woman of the neighbourhood', declared one medical supporter of the movement in 1870. 'She should, if time permits, be sent for a few months to a good county hospital, where, if she is quick to learn, she will pick up a great deal of useful information. Her homely, country manner, will be more appreciated by the patients than that of a professed trained nurse.'[76]

Elsewhere a desire to promote the values of professional nursing aroused the philanthropic instincts of the wives and daughters of the landed classes and led them to recruit private nurses to cater for 'their' cottagers. Among them was Lady Georgina Vernon of Hanbury, Worcestershire, who accompanied the nurse on visits to patients on the estate. According to the nurse's diary, covering the period 1867 – 75, the medical aid she rendered consisted of poulticing, bandaging, and general first aid – as well as laying out the dead. She distributed medicaments, including quinine, linseed, 'ointment' and cod-liver oil, and supplemented these with gin, brandy, porter, port, eggs, chops, rabbits and tea: 'took wine for Mrs. Wardle's child suffering from abscesses', reads one diary entry.[77] From time to time, doubtless with Lady Georgina's approval, she also supplied blankets, clothing, and admission tickets to the local infirmary. But although clearly a valued member of the community, who often 'stayed all night' with her patients, she was not, in essence, very different from the old-style village nurses of her day, who lent a hand to their neighbours. There is no evidence that she had received any formal training.

Meanwhile, in the towns the district nursing service was growing rapidly, following its introduction in Liverpool in 1859. Its main purpose was to care for the sick poor in their home, but until the 1880s its impact in country districts was limited.[78] Then in 1883 came the first major initiative, when Miss Bertha Broadwood set up the Holt-Ockley system of cottage nursing around her home parish of Ockley. It was run on provident lines, with the subscribers entitled to the services of a nurse when sick. The nurses themselves were women 'of the village class', who were given a short training in maternity and district nursing at a special training centre established at Plaistow in London. They did not attend surgical operations, and the help they gave when they returned to the villages was largely domestic. Many lived in with the patients while they cared for them. 'The cottage nurse is one of the humblest of the great army of nurses that are fighting . . . the three D's – dirt, drink . . . and disease', declared Miss Broadwood in 1909. By that date her organization had 137 branches in England and Wales, plus forty more which were unaffiliated, and employed a nursing staff of around 800; about 4 per cent of these were qualified midwives.[79]

A year after Miss Broadwood's scheme was established, Mrs Elizabeth Malleson of Dixton Manor, Gloucestershire, took a similar step, although in her case she was concerned to employ a trained worker. When she first moved to Gloucestershire from London at the beginning of the 1880s she was shocked at the general indifference towards the safety and well-being of cottage wives during their confinements. The low calibre of the local midwives or 'handywomen' aggravated the situation. Many of them combined their midwifery duties with labour in the fields or other manual work. According to Mrs Malleson, these 'handywomen' were illiterate, 'by no means always sober, and absolutely ignorant of the most elementary rules of hygiene or of sick-nursing'.[80] She may have exaggerated their deficiencies in order to underline the improvements she subsequently introduced, but, in any event, in 1884 she decided to recruit a trained nurse and midwife for the nearby village of Gotherington. In September of the following year 'Nurse Mary' took up her post. At first the village women regarded her ministrations with some suspicion, but her willingness to attend patients in neighbouring parishes in all weathers and her 'kindly, energetic, devoted' character soon won them over.[81]

Mrs Malleson, like Miss Broadwood before her, was anxious to extend her activities beyond her own locality. She canvassed for the formation of 'an Association to supply Trained Midwives and Sick Nurses (for non-infectious cases) in districts remote from medical aid', and invited ladies interested in such a scheme to contact her. A number did, especially from Gloucestershire and Worcestershire; among them was her neighbour, Lady Hicks-Beach from Winchcombe, wife of the chancellor of the exchequer. By 1890 she and Lady Hicks-Beach had not only gained widespread support among members of the landed classes but had helped to establish the Rural Nursing Association to 'promote the employment of trained Midwives and Nurses in Country Districts, in co-operation with existing Nursing Organizations'. Mrs Malleson became honorary secretary of the new organization, and from an early stage it was agreed that household chores were to be excluded from the nurse's duties. 'In some places, by the bounty of the rich, all nursing was given free to the poor; in others, some voluntary contribution was expected in return for the Nurse's services', declared the third Report in 1893.[82]

But important though these developments were, the main impetus towards the creation of a comprehensive district nursing service came in 1887, when Queen Victoria agreed to devote £70,000 which had been given by the women of England towards her Golden Jubilee to this cause. Two years later Queen Victoria's Jubilee Institute for Nurses was incorporated. Its importance lay not only in its broad scope but in its emphasis on the importance of training for all 'Queen's nurses'. This involved a year's general training in a hospital (later increased to two years), plus six months' experience of district nursing, gained under supervision; and, for those working in country areas, there must be at least three months' approved training in midwifery, leading to the London Obstetrical Society's midwifery qualification or some other appropriate certificate. A distinctive uniform had to be worn, as well as a special badge and brassard. Queen's nurses were forbidden to interfere with the religious opinions of their patients and warned that they must work under the direction of a medical man.[83] Their professional standing was emphasized by the requirement that they be provided with a home of their own by the district associations which employed them. A salary of at least £30 a year was recommended, and a uniform allowance had also to be made.

As the influence of the Queen's Institute spread, a number of local organizations became affiliated to it, including, in 1891, Mrs Malleson's Rural Nursing Association, which now became its 'Rural District Branch'. By 1893, thirty-two of its nurses had been admitted to the Queen's Roll.[84]

Elsewhere, an increasing awareness of the needs of the poor further encouraged the spread of district nursing associations. Many were led by wives and daughters of the aristocracy and gentry, and this attracted the attention of socially ambitious middle-class ladies, anxious to move in such elevated circles. In Hampshire, where a County Nursing Association was formed in 1891, it had the active support of the Countess of Selborne and the Marchioness of Winchester. In Lincolnshire the County Association set up in 1894 had as its President the Countess of Winchelsea.

Many of these local organizations, however, lacked the funds to recruit a qualified 'Queen's nurse'. Hampshire, for example, had no Queen's nurses in its employ as late as 1898, almost all of the twenty-eight women at work in that year being of the 'village nurse' type. That meant they had a qualification in midwifery only. The salaries paid to them varied between £25 and £60 a year, and they included Mrs Egan, a soldier's wife, from Amport. She had been trained in midwifery at an Aldershot hospital, and, according to a report by a Queen's Institute inspector in July 1892, the district she covered was large and scattered:

> Since her appointment in March 1891, she has had 20 midwifery cases. . . . Besides her work in this special branch, she undertakes when her time is not fully occupied, cases of general illness. . . . Nurse Egan lives in her own home. She goes out to her work as a rule about nine in the morning, but as she is liable to be called out at any hour of the day or night, no fixed time can be stated. She has a daughter who sees to her housework, which leaves her free for her nursing duties. She receives 15/− a week and house rent free . . . Once a week she goes to the Lady Manager [of her local association] who hears from her about her cases. . . . Nurse Egan has been supplied with a donkey cart to help her in the great distances she has to go. It is not an expeditious way of getting about, but it rests her and prevents her being too tired.[85]

Subsequently bicycles became the preferred mode of transport for district nurses. Unlike donkeys they did not tire, and they were quicker and cheaper to run. By the early 1900s an ability to ride a bicycle was regarded as an essential prerequisite for many district nurses and midwives.[86]

As the report on Nurse Egan suggests, the district nurse's position could be one of some delicacy. At all times she had to maintain her professional integrity, and yet she was expected to submit to the supervision of a 'lady manager' or similar local patron. In some of the smaller associations this outside influence could be considerable. At

Appleby and Bongate in Westmorland, the secretary of the association was Lady Hothfield of Appleby Castle. In January 1895, she initiated the service by recruiting Queen's Nurse Annie Backer, who had previously worked in Manchester. Miss Backer was paid £30 a year, plus a uniform allowance of £4, and 11s. a week for her board. She lived in the castle lodge, with the lodgekeeper as her landlady, and her washing was done at the castle laundry. It is clear that her professional duties were closely supervised by Lady Hothfield, who was financing the venture.[87]

In such circumstances it is not surprising that many district nurses (like country teachers) experienced a sense of loneliness, cut off as they were from the companionship of social equals. This, coupled with their relatively low salaries, led many to resign their posts after a short period in office. Thus during 1901 alone there were 130 resignations of Queen's nurses, compared to a total of 568 on the roll at the end of that year. A substantial proportion gave as their reason for leaving that they were taking up 'other work' or assuming 'Home Duties'; a smaller number were entering 'private nursing' or 'hospitals'; while marriage or poor health accounted for most of the remainder. Adding to their sense of unease was the fact that some of the nurses also faced hostility from local doctors. This was particularly true of midwifery cases, but district nursing, too, had its opponents. Feelings ran especially high when 'educated' middle-class women were engaged, as happened in some instances. The doctors were concerned that the recruitment of nurses as socially established as themselves would upset the traditional relationship of superior and subordinate which had hitherto applied between the GP and a nurse. They were also anxious that the nurse's ministrations might cut their income. In 1908, the Penwith Medical Union, for example, complained that nurses were attending to minor cuts and burns, and thus depriving doctors of work.[88] And at Wrangle, Lincolnshire, as late as the First World War, one local doctor refused even to meet the district nurse, let alone work with her.[89]

It was to reduce the feeling of isolation which this kind of situation induced that in 1904 the *Queen's Nurses Magazine* was established, to form a link among members of the profession. By that date the total of Queen's nurses in England and Wales had climbed to almost 800 (excluding the hundreds of 'Village' and 'Cottage' staff who were insufficiently qualified to gain full Queen's status).[90] In an early issue, a district nurse from Kent described her experiences, and the opposition she had at first encountered from the principal doctor. He had thought 'a nurse going round' would lead to 'gossip and chatter', but when he discovered his mistake, he became a staunch supporter:

> My work extended over a radius of two miles, and there was a . . . little Welsh pony for me to drive. He was kept at the doctor's stables, so I heard of any fresh cases at the surgery before starting each morning. . . .
>
> The first winter, while people were still rather afraid of having a strange nurse when they were ill, I got to know as many as possible . . . by helping at mothers' meetings, Sunday school, joining the choral class and working parties . . . There were many things outside nursing work that helped to fill in my time. I escorted girls to concerts and various meetings when chaperones were scarce, or saw them home after church . . . Lectures of all sorts I attended, when work permitted . . . and gave some extra practices to an ambulance class.[91]

In this way she soon became absorbed into the life of her community.

But a colleague working in rural Wales found assimilation more difficult. She was shocked at the low standard of hygiene which prevailed, and as a first step decided to get one person in each village in her district to learn 'nurse's ways' in this regard. She also gave lectures to mothers on 'fresh air' and similar topics.[92] In doing this she was following Florence Nightingale's advice that the district nurse should be both a nurse and a 'sanitary reformer' – a view with which the Queen's Institute fully concurred.[93]

A particular problem for nurses in rural areas was the spasmodic nature of the work. Thus in July 1899, the Nailsworth District Nursing Association in Gloucestershire complained that between 28 March and 8 July in that year, the nurse had paid only 732 visits, 'making an average of 43 per week; this has been an unusually low average. . . . It was agreed by the Committee that the Secy. should point out to Nurse Fulton that they would be glad to see more maternity cases on her report.'[94] Quite how she was to achieve this they did not say, especially as their own rules laid down that she could only attend maternity cases 'under a Doctor'.[95] Over the months the issue continued to fester, with further complaints registered in June 1900 because Nurse Fulton had allowed her total visits to slump to 467

PLATE 30   *District nurse out on her rounds with a donkey cart, c.1900.*
(Queen's Nursing Institute, London)

between 26 March and 14 June in that year. Perhaps not surprisingly, the following month she resigned, and on the day she left, a placard was displayed outside one of the village shops, claiming that she had taken maternity cases without the authorization of the local doctor. This was strongly denied by the Committee, but it would appear that Nurse Fulton had been trapped between the need to increase her patient load (especially of maternity cases) to please the Committee and the hostility of the medical profession if she exceeded her specified role. Small wonder that she preferred to seek a post as matron in an Isolation Hospital.[96]

It was, indeed, over the midwifery issue that relations between doctors and their district nurses were most strained. By the end of the nineteenth century increasing numbers of women were coming forward who had passed the examinations of the London Obstetrical Society (first introduced in 1872) or had obtained a similar professional qualification. A number of these new entrants came from the established middle classes, either because, as spinsters, they had to earn their own living, or because they saw the work as a charitable duty, designed to reduce the high infant and maternal mortality among the poor. Some were anxious for their calling to be recognized as a respected female occupation, and to this end to secure the elimination of the untrained old-style midwives, whom they blamed for many avoidable maternal deaths. Hence they began to press for professional regulation and the introduction of a system of registration to distinguish between qualified and unqualified practitioners.[97] They also argued that since they were working with labouring families who could not afford doctors' fees they were in no way interfering with the medical profession's role in midwifery matters.[98]

However, most doctors saw things differently. Some considered the women's agitation a feminist plot to drive men out of midwifery altogether. Others disputed the fact that a high proportion of child-bearing women could not afford the services of a doctor. They argued that the minority who genuinely could not pay a fee could be attended by the poor law medical officer. The anger these men felt towards the midwives was expressed by Dr McCook Weir, a GP from Mortlake, in a letter to the *British Medical Journal*. The professional nurse, he declared bitterly, 'with her thermometer and her tongue' was bad enough, but the certificated midwife was an 'outrage' against the medical practitioner.[99]

So it was that Alice Gregory, a daughter of the dean of St Paul's and subsequently a noted figure in the midwifery world, had to promise local doctors in Somerset that she would not 'attend the wives of tradesmen, clerks, farmers or firemen, or any woman who had previously been attended by a doctor, without the latter's sanction'.[100]

Still more seriously, some GPs refused to attend cases of abnormal labour, even though these were outside the midwives' agreed sphere of duties. In some rural areas medical opposition was so severe that trained midwives working in private practice or employed by maternity charities preferred to move away rather than risk being left with responsibility for abnormal cases on their own.[101]

However, the adverse publicity which this approach gave to the medical profession boosted the campaign of those doctors and midwives anxious for the proper regulation of midwifery and for the drawing up of a register of qualified practitioners. They achieved their aim in 1902 with the passage of the Midwives Act. This created a Central Midwives Board to oversee the profession and to organize the relevant qualifying examinations. From 1905, only women certified under the Act were allowed to use the name or title of midwife, and from 1910 it became illegal for any woman 'habitually and for gain' to attend mothers in childbirth, unless she was duly certified or was acting under the direction of a qualified medical practitioner. Certification could be secured by existing midwives either through success in the examinations of the Obstetrical Society or some other recognized body, or, for the large army of unqualified women, by gaining recognition as 'bona fide' practitioners. This meant they had been at work for at least a year at the time of the Act's passage and possessed a good character. It was intended as a once and for all concession. Thereafter those who wished to be certified midwives had to pass the examinations of the Central Midwives Board. Regulation of the service at local level was put in the hands of the county councils, and each year those proposing to practise in a given area had to apply to the relevant council for authorization.[102]

Unfortunately, despite the Act's good intentions, difficulties remained, especially in rural areas. One problem was the large number of untrained women who gained certification as 'bona fide' practitioners. In 1905, of 22,308 names on the Midwives Roll, 7,465 had passed the Obstetrical Society's examinations, 2,322 held hospital certificates – and 12,521 were in 'bona fide practice'. Many of these latter were illiterate and had difficulty in maintaining their records. Some were unable to take patients' temperature because they could not read the thermometer, even after instruction. All six 'bona fides' warned for inefficiency by the Hampshire Midwives Act Committee in April 1909 were unable to use a thermometer.[103] Another woman's name was removed from the Roll because, despite repeated warnings, she had failed to provide herself with a regulation bag and appliances and would not wear a dress of washable material, as she was required to do.[104] Occasionally the Sarah Gamp image reared its head, as when an Itchen midwife was charged with misconduct in 1910 because she was 'Intoxicated on arrival', which led to 'complete neglect of duties in connection with [the] case'.[105]

Gradually the number of incompetents fell, as women were struck off the roll or were forced to abandon practice by increasing age.[106] By March 1909, when the number of certified midwives had risen to

27,234, the number of 'bona fide' practitioners had shrunk to 11,636.[107] The rest had all obtained some formal qualification.

This changing pattern was reflected at county level. In Somerset, where 81 trained and 125 bona fide midwives had been practising in 1907, these totals had altered to 155 and 102, respectively, by 1911 – although even then almost a fifth of the county's maternity cases were being attended by 'bona fides'. Likewise in Lincolnshire, 18 of the 41 midwives at work in 1914 were 'bona fides', compared to 23 who were trained.[108]

Alongside these certified but unqualified midwives, however, there were women still practising without any authority. In 1910, the Oxfordshire midwives' inspector estimated that 106 of them were at work in the county, compared to 111 certified women (of whom 62 were trained and the rest were bona fides).[109] Indeed, a trained Hertfordshire practitioner sourly observed that mothers who were 'not sober and clean' chose the unauthorized women because qualified midwives made them 'clean up their places, and do not let them have a lot of drink'.[110] Some of the unqualified were also favoured because of their greater 'churchyard luck' in securing the early death of an unwanted infant.

Nevertheless, local authorities were slow to prosecute such women. Partly this was because of difficulty in collecting evidence that the law had been flouted and in persuading magistrates to take the prohibition seriously.[111] Thus a Hampshire woman charged at Aldershot in 1911 with practising illegally was fined a mere 2s. 6d. – a penalty which her fees would have more than covered.[112] Sometimes, too, the shortage of certified midwives made the continued use of 'handywomen' necessary if mothers were not to be left without assistance. To rectify this, a number of county councils, including Oxfordshire and Bedfordshire, offered scholarships to potential midwives to enable them to train.[113] But in other areas, including parts of Wales, the shortage of qualified women was so serious that the legislation was a virtual dead letter. It was, significantly, in the principality, and in the English rural counties of Westmorland, Cambridgeshire and Herefordshire, that the highest maternal death rates from puerperal sepsis and accidents of childbirth occurred, according to a survey of 1907.[114]

So untrained nurses and midwives continued to practise in the villages alongside their certificated, professional counterparts up to the First World War. Unlike in elementary education, where government funding of schools was in operation by the 1830s, the state did little to regulate nursing apart from the establishment of minimal machinery for midwife registration and the provision of poor law medical care.

9

Epilogue

My husband used to bring ½ lb. of pork home for Sundays, and I have seen him divide it up amongst his children and not take a piece for himself. . . . I cannot tell you how we clothed our children. I have collected sticks and made a fire, bought a half-pennyworth of soap and washed the children's clothes on Saturday night and dried them ready for Sunday morning. Now the young people dress like ladies. . . . Ah! times have altered.

Mrs Wilkins, aged seventy-five, a labourer's wife in *The Hungry Forties*
(T. Fisher Unwin, London, 1904), comparing life in the 1840s and the
early 1850s with 1904

Despite the occasional friction which occurred in some country districts between teachers, nurses, midwives and those who considered themselves their social superiors, by the First World War the professional status of all three groups had been recognized. Admittedly, a number of untrained women still clung on the fringes of the occupations, but it was clear that the future lay with the qualified practitioner. 'Progressive women to-day . . . realise that social service needs labour of a highly skilled variety', wrote Edith Morley in 1914, 'and they therefore demand . . . training for their work as a guarantee of their efficiency . . . and . . . monetary payment and security of tenure as guarantees to them of economic independence.'[1] In the decades which lay ahead that view gained increasing support.

However, for *most* country women the Victorian era represented a period of both progress and retreat. There was progress for the minority who were beginning to penetrate the professions and were being elected to minor political office in local government; but retreat for the many who, under the influence of technology and the prevailing domestic ideology, were increasingly restricted to hearth and home. Even some feminists came to accept the 'naturalness' of the separate spheres philosophy, and the sexual division of labour which was an integral part of it. Frances Power Cobbe, for example, saw reproduction as the principal female function: 'a Mother . . . serves the community in the very best and highest way . . . by giving birth to healthy children . . . in my judgment it is a misfortune . . . when a woman . . . is lured by any generous ambition to add . . . any other systematic work; either as breadwinner to the family, or as philanthropist or politician.'[2] Such arguments ignored the fact that for a number of working-class women such an option was economically impossible. Poverty demanded that they must work. But it created a role model to which they were encouraged to aspire, and it further widened the gap between the lady of leisure and the working girl.

For those in employment, domestic service remained the major single occupation throughout the period, in both urban and rural areas, followed by dressmaking, tailoring and associated trades. The decline in cottage industries and the reduction in female land work during the second half of the nineteenth century made it especially difficult for countrywomen to find alternative employment.

On a brighter note, within the home, improvements in living standards, as a result of the sharp falls in food and consumer good prices in the final quarter of the century, had eased the lot of most village wives, although much poverty remained, especially in families with young children.[3] And although contraception was beginning to be practised, fertility rates among the labouring classes remained well above the all-class average up to the First World War.[4]

Perhaps most significant of all, however, was the alteration in the urban/rural population balance, as migration from the villages gathered pace in the second half of the nineteenth century. When Queen Victoria ascended the throne in 1837 the majority of people still lived in the countryside. By 1901, three-quarters of the population lived in urban areas, and among females alone the proportion was approaching four-fifths. The remoter districts were most affected by this population shift, with parts of Wales, Cornwall, Huntingdon and the border counties of Hereford and Shropshire suffering an absolute decline in numbers during the period.[5] The main cause of the outflow was the increasing size and scope of town employment, at a time when job opportunities in the villages were being cut back. The fact that there was more to do in towns during leisure hours was a further attraction.[6]

The last three decades of the nineteenth century also saw a substantial emigration of male farm workers to the colonies and the United States of America, and a large proportion of these took wives and daughters with them.[7] But the majority of women who left the villages migrated to towns in Britain rather than to homes overseas. And, ironically, whilst this outward movement of country people was under way, transport improvements were encouraging a number of middle-class town families to settle in rural areas. They came to parishes on the fringes of the great conurbations, where they could enjoy the fresh air, scenery and other amenities which they associated with village life. The contrast between their economic and social attitudes and those of the traditional inhabitants served to underline the limitations of rural existence for the lower orders. George Sturt, whose family had run a wheelwright's business in Farnham, Surrey, for generations, referred angrily to these 'resident trippers', who had disturbed the old community ways. They sought to impose 'a form of subtopian "country" life which showed no continuity at all with what had gone before'.[8] This was especially true of the female section of the population: 'middle-class domesticity, instead of setting cottage women on the road to middle-class culture of mind and body, has side-tracked them – has made of them charwomen and laundresses, so that other women may shirk these duties and be "cultured".'[9]

But however much Sturt, and those who thought like him, might rail against these developments, they were powerless to stop them. The growth of suburbia and the burgeoning influence of the new-style middle-class 'countrywomen' which accompanied it were destined to increase and strengthen in the decades that lay ahead.[10]

Appendix 1

Declared Employment of Female Villagers in Nine Specimen Rural Communities, 1871

	Wilburton, Cambs.	Helmingham, Suffolk	Stonesfield, Oxon.	Yarnton, Oxon.
Total female population (all ages)	265	143	284	144
Farmers	–	1	–	2
Agricultural labourers and farm servants	2	–	1	2
Domestic servants and dairymaids	21	28	18	16
Governesses	1	1	–	1
Dressmakers etc.	3	–	8	4
Nurses	–	–	–	1
Charwomen	2	–	1	–
Shopkeepers and assistants	–	–	–	–
Laundresses	–	1	3	2
Straw plaiters	–	–	–	–
Lacemakers	–	–	–	–
Glovemakers	–	1	120	1
Schoolmistresses	1	1	1	1
Miscellaneous	–	–	2	1
% of females in work	11.3	23.1	54.2	21.5

Source: Calculated from census returns at the Public Record Office

(Appendix 1 contd.)

Ibberton, Dorset	Kilham, Northum.	Branxton, Northum.	Great Horwood, Bucks.	Ivinghoe, Bucks.
121	108	121	388	456
—	—	—	—	—
—	23	18	—	—
12	12	18	14	10
—	1	—	—	—
2	1	2	13	13
1	—	—	2	1
—	—	—	4	3
3	—	—	—	2
2	—	—	1	—
—	—	—	3	275
—	—	—	160	1
11	—	—	—	—
1	—	—	2	2
1	—	1	3	4
27.2	34.2	32.2	52.1	68.2

Appendix 2

Analysis of Household Size in Twelve Specimen Rural Communities, 1861–1881

Census year and community	*Household size — % of households*					
	1 member	*2 members*	*3 members*	*4 members*	*5 members*	*6 members or above*
1861						
Mapledurham, Oxon.	11.5	10.6	14.4	18.3	16.3	28.9
Elmdon, Essex	6.0	23.0	17.0	19.0	8.0	27.0
1871						
Yarnton, Oxon.	7.2	17.4	14.5	20.3	10.2	30.4
Stonesfield, Oxon.	4.3	12.0	22.2	17.1	12.8	31.6
Kilham, Northum.	0.0	2.7	13.9	11.1	27.8	44.5
Lanton, Northum.	12.5	6.2	31.4	12.5	12.5	24.9
Ibberton, Dorset	4.1	18.4	20.4	6.1	16.3	34.7
Sutton Courtenay, Berks.	7.9	20.4	18.3	12.9	16.3	24.2
Ivinghoe, Bucks.	11.2	14.8	15.3	14.8	12.2	31.7
Ivinghoe Aston, Bucks.	5.6	8.5	15.5	25.4	14.1	30.9
Lower Heyford, Oxon. [a]	4.5	13.3	20.0	14.5	16.7	31.0
1881						
Lower Heyford, Oxon. [a]	6.3	17.7	19.0	15.2	8.9	32.9
Juniper Hill, Oxon. (hamlet) [b]	9.7	22.6	19.3	12.9	16.1	19.4

a   Included in two censuses for purposes of general comparison.

b   Flora Thompson, who lived at Juniper Hill in the 1870s and 1880s, wrote of it in disguised form in *Lark Rise to Candleford* (Penguin, Harmondsworth, 1979 paperback edn.), where she christened it Lark Rise. She noted of the bedroom arrangements that where there was only one room, 'it had to be divided by a screen or curtain to accommodate parents and children. Often the big boys of a family slept downstairs . . . Still it was often a tight fit' (pp. 18–19).

Sources: Census returns at the Public Record Office; Jean Robin, *Elmdon: Continuity and Change in a North-West Essex Village* (Cambridge University Press, Cambridge, 1980).

Appendix 3

Unmarried Girls aged 15–24 in Seven Specimen Rural Communities, 1871

Community	Total female population	% of female population comprising unmarried girls 15–24	% of unmarried girls aged 15–24 living at home	% of unmarried girls aged 15–24 with jobs
Kilham, Northum.	108	24.1	80.7	96.0[a]
Lower Heyford, Oxon.	218	12.8	60.7	50.0[b]
Stonesfield, Oxon.	284	12.3	85.7	85.7[c]
Ibberton, Dorset	121	15.7	68.4	73.6[d]
Ivinghoe, Bucks.	456	16.7	89.4	92.1[e]
Ivinghoe Aston, Bucks.	225	8.9	80.0	95.0[f]
Sutton Courtenay, Berks.	502	13.5	86.8	69.1[g]

NB In England and Wales as a whole at this time, 18.4 per cent of the total female population (married and unmarried) was aged 15–24.

a   Of the twenty-four girls with jobs, seventeen worked on the land, and five were in service, one was a dressmaker and one was a governess.

b   All the workers were in service. Of fourteen girls without jobs, five were members of farming families, two daughters of a carpenter and ironmonger, one was the stationmaster's daughter and one was a slate-digger's daughter.

c   Twenty-two of the girls with jobs were gloveresses, two were dressmakers and six were servants. The five without jobs comprised three members of farming families, the clergyman's daughter and a member of a grocer's family.

d   Half the fourteen girls with jobs were domestic servants, three kept a shop jointly, three were gloveresses and one was a seamstress.

e   Of seventy girls with jobs, fifty-eight were straw plaiters, seven were maids, two were dressmakers, two were milliners and one was a teacher. Of the six without specific jobs, four were farmers' daughters and one a licensed victualler's daughter.

f   Of nineteen girls, thirteen were plaiters, two dressmakers, three maids and one a schoolmistress.

g   Of forty-seven girls working, twenty-four were in the ready-made clothing trade based on nearby Abingdon, five worked in a village paper mill, eleven were maids, one was a dressmaker and one a laundress. Others included a music teacher and a schoolmistress. Of the twenty-one girls without jobs, six were members of farming families, four of innkeepers' families, two were daughters of butchers and drapers and seven were from gentry or professional families.

Source: Census returns at the Public Record Office.

Appendix 4

Marriage Patterns in Fourteen Specimen Rural Parishes, 1851–1881

Census year and community	Total number of married couples in residence on census night	% where both partners were born in parish	% where the husband only was born in parish	% where the wife only was born in parish	% where neither partner was born in parish
1851					
Great Horwood, Bucks.[a]	131	26.7	39.6	9.2	24.5
Wilburton, Cambs.[a]	90	15.5	35.5	16.7	32.3
Lower Heyford, Oxon.[a]	73	19.2	38.3	8.3	34.2
Drayton, Berks.[a]	89	22.5	40.4	10.1	27.0
Sutton Courtenay, Berks.	150	27.3	26.0	8.0	38.7
Mapledurham, Oxon.	83	16.9	21.7	12.0	49.4
1861					
Cottisford, Oxon.	51	3.9	52.9	7.8	35.4
Elmdon, Essex	86	38.0	44.0	4.0	14.0
1871					
Stonesfield, Oxon.	84	33.3	32.1	14.3	20.3
Kilham, Northum.	25	0.0	4.0	12.0	84.0
Lanton, Northum.	10	0.0	20.0	0.0	80.0
Yarnton, Oxon.	51	13.7	39.2	5.9	41.2
Ibberton, Dorset	41	19.5	26.9	7.3	46.3
1881					
Great Horwood, Bucks.[a]	107	28.1	29.9	17.7	24.3
Wilburton, Cambs.[a]	87	24.1	36.8	9.2	29.9
Lower Heyford, Oxon.[a]	57	10.5	38.6	14.0	36.9
Drayton, Berks.[a]	111	16.2	36.0	18.9	28.9
Ivinghoe Aston, Bucks.	56	44.6	24.5	10.9	20.0

NB In the two Northumberland parishes, the scattered nature of the population and the widespread use of hiring fairs to recruit workers on the land account for the large number of 'out' marriages; many residents were born in Scotland.

a   Parishes included in two censuses for purposes of general comparison.

Source: Census returns at the Public Record Office; Jean Robin, *Elmdon: Continuity and Change in a North-West Essex Village, 1861–1964* (Cambridge University Press, Cambridge, 1980), p. 27.

Appendix 5

Illegitimacy Rates, Birth Rates, and Under-Age Marriages in Twelve Specimen Rural Counties, 1890–1900

	Illegitimate births per 1,000 births: average for 1890–9	Birth rate per 1,000 living: average for 1890–9	% of women marrying in 1900 who were not of full age (i.e. under 21)
England and Wales	42	30.0	16.3
Counties with high illegitimacy rates			
Shropshire	72	26.8	10.1
Herefordshire	70	26.0	7.7
Cumberland	69	29.9	14.6
North Wales	65	27.0	8.1
Norfolk	65	28.0	15.6
Westmorland	62	25.1	9.9
Counties with low illegitimacy rates			
Essex	29	30.5	17.4
Somerset	36	27.1	12.2
Gloucestershire	39	27.3	13.2
Wiltshire	40	26.6	11.8
Devon	40	25.8	13.0
Hampshire	41	26.6	14.9

NB The *lowest* illegitimacy rates were found in urban areas and mining communities, where early marriage was common. In Middlesex, an illegitimacy rate of thirty was recorded in the 1890s and in Monmouth of thirty-one. Under-age marriages comprised 14.9 per cent and 20.8 per cent of females marrying, respectively, in those counties in 1900.

Source: 63rd *Annual Report of the Registrar-General of Births, Deaths and Marriages in England for 1900*, pp. 1901, vol. XV, p. lx.

Appendix 6

Women and the Settlement Laws

From: Bicester Poor Law Union Minute Book, T/G.II/1/17 – 18, at Oxfordshire Record Office

1871

14 July: The Clerk was directed . . . to write to St Neots Union and state that Sarah Baldock the widow of James Baldock has become chargeable to this Union about a month, to state the particulars of her husband's settlement in that Union and inquire if they will receive her without an order of Removal.

21 July: The Clerk was . . . directed to write to the Towcester Union and request that Board to relieve Elizabeth Moss who is about to reside with John White of Whittlebury – to the amount of 2/6d. per week which will be repaid by this Union.

28 July: A letter from St Neots Union was read accepting Sarah Baldock as belonging to that Union. The Master of the Workhouse was directed to remove her thereto. . . .

A letter from the Towcester Union was read stating that they were willing to accede to the request of this Board to pay 2/6d. per week to Elizabeth Moss upon the usual conditions, viz. that the Guardians of this Union repay (in addition to the 2/6d. weekly) all sums of money expended by that Union for Medical relief and Funeral expenses on account of this person.

The Clerk was directed to inquire with reference to the payment of Medical Relief . . . if this applies to extra fees only or for General Medical Attendance.

8 September: An order for the removal of Ann Matthews from the parish of St George in the East to this Union was read and it was resolved she be accepted.

20 October: The Clerk was directed to write . . . to the Berkhampstead Union requesting to be informed of the circumstances of Margaret Baylis a Pauper chargeable to this Union and who has one child dependent upon her. . . .

1872

16 February: An order for the Removal of Ellen Walker and her six children from Oxford Poor Law Incorporation to this Union was read to the Board.

19 April: A letter from the Edmonton Union was read stating that Mary Ann Auger had been deserted by her Husband and with her two children had become chargeable to that Union and enquiring if they would be received by this Board without an order of Removal.

The matter was deferred for inquiry by the Relieving Officer as to the Settlement of the Pauper.

An Account from the Towcester Union was read claiming £4 2s. 6d. relief advanced to Elizabeth Moss from the 9th day of August 1871 to 23rd March 1872.

It was ordered to be deferred for inquiry.

26 April: An Account from the Towcester Union for Non Resident Relief afforded to Elizabeth Moss belonging to this Union but residing at Whittlebury was read. The Clerk was directed to state that at the time the application for relief was requested to be afforded her at Whittlebury it was granted to her friends on the condition that no additional relief should be applied for and if a nurse was required the person with whom she lived would attend to her without any further cost, and to forward an order for her admission into the

Union Workhouse and also further to inquire if the charge of £4 2s. 6d. is correct.

3 May: A letter was read from the Aylesbury Union stating that Sarah Blake, wife of William Blake belonging to the parish of Boarstall in this Union has in consequence of the desertion of her husband become chargeable to that Union and inquiring if this Board would receive her without an order of Removal.

The Clerk was directed to write and state that the Board were willing to receive the Pauper without such order of Removal.

An Account from the Berkhampstead Union was read for Non Settled Relief afforded to Margaret Baylis belonging to this Union to Lady Day last: the account was allowed and the Clerk was directed to write to that Union and state that for the future the relief be discontinued on behalf of this Union.

The Clerk was directed to write to the Towcester Union and inquire if Elizabeth Moss is fit to be removed to this Union House and to inclose a Cheque for £4 12s. 6d. and to explain the error made by them in the adding up of the total amount . . .

10 May: A letter from the Edmonton Union was read forwarding particulars of the case of Mary Auger chargeable to that Union.

The Clerk was directed to write and state that this Board will receive her without an order of Removal.

A letter from the Towcester Union was read inclosing a receipt for £4 12s. 6d. the amount of Relief afforded to Elizabeth Moss and stating that the Pauper was seen today, that she was better, and the Nurse had been discontinued and she is able now to be removed to Bicester and that she appeared to have been almost a proper subject for a Lunatic Asylum where the Nurse was allowed. . . .

11 October: Proceedings were directed to be taken against John Judd for leaving his Wife and Family chargeable to this Union.

Notes

PP = Parliamentary Papers

CHAPTER 1 INTRODUCTION: WOMEN IN THE VILLAGE COMMUNITY

1 Edwin Grey, *Cottage Life in a Hertfordshire Village* (Harpenden & District Local History Society, Harpenden, Herts, 1977 edn), pp. 144–5.

2 *1901 Census of Population: Occupations*, PP 1903, vol. LXXXIV, pp. 190–1.

3 Calculated from *1901 Census of Population: Occupations*, pp. 187 and 220. Of the rural work force, 23.4 per cent was female, compared to 29 per cent of the labour force of England and Wales as a whole in 1901.

4 Louisa M. Hubbard, *Work for Ladies in Elementary Schools* (Longmans, Green & Co., London, n.d. [1872]), Preface by James Kay-Shuttleworth, p. viii.

5 Margaret Hewitt, *Wives and Mothers in Victorian Industry* (Greenwood Press, Westport, Connecticut, 1975 edn), p. 3. The book was first published in 1957.

6 Calculated from *Population Census (England and Wales) 1911, Vol. X, Occupations and Industries*, PP 1913, vol. LXXIX, p. 14.

7 *Reports of Special Assistant Poor Law Commissioners on the Employment of Women and Children in Agriculture*, PP 1843, vol. XII, 'Report by Mr Alfred Austin on the Counties of Wilts, Dorset, Devon, and Somerset', pp. 27–8.

8 Hewitt, *Wives and Mothers*, p. 3.

9 *First Report of the Royal Commission on the Employment of Children, Young Persons and Women in Agriculture*, PP 1867–8, vol. XVII, 'Report by the Rev. James Fraser', p. 16.

10 *Second Report of the Royal Commission on the Employment of Children, Young Persons and Women in Agriculture*, PP 1868–9, vol. XIII, 'Mr Culley's Evidence on Berkshire', p. 373.

11 See certificate displayed in King John's House, Romsey, Hants.

12 *General Report of the 1871 Census of Population*, PP 1873, vol. LXXI, part II, p. xli.

13 Munby diaries at Trinity College, Cambridge, vol. 21, entry for 31 August 1863, f. 241.

14 Arthur Munby, *Verses New and Old* (Bell & Daldy, London, 1865), p. 95.

15 [A. J. Munby], *Dorothy: A Country Story in Elegaic Verse* (C. Kegan Paul & Co., London, 1880), Preface, pp. ix and xiii.

16 George Sturt, *Lucy Bettesworth* (Caliban Books, Firle, Sussex, 1978 edn), pp. 61–2 and 69–70.

17 Flora Thompson, *Lark Rise to Candleford* (Penguin Books, Harmondsworth, 1979 edn), p. 58.

18 P. L. R. Horn, 'Agricultural Labourers' Trade Unionism in Four Midland Counties (1860–1900)', Leicester University PhD thesis, 1968, pp. 155–6.

19 Clementina Black (ed.), *Married Women's Work* (Virago, London, 1983 edn), pp. 247 and 250. For similar conclusions by urban researchers at around the same time, see Carol Dyhouse, *Feminism and the Family in England 1880–1939* (Basil Blackwell, Oxford, 1989), pp. 85–6.

20 Information provided by Mrs Wiggins of Leafield in interviews with the author in May and June 1988.

21 Flora Thompson, 'Old Queenie', *The Lady*, 29 April 1937, p. 751.

22 Mary Chamberlain, *Fenwomen: A Portrait of Women in an English Village* (Routledge & Kegan Paul, London, 1983 edn), p. 12. For an example of the neglect of the female perspective see, for instance, Howard Newby, *Country Life: A Social History of Rural England* (Weidenfeld & Nicolson, London, 1987); this shows a woman worker on the dust jacket but makes little mention of females in the text.

23 Richard Jefferies, *The Toilers of the Field* (Macdonald Futura, London, 1981 edn), p. 83. The book was first published in 1892.

24 Thompson, *Lark Rise*, p. 166.

25 Chamberlain, *Fenwomen*, pp. 33–4.

26 *Report of the Committee of Council on Education (England and Wales), 1882–83*, PP 1883, vol. XXV, 'Mr Burrow's General Report for 1882 on the Newton Abbot district', pp. 270–1.

27 *Report of the Committee of Council, 1882–83*, 'Mr H. W. G. Markheim's General Report for 1882 on the Northallerton district', pp. 390–1.

28 Dyhouse, *Feminism and the Family*, p. 127. The commentator was particularly anxious to ensure a plentiful supply of domestic servants.

29 *Sixty-third Annual Report of the Registrar-General of Births, Deaths and Marriages in England*, PP 1901, vol. XV, p. lx. For discussion of the deficiencies of working-class mothers in bringing up children see, for example, *Report of the Inter-Departmental Committee on Physical Deterioration*, PP 1904, vol. XXXII, Evidence, Q.5498 and Q.6669-70.

30 Pamela Horn, *The Victorian and Edwardian Schoolchild* (Alan Sutton, Gloucester, 1989), pp. 53–4.

31 Patricia Hollis, *Ladies Elect: Women in English Local Government 1865–1914* (Clarendon Press, Oxford, 1987), pp. 232–3.

32 Hollis, *Ladies Elect*, p. 134.

33 Hollis, *Ladies Elect*, p. 134; Marion Johnson, *Derbyshire Village Schools in the Nineteenth Century* (David & Charles, Newton Abbot, 1970), p. 137.

34 Richard Heath, *The Victorian Peasant*, ed. Keith Dockray (Alan Sutton, Gloucester, 1989), p. 194. This analysis by Heath was first included in an article in the *Contemporary Review* of 1895.

35 Hollis, *Ladies Elect*, pp. 241–2; Elmy MSS. at the British Library, Add. MSS. 47, 450, f. 198.

36 George Edwards, *From Crow-Scaring to Westminster* (National Union of Agricultural Workers, London, 1957 edn), pp. 68–9.

37 See 1871 census return for Yarnton, at the Public Record Office, RG.10.1449.

38 Charles Booth, *The Aged Poor in England and Wales* (Macmillan & Co., London, 1894), p. 355.

39 Booth, *The Aged Poor*, p. 414.

40 Booth, *The Aged Poor*, p. 380.

41 Thompson, *Lark Rise*, pp. 96–7.

42 *Jackson's Oxford Journal*, 9 January 1909.

43 Pat Jalland, *Women, Marriage and Politics, 1860–1914* (Oxford University Press, Oxford, 1988, paperback edn), p. 253.

44 David Jenkins, *The Agricultural Community in South-West Wales at the Turn of the Twentieth Century* (University of Wales Press, Cardiff, 1971), pp. 44 and 143.

45 Grey, *Cottage Life*, p. 26.

46 Pamela Horn, *The Changing Countryside in Victorian and Edwardian England and Wales* (Athlone Press, London, 1984), p. 181. For examples of witchcraft in Oxfordshire, see Percy Manning, 'Stray Notes on Oxfordshire Folklore', *Folklore*, XIII, 3 (29 September 1902), p. 290, and Manning MSS., at the Bodleian Library, Oxford, MS.Top.Oxon.d.1972, p. 76.

47 Enid Porter, *Cambridgeshire Customs and Folklore* (Routledge & Kegan Paul, London, 1969), pp. 174–82.

CHAPTER 2   FAMILY LIFE AND MORALITY

1 Joseph Arch, *The Story of His Life Told by Himself* (Hutchinson & Co., London, 1898), pp. 23–4.
2 Arch, *The Story of His Life*, pp. 10 and 24.
3 Sybil Marshall, *Fenland Chronicle* (Cambridge University Press, Cambridge, 1980, paperback edn), p. 260.
4 Marshall, *Fenland Chronicle*, pp. 262–3.
5 Pamela Horn, *The Changing Countryside in Victorian and Edwardian England and Wales* (Athlone Press, London, 1984), pp. 135–6.
6 Arch, *The Story of His Life*, p. 78.
7 Calendar of Prisoners: Quarter Sessions QSP.I/5, 16 October 1854, and QSP.I/7, 29 June 1868; List of Prisoners in the House of Correction with Calendar of Prisoners for the Quarter Sessions, 1 July 1867; all at Oxfordshire Record Office.
8 'Agricultural Gangs' [no author given], *Quarterly Review*, 123 (1867), p. 184.
9 Marshall, *Fenland Chronicle*, pp. 224–6.
10 *Second Report of the Royal Commission on the Employment of Children, Young Persons and Women in Agriculture*, PP 1868–9, vol. XIII, Evidence, pp. 345–6. Hereafter cited as *1868–9 Report*.
11 *First Report of the Royal Commission on the Employment of Children, Young Persons and Women in Agriculture*, PP 1867–8, vol. XVII, p. 35. Hereafter cited as *1867–8 Report*.
12 *1867–8 Report*, p. 65, and Evidence, p. 234; Richard Heath, *The English Peasant* (T. Fisher Unwin, London, 1893), p. 211.
13 *Within Living Memory: A Collection of Norfolk Reminiscences* (Norfolk Federation of Women's Institutes, printed at Stone Ferry, King's Lynn, Norfolk, 1971), p. 14.
14 Marshall, *Fenland Chronicle*, p. 220.
15 *Report of the Inter-Departmental Committee on Physical Deterioration*, PP 1904, vol. XXXII, Evidence of Mrs Arthur Lyttelton, p. 213, Q. 5371.
16 *1868–9 Report*, Evidence, pp. 15–16.
17 D. Haworth and W. M. Comber (eds), *Cheshire Village Memories* (Cheshire Federation of Women's Institutes, County Office of the Cheshire Federation of Women's Institutes, Malpas, 1969), pp. 28 and

56; Enid Porter, *Cambridgeshire Customs and Folklore* (Routledge & Kegan Paul, London, 1969), p. 360; *Within Living Memory*, p. 11.

18 Walter Rose, *Good Neighbours* (Country Club, London, 1969 edn), pp. 71–3; Horn, *The Changing Countryside*, pp. 110–11.

19 Heath, *The English Peasant*, p. 182.

20 *1867–8 Report*, Evidence, p. 234.

21 Flora Thompson, *Lark Rise to Candleford* (Penguin Books, Harmondsworth, 1979 edn), pp. 24–5.

22 *Within Living Memory*, p. 17; Charles Kightly, *Country Voices: Life and Lore in Farm and Village* (Thames & Hudson, London, 1984), p. 77.

23 *Royal Commission on Labour: The Agricultural Labourer*, PP 1893–4, vol. XXV, 'Report by Mr Cecil Chapman', p. 44.

24 Pamela Horn, *Labouring Life in the Victorian Countryside* (Alan Sutton, Gloucester, 1987, paperback edn), p. 25; Charlotte M. Yonge, *An Old Woman's Outlook in a Hampshire Village* (Macmillan & Co., 1892), p. 2.

25 B. Seebohm Rowntree and May Kendall, *How the Labourer Lives* (Thomas Nelson & Sons, London, 1917, 2nd edn), pp. 113–15.

26 Rowntree and Kendall, *How the Labourer Lives*, pp. 159–64.

27 Rowntree and Kendall, *How the Labourer Lives*, p. 54.

28 Margaret Llewelyn Davies (ed.), *Life As We Have Known It* (Virago, London, 1977 edn), pp. 56–7.

29 See census returns at the Public Record Office: Wilburton, 1851: H.O.107/1764 and 1881: RG.11/1682.

30 P. J. Perry, 'Working-Class Isolation and Mobility in Rural Dorset, 1837–1936: A Study of Marriage Distances', *Transactions of the Institute of British Geographers*, 46 (1969), p. 131.

31 John R. Gillis, *For Better, For Worse: British Marriages, 1600 to the Present* (Oxford University Press, Oxford, 1985), p. 122; Horn, *Labouring Life in the Victorian Countryside*, p. 2.

32 Horn, *The Changing Countryside*, p. 127.

33 *Sixth Report of the Children's Employment Commission*, PP 1867, vol. XVI, Evidence with Mr F. D. Longe's report, p. 53; Angus McLaren, *Birth Control in Nineteenth-Century England* (Croom Helm, London, 1978), pp. 135, 203 and 228.

34 *Seventh Report of the Medical Officer of the Privy Council*, PP 1865, vol. XXVI, 'Inquiry on the State of the Dwellings of Rural Labourers by Dr H. J. Hunter', p. 146.

35 *1868–9 Report*, Evidence, p. 13.

36 *1868–9 Report*, p. 141.

37 Albert Leffingwell, *Illegitimacy and the Influence of Seasons upon Conduct* (Swan Sonnenschein, London, 1892), p. 33.

38 Herbert B. J. Armstrong (ed.), *A Norfolk Diary: Passages from the Diary of the Rev. B. J. Armstrong, Vicar of East Dereham 1850–88* (George G. Harrap & Co., London, 1949), p. 87.

39 Horn, *The Changing Countryside*, p. 126; *Third Report of the Royal Commission on the Employment of Children, Young Persons and Women in Agriculture*, PP 1870, vol. XIII, pp. 42–3. 'Bundling' had also been imported into parts of Cambridgeshire by itinerant workers in the nineteenth century: Porter, *Cambridgeshire Customs*, pp. 3–5.

40 George Ewart Evans, *Where Beards Wag All* (Faber & Faber, London, 1970), p. 122; Owen Chadwick, *Victorian Miniature* (Hodder & Stoughton, London, 1960), p. 74.

41 Calendar of Prisoners at Oxford Assizes in 1855 and 1858: QSP.I/5, at Oxfordshire Record Office.

42 Susan Oldacre, *The Blacksmith's Daughter* (Alan Sutton, Gloucester, 1985), pp. 25–6, 77 and 101–2.

43 [Mary Ann Hearn] Marianne Farningham, *A Working Woman's Life* (James Clarke & Co., London, 1907), pp. 44, 46, 48, 50 and 66; Deborah Gorham, *The Victorian Girl and the Feminine Ideal* (Croom Helm, London, 1982), pp. 143–7 and 151. Miss Hearn wrote under the pseudonym of Marianne Farningham — the name of her native village.

44 *The Autobiography of Mary Smith, Schoolmistress and Nonconformist* (Bemrose & Son, London, 1892), pp. 1, 4, 41, 50–65, 70–1 and 96–9.

45 Oldacre, *The Blacksmith's Daughter*, pp. 83 and 102.

46 Jean Robin, *Elmdon: Continuity and Change in a North-West Essex Village, 1861–1964* (Cambridge University Press, Cambridge, 1980), pp. 144–6.

47 See parish register transcripts for these villages at Oxfordshire Record Office.

48 Robin, *Elmdon*, p. 146.

49 David Jenkins, *The Agricultural Community in South-West Wales at the Turn of the Twentieth Century* (University of Wales Press, Cardiff, 1971), p. 130.

50 Bidding Letter in the Welsh Folk Museum Library, 2366/10(a).

51 S. Minwel Tibbott, 'Liberality and Hospitality: Food as Communication in Wales', *Folk Life*, 24 (1985–6), p. 48.

52 Bidding Account of Thomas Thomas of Llwynhelyg from Brynmor Thomas Collection at the Welsh Folk Museum, 2366/1.

53 Jenkins, *The Agricultural Community*, p. 190.

54 Porter, *Cambridgeshire Customs*, p. 2.

55 *The Labourers' Union Chronicle*, 4 October 1873, p. 6.

56 *1868–9 Report*, p. 141.

57 Pamela Horn (ed.), *Oxfordshire Village Life: The Diaries of George James Dew (1846–1928), Relieving Officer* (Beacon Publications, Sutton Courtenay, 1983), p. 35, entry for 7 September 1872.

58 *Hexham Herald*, 12 November 1870.

59 Robert W. Malcolmson, *Popular Recreations in English Society 1700–1850* (Cambridge University Press, Cambridge, 1979, paperback edn), p. 78.

60 Margaret Fuller, *West Country Friendly Societies* (University of Reading, Reading, 1964), p. 155.

61 Elizabeth W. Otter, *A Southwell Maid's Diary* (privately printed, [no place of publication given], July 1930), p. 12. A copy of the booklet is held at Dorset Record Office.

62 Chris Wrigley (ed.), *William Barnes: The Dorset Poet* (The Dovecote Press, Wimborne, 1984), pp. 64–5.

CHAPTER 3 WIVES AND DAUGHTERS OF THE COUNTRY HOUSE

1 Calculated from John Bateman, *The Great Landowners of Great Britain and Ireland: A List of All Owners of Three Thousand Acres and Upwards, Worth £3,000 a Year* (Harrison & Sons, London, 1878), *passim*. Only owners with land in England and Wales have been taken into account.

2 Bateman, *The Great Landowners*, and also reprint of the 1883 text, with an introduction by David Spring (Leicester University Press, Leicester, 1971), p. 480; R. J. Olney, *Lincolnshire Politics, 1832–1885* (Oxford University Press, London, 1973), pp. 19 and 113, for the influence of the Willoughby d'Eresby family and their marital connections.

3 Bateman, *The Great Landowners*, 1878 and 1883 edns, p. 236; W. D. Rubinstein, *Men of Property* (Croom Helm, London, 1981), p. 253.

4 Lawrence Stone and Jeanne C. Fawtier Stone, *An Open Elite? England 1540–1880* (Clarendon Press, Oxford, 1984), pp. 105 and 188–19.

5 Quoted in Stone and Fawtier Stone, *An Open Elite?*, p. 98.

6 Lady Maud Selborne's Childhood Recollections in the Bodleian Library, Oxford, MS.Eng.misc.e.964, f. 7–8.

7 Alice Fairfax-Lucy (ed.), *Mistress of Charlecote: The Memoirs of Mary Elizabeth Lucy* (Victor Gollancz, London, 1985), p. 137.

8   Charles Roberts, *The Radical Countess: The History of the Life of Rosalind Countess of Carlisle* (Steel Brothers (Carlisle), Carlisle, 1962), p. 115.

9   Carrington diaries in the Bodleian Library, MS.Film 1097 and 1100, entries for 24 May 1880 and 5 June 1895.

10 Consuelo Vanderbilt Balsan, *The Glitter and the Gold* (George Mann, Maidstone, 1973 edn), p. 25.

11 F. M. L. Thompson, *English Landed Society in the Nineteenth Century* (Routledge & Kegan Paul, London, 1963), p. 99.

12 *The Referee*, 29 February 1880; Frances, Countess of Warwick, *Life's Ebb and Flow* (William Morrow & Co., New York, 1929 edn), pp. 24–8.

13 Bateman, *The Great Landowners*, 1883, p. 59. In the 1878 edition the properties had been credited to his wife.

14 David N. Thomas, 'Marriage Patterns in the British Peerage in the Eighteenth and Nineteenth Centuries', London University MPhil thesis, 1969, pp. 129–37.

15 Pat Jalland, *Women, Marriage and Politics, 1860–1914* (Oxford University Press, Oxford, 1988, paperback edn), pp. 66–7 and 69; Christopher Simon Sykes, *Country House Camera* (Book Club Associations, London, 1980 edn), p. 153.

16 Vanderbilt Balsan, *The Glitter and the Gold*, pp. 33, 38-40; Sykes, *Country House Camera*, p. 162.

17 M. Corelli, *Free Opinions* (1905), p. 119, quoted in Thomas, 'Marriage Patterns in the British Peerage', p. 136.

18 Jalland, *Women, Marriage and Politics*, pp. 23–4 and 32.

19 Jalland, *Women, Marriage and Politics*, pp. 63–4.

20 L. E. Charlton (ed.), *The Recollections of a Northumbrian Lady 1815–1866, being the Memoirs of Barbara Charlton* (Jonathan Cape, London, 1949), pp. 100–1. For details of the size of the Hesleyside estate see Bateman, *The Great Landowners*, 1883, p. 85.

21 Georgina Battiscombe, *Mrs. Gladstone* (Constable, London, 1956), p. 16.

22 Jean Robin, *Elmdon: Continuity and Change in a North-West Essex Village, 1861–1964* (Cambridge University Press, Cambridge, 1980), p. 141; Viscountess Ridley (ed.), *Cecilia: The Life and Letters of Cecilia Ridley (1819–1845)* (Rupert Hart-Davis, London, 1958), pp. 41 and 92.

23 The Earl of Bessborough (ed.), *Lady Charlotte Guest: Extracts from her Journal, 1833–52* (John Murray, London, 1950), pp. 4–5.

24 Revel Guest and Angela V. John, *Lady Charlotte: A Biography of the*

Nineteenth Century (Weidenfeld & Nicolson, London, 1989), pp. 78–80.

25 Bessborough, *Lady Charlotte Guest*, p. 38; Guest and John, *Lady Charlotte*, p. 81.

26 The Carrington Diaries, MS.Film 1097, entry for 19 January 1877.

27 The Carrington Diaries, MS.Film 1097, entry for 2 February 1877.

28 Charles Kightly, *Country Voices: Life and Lore in Farm and Village* (Thames & Hudson, London, 1984), p. 172.

29 Quoted in Jessica Gerard, 'Lady Bountiful: Women of the Landed Classes and Rural Philanthropy', *Victorian Studies*, 30, 2 (winter, 1987), p. 205.

30 Gerard, 'Lady Bountiful', p. 196.

31 Charlotte M. Yonge, *An Old Woman's Outlook in a Hampshire Village* (Macmillan & Co., London, 1892), p. 280.

32 The Rev. C. Kingsley, 'The Country Parish', in *Lectures to Ladies on Practical Subjects* (Macmillan & Co., Cambridge, 1855), pp. 53–5.

33 John Burnett (ed.), *Destiny Obscure* (Penguin Books, Harmondsworth, 1984), pp. 289 and 293; Gerard, 'Lady Bountiful', p. 200.

34 Roberts, *The Radical Countess*, pp. 60–4.

35 Mary Carbery, *Happy World. The Story of a Victorian Childhood* (Longmans, Green & Co., London, 1941), p. 49.

36 D. Haworth and W. M. Comber (eds), *Cheshire Village Memories* (Cheshire Federation of Women's Institutes, County Office of the Cheshire Federation of Women's Institutes, Malpas, 1969), p. 54.

37 Gerard, 'Lady Bountiful', p. 193.

38 Georgina Battiscombe, *Charlotte Mary Yonge. The Story of an Uneventful Life* (Constable & Co., London, 1943), pp. 57, 61 and 167.

39 Rachel Weigall, *Lady Rose Weigall* (John Murray, London, 1923), p. 58.

40 *A Pattern of Hundreds* (Buckinghamshire Federation of Women's Institutes, Chalfont St Giles, 1975), p. 17.

41 George Ewart Evans, *Where Beards Wag All* (Faber & Faber, London, 1970), p. 122; Gerard, 'Lady Bountiful', p. 198.

42 Frances, Countess of Warwick, *Afterthoughts* (Cassell & Co., London, 1931), pp. 242–3.

43 Evans, *Where Beards Wag All*, p. 123 (though Evans notes that among some, there was an 'underlying, smouldering resentment' against the social control exercised).

44 Ridley, *Cecilia*, p. 141.

45 MSS.D.D.Dashwood (Bucks) G.3/36/2 at the Bodleian Library.

46 Guest and John, *Lady Charlotte*, p. 67.

47 *Second Report of the Royal Commission on the Employment of Children, Young Persons and Women in Agriculture*, PP 1868–9, vol. XIII, Evidence, pp. 355–6.

48 Sturges Bourne–Dyson correspondence at Hampshire Record Office, 9M55.F.31; 1861 Census Return for Testwood House at the Public Record Office, RG.9.672.

49 MSS.D.D.Dashwood (Bucks) G.36/5, letter dated 11 April [1851], and MSS.D.D.Dashwood (Bucks) G.3/33/10a, letter dated 16 April [1851].

50 Gerard, 'Lady Bountiful', p. 206.

51 Elmy MSS at the British Library, Additional MSS. 47, 450, ff. 152, 162, 164 and 170.

52 Elmy MSS at the British Library, Additional MSS. 47, 450, f. 170, letter dated 7 January 1895.

53 *Parish, District and Town Councils' Gazette*, 12 January 1895, p. 98.

54 Edith Olivier, *Four Victorian Ladies of Wiltshire* (Faber & Faber, London, 1945), pp. 9–10.

55 The Marchioness of Londonderry, *Retrospect* (Frederick Muller, London, 1938), p. 101 (Lady Londonderry was born in 1878); Sykes, *Country House Camera*, pp. 13–14.

56 The Carrington Diaries, MS.Film 1097, entry for 22 January 1877.

57 John Bailey (ed.), *The Diary of Lady Frederick Cavendish* (John Murray, London, 1927), vol. 1, p. 124.

58 *Country Life*, 16 December 1899, p. 783.

59 Richard Greville Verney, Lord Willoughby de Broke, *The Passing Years* (Constable & Co., London, 1924), pp. 38–40.

60 Ridley, *Cecilia*, pp. 89 and 104.

61 Sykes, *Country House Camera*, p. 22.

62 Battiscombe, *Mrs. Gladstone*, p. 80.

63 The Countess of Cardigan and Lancastre, *My Recollections* (Evelyn Nash, London, 1909), pp. 53–9.

64 Ralph Nevill (ed.), *The Reminiscences of Lady Dorothy Nevill* (Thomas Nelson & Sons, London, Edinburgh and Dublin, n.d. [c.1906]), p. 126.

65 Noel Streatfeild (ed.), *The Day Before Yesterday* (Collins, London, 1956), p. 106.

66 Streatfeild, *The Day Before Yesterday*, p. 109.

67 *Country Life*, 30 December 1899, p. 852.

68 Jalland, *Women, Marriage and Politics*, p. 4.

69 MSS.D.D.Dashwood (Bucks.) G.3/33/7, 8, 9 at the Bodleian Library, n.d., c.1851.

70 Sturges Bourne–Dyson correspondence at Hampshire Record Office,

9M55.F.30, letter written in 1857, and 9M55.F.31, letter written c.1858.

71 MSSD.D.Dashwood (Bucks) G.3.33/2a, letter dated January 1842.

72 Charlton, *The Recollections of a Northumbrian Lady*, p. 176.

73 Jalland, *Women, Marriage and Politics*, p. 23.

74 Osbert Sitwell (ed.), *Two Generations* (Macmillan & Co., London, 1940), p. 277.

75 Sitwell, *Two Generations*, p. 293.

76 Cecil Woodham-Smith, *Florence Nightingale* (Penguin Books, Harmondsworth, 1955 edn), p. 36; Sarah Gristwood, *Recording Angels: The Secret World of Women's Diaries* (Harrap, London, 1988), p. 17.

77 Woodham-Smith, *Florence Nightingale*, p. 53.

78 Woodham-Smith, *Florence Nightingale*, p. 54.

79 Woodham-Smith, *Florence Nightingale*, p. 54.

80 Ray Strachey, *The Cause* (Virago, London, 1978 edn), pp. 396–415 *passim*. This long appendix quotes from Florence Nightingale's writings.

81 Ralph G. Martin, *Lady Randolph Churchill: A Biography, 1854–1895* (Literary Guild, London, 1969 edn), pp. 88 and 166.

82 Roberts, *The Radical Countess*, pp. 56–7.

83 Jalland, *Women, Marriage and Politics*, pp. 238–9; Selborne MSS. at the Bodleian Library, letters written to Roundell Palmer by Lady Selborne, advising her son on political matters, MS.Eng.Lit.c.978, f. 20, letter dated 25 June [1908].

84 Owen Chadwick, *Victorian Miniature* (Hodder & Stoughton, London, 1960), pp. 68–70.

85 Vanderbilt Balsan, *The Glitter and the Gold*, pp. 84–5.

86 Vanderbilt Balsan, *The Glitter and the Gold*, p. 62.

87 Streatfeild, *The Day Before Yesterday*, pp. 118–19.

88 Ridley, *Cecilia*, pp. 106 and 187.

89 Bailey, *The Diary of Lady Frederick Cavendish*, vol. 2, p. 18.

90 Bailey, *The Diary of Lady Frederick Cavendish*, vol. 2, p. 36.

91 Diary of Louisa Yorke of Erddig for 1902 at Clwyd Record Office, D.E.2816, entries for 1 and 17 July.

92 Diary of Louisa Yorke of Erddig for 1902, entry for 5 September.

93 Bailey, *The Diary of Lady Frederick Cavendish*, vol. 1, p. 263, entry for 17 May 1865, less than a year after her marriage.

94 See Guest and John, *Lady Charlotte*, p. 33.

95 Janet Horowitz Murray, *Strong-Minded Women* (Penguin Books, Harmondsworth, 1984), p. 144.

96 Battiscombe, *Mrs. Gladstone*, pp. 108–10; Jalland, *Women, Marriage*

and Politics, pp. 176–7; Ridley, *Cecilia*, pp. 126 and 199.

97 Jalland, *Women, Marriage and Politics*, p. 168.

98 Roberts, *The Radical Countess*, p. 68; Chadwick, *Victorian Miniature*, pp. 147–8.

99 Olivier, *Four Victorian Ladies*, pp. 53–4.

100 Angus McLaren, *Birth Control in Nineteenth-Century England* (Croom Helm, London, 1978), p. 11; Jalland, *Women, Marriage and Politics*, p. 175.

101 Josephine Kamm, *How Different from Us. A Biography of Miss Buss and Miss Beale* (Bodley Head, London, 1958), pp. 55 and 63–4.

102 Carol Dyhouse, *Girls Growing Up in Late Victorian and Edwardian England* (Routledge & Kegan Paul, London, 1981), p. 183.

103 Dyhouse, *Girls Growing Up*, pp. 40, 41 and 56.

104 Lady Maud Selborne's Childhood Recollections, f. 16.

105 Adeline Hartcup, *Children of the Great Country Houses* (Sidgwick & Jackson, London, 1982), p. 60.

106 Bailey, *The Diary of Lady Frederick Cavendish*, vol. 1, pp. 36–7.

107 Thea Thompson, *Edwardian Childhoods* (Routledge & Kegan Paul, London, 1981), pp. 222–3; Pamela Horn, 'The Victorian Governess', *History of Education*, 18, 4 (1989), p. 342.

108 Quoted in Jill Franklin, *The Gentleman's Country House and its Plan, 1835–1914* (Routledge & Kegan Paul, London, 1981), p. 40.

109 Carol Dyhouse, *Feminism and the Family in England, 1880–1939* (Basil Blackwell, Oxford, 1989), p. 195. For the Married Women's Property Acts see Lee Holcombe, 'Victorian Wives and Property Reform', in Martha Vicinus (ed.), *A Widening Sphere* (Indiana University Press, Bloomington, Indiana, & London, 1977), pp. 7–25.

110 Jalland, *Women, Marriage and Politics*, p. 60.

111 Quoted in Jalland, *Women, Marriage and Politics*, p. 61.

112 See letters to G. H. (later Sir George H.) Dashwood from his sister-in-law, Anne, wife of the Rev. Henry Dashwood, for 1844–5, in MSS.D.D.Dashwood (Bucks.), G.3/20/2–7a.

113 See letters to Sir George H. Dashwood from Mrs Henry Dashwood in MSS.D.D.Dashwood (Bucks.) G.3/20/8–13a.

114 Guest and John, *Lady Charlotte*, pp. 145–7.

115 Bessborough, *Lady Charlotte Guest*, pp. 168 and 225.

116 Bessborough, *Lady Charlotte Guest*, p. 252.

117 Guest and John, *Lady Charlotte*, p. 189.

118 Edith, Marchioness of Londonderry, *Frances Anne: The Life and Times of Frances Anne, Marchioness of Londonderry and her husband Charles, Third Marquess of Londonderry* (Macmillan & Co., London, 1958), p. 286.

119 Londonderry, *Frances Anne*, pp. 268 and 301.

120 Mrs James de Rothschild, *The Rothschilds at Waddesdon Manor* (Collins, London, 1979), pp. 75–8.

121 Roberts, *The Radical Countess*, pp. 136–7.

122 Roberts, *The Radical Countess*, pp. 139–40 and 150.

123 See, for example, her entry in the *Dictionary of National Biography*; she was one of the relatively few women to gain an early entry in this work. Her anti-game writings included *The Horrors of Sport*, published in 1905. And see McLaren, *Birth Control*, p. 211.

124 Francesca M. Wilson, *Rebel Daughter of a Country House: The Life of Eglantyne Jebb* (Allen & Unwin, London, 1967), pp. 80–1.

125 Joan N. Burstyn, *Victorian Education and the Ideal of Womanhood* (Rutgers University Press, New Brunswick, New Jersey, 1984), p. 135.

126 Patricia Hollis, *Ladies Elect: Women in English Local Government, 1865–1914* (Clarendon Press, Oxford, 1987), p. 368; *Parish, District and Town Councils Gazette*, 5 January 1895.

127 *Country Life*, 11 November 1899, p. 578. Dairying and poultry-keeping were identified as especially suitable for women.

128 Letter Books of the Lady Warwick Hostel at Reading University Library, WAR.5/1/2, ff. 65 and 358.

129 Pamela Horn, *Rural Life in England in the First World War* (Gill & Macmillan, Dublin, 1984), p. 41. Olive Banks's researches suggest that relatively few of the early feminists were from a landed background: see Olive Banks, *Becoming a Feminist: The Social Origins of 'First Wave' Feminism* (Wheatsheaf Books, Brighton, 1986), p. 18.

CHAPTER 4 PROFESSIONAL FAMILIES

1 George Eliot, *Middlemarch: A Study of Provincial Life* (William Blackwood & Sons, Edinburgh & London, 1890 edn), p. 169. The book was first published in 1871–2.

2 Jean Donnison, *Midwives and Medical Men: A History of the Struggle for the Control of Childbirth* (Historical Publications, New Barnet, Herts, and London, 1988), pp. 70–1.

3 Noel Streatfeild, *A Vicarage Family* (Collins, London, 1963), p. 77. The comment was made by Noel Streatfeild's grandmother early in the twentieth century.

4 W. J. Reader, *Professional Men* (Weidenfeld & Nicolson, London, 1966), p. 68.

5 Quoted in Reader, *Professional Men*, p. 69.

6 Richard Jefferies, *Hodge and His Masters* (Macgibbon & Kee, London, 1966 edn), vol. II, p. 9. The book was first published in 1880.

7 Leonore Davidoff and Catherine Hall, *Family Fortunes: Men and Women of the English Middle Class, 1780–1850* (Hutchinson, London, 1987), p. 283.

8 David N. Thomas, 'Marriage Patterns in the British Peerage in the Eighteenth and Nineteenth Centuries', London University MPhil thesis, 1969, p. 162.

9 Elizabeth C. Gaskell, *Wives and Daughters* (Oxford University Press, London, 1936, World's Classics edn), pp. 115–16. The book was first published in 1866.

10 Quoted in Pamela Horn, *The Changing Countryside in Victorian and Edwardian England and Wales* (Athlone Press, London, 1984), pp. 155–6.

11 Donnison, *Midwives and Medical Men*, p. 58.

12 Horn, *The Changing Countryside*, p. 155.

13 *The Lancet*, 21 June 1879, p. 900.

14 Anthony Trollope, *Doctor Thorne* (Oxford University Press, London, 1956, World's Classics edn), pp. 466–9. The book was first published in 1858. It was symptomatic of the general approach that Trollope makes the snobbish Lady de Courcy deplore 'the idea of Mr. Gresham, a country gentleman of good estate . . . , making a confidant of a country doctor' (p. 47).

15 Thomas, 'Marriage Patterns in the British Peerage', p. 161.

16 Patricia Hollis, *Ladies Elect: Women in English Local Government 1865–1914* (Clarendon Press, Oxford, 1987), pp. 365–6.

17 See census returns for Ivinghoe at the Public Record Office, for 1851, H.O.107.1756, and 1871, R.G.10.1564; Kenneth D. Brown, *A Social History of the Nonconformist Ministry in England and Wales, 1800–1930* (Clarendon Press, Oxford, 1988), pp. 154 and 157.

18 Brown, *A Social History*, p. 159.

19 Brown, *A Social History*, p. 151.

20 Brown, *A Social History*, p. 179.

21 Brown, *A Social History*, pp. 173–4.

22 Owen Chadwick, *The Victorian Church* (Adam and Charles Black, London, 1972, 2nd edn), part II, pp. 181–2.

23 George Eliot, *Felix Holt, The Radical* (William Blackwood & Sons, Edinburgh & London, 1901), pp. 111–12. The book was first published in 1866.

24 J. A. Robinson (ed.), *The Ames Correspondence* (Norfolk Record Society, 1962), vol. XXXI, p. 44, letter dated 8 January 1839.

25 Pamela Horn (ed.), *Oxfordshire Country Life in the 1860s: The Early Diaries of George James Dew (1846–1928), of Lower Heyford* (Beacon Publications, Sutton Courtenay, 1986), p. 67.

26 Owen Chadwick, *Victorian Miniature* (Hodder & Stoughton, London, 1960), pp. 179–80.

27 Joseph Ritson, *The Romance of Primitive Methodism* (Edwin Dalton, London, 1909), p. 152.

28 Brown, *A Social History*, p. 17. In 1850, the Primitive Methodists had a membership of 104,762, and the Bible Christian Methodists numbered 10,146 members two years later. By contrast, the main body of Wesleyan Methodists numbered 358,277 in Great Britain in 1850. See Robert F. Wearmouth, *Methodism and the Working-Class Movements of England 1800–1850* (Epworth Press, London, 1947), p. 3.

29 James Obelkevich, *Religion and Rural Society: South Lindsey, 1825–1875* (Clarendon Press, Oxford, 1976), p. 244.

30 Ruth Hillyer, 'The Parson's Wife in History', London University MPhil thesis, 1971, p. 111.

31 Aubrey Moore, *A Son of the Rectory* (Alan Sutton, Gloucester, 1982), p. 16.

32 See 1861 population census return for Old Alresford at the Public Record Office, R.G.9.703.

33 Joyce Coombs, *George and Mary Sumner: Their Life and Times* (Sumner Press, London, 1965), p. 62.

34 Anne Hopkinson, 'Mary Sumner and the Mothers' Union – 100 Years On', *Hampshire* (March 1976), p. 50.

35 Brenda Colloms, *Charles Kingsley: The Lion of Eversley* (Constable, London, 1975), p. 77. For the Kingsley timetable see Susan Chitty, *The Beast and the Monk: A Life of Charles Kingsley* (Hodder & Stoughton, London, 1974), p. 97.

36 A. Tindal Hart, *The Curate's Lot* (Country Book Club, Newton Abbot, 1971 edn), p. 145.

37 Hillyer, 'The Parson's Wife', p. 544.

38 Hillyer, 'The Parson's Wife', p. 544.

39 Dorothy Thompson, *Sophia's Son: The Story of a Suffolk Parson, The Rev. Henry Thompson, MA., His Life and Times, 1841–1916* (Terence Dalton, Lavenham, Suffolk, 1969), p. 92.

40 Thompson, *Sophia's Son*, p. 110.

41 Chadwick, *The Victorian Church*, p. 169.

42 Jefferies, *Hodge and His Masters*, vol. I, p. 153.

43 Pamela Horn, *The Tithe War in Pembrokeshire* (Preseli Printers,

Fishguard, 1982), p. 7; R. E. Prothero, *The Anti-Tithe Agitation in Wales* (London, pamphlet, 1889), pp. 13–14.

44 Horn, *The Tithe War*, p. 6.

45 Mary Paley Marshall, *What I Remember* (Cambridge University Press, Cambridge, 1947), pp. 5 and 8.

46 Emma Hardy, *Some Recollections* (Oxford University Press, London, 1961), p. 45; *Crockford's Clerical Directory* (Horace Cox, London, 1872).

47 Hardy, *Some Recollections*, p. 53.

48 'Deborah Primrose' [Mrs R. L. Ottley], *A Modern Boeotia* (Methuen & Co., London, 1904), pp. 4, 6–10 and 52.

49 'Primrose', *A Modern Boeotia*; information provided by Wiltshire Local History Library at Trowbridge.

50 Elizabeth C. Gaskell, *The Life of Charlotte Brontë* (Oxford University Press, London, 1961, World's Classics edn), pp. 146–7 (first published 1857); Brenda Colloms, *Victorian Country Parsons* (Constable, London, 1977), p. 85.

51 Letter from T. J. Scott, rector of Marksbury, to the Archbishop of Canterbury, in Lambeth Palace Library, Benson MSS. 171, ff. 95–7.

52 Louisa Scott's diaries at Clwyd Record Office, D/E/2816, for this and other diary entries. For a brief account of Louisa's life and family background see Pamela Horn, 'The Last Mistress of Erddig', *Out of Town* (April 1987), pp. 12–14.

53 Diary of Caroline Blanche Smith of West Stafford Rectory, Dorchester, for 1881, at Dorset Record Office, D.500/25.

54 At the end of the Victorian era, clergy daughters were less likely to marry into the aristocracy than they had been earlier in the century. See Thomas, 'Marriage Patterns in the British Peerage', p. 161.

55 Moore, *A Son of the Rectory*, pp. 43, 49 and 51.

56 Diary of Mary Drew at the British Library, Additional MSS. 46, 262; Pat Jalland, *Women, Marriage and Politics 1860–1914* (Oxford University Press, Oxford, 1988, paperback edn), pp. 100–2.

57 Hillyer, 'The Parson's Wife', p. 546.

58 Hillyer, 'The Parson's Wife', p. 543.

59 *Reports of Special Assistant Poor Law Commissioners on the Employment of Women and Children in Agriculture*, PP 1843, vol. XII, pp. 151 and 195–6.

60 Pamela Horn, *The Victorian Country Child* (Alan Sutton, Gloucester, 1985), pp. 135 and 143.

61 Horn, *The Victorian Country Child*, pp. 147 and 148.

62 Clifford B. Freeman, *Mary Simpson of Boynton Vicarage: Teacher of Ploughboys and Critic of Methodism* (East Yorkshire Local History

Society, 1972), p. 21.

63 Freeman, *Mary Simpson*, p. 14.

64 Freeman, *Mary Simpson*, pp. 18 and 23–7; Horn, *The Victorian Country Child*, p. 89.

65 Davidoff and Hall, *Family Fortunes*, p. 124.

66 Coombs, *George and Mary Sumner*, pp. 63 and 81–2; Hopkinson, 'Mary Sumner', p. 50.

67 Coombs, *George and Mary Sumner*, p. 90; Violet B. Lancaster, *Mary Sumner* (The Mothers' Union, London, 1960 edn), p. 10.

68 Mrs Acland, 'Our Difficulties', *Mothers' Union Journal* (July 1893) for the advice on the dangers of debt; *Mothers' Union Journal* (October 1896) for circulation figure.

69 Mrs Horace Porter, *Mary Sumner: Her Life and Work* (The Mothers' Union, London, 1950, 3rd edn), pp. 36–42.

70 *Handbook and Central Report of the Mothers' Union for 1903* gives details of membership and associateship.

71 Porter, *Mary Sumner*, pp. 59–61.

72 Hillyer, 'The Parson's Wife', pp. 547–8. A parish branch of the Mothers' Union was formed at Great Gaddesden in 1891.

73 Pamela Horn, 'The Rising Lark', *Out of Town* (March 1987), p. 56; Flora Thompson, *Lark Rise to Candleford* (Penguin Books, Harmondsworth, 1979 edn), pp. 133 and 162.

74 Thompson, *Lark Rise to Candleford*, p. 221.

75 Thompson, *Lark Rise to Candleford*, pp. 221–2.

76 Joseph Arch, *The Story of His Life Told by Himself* (Hutchinson & Co., London, 1898), pp. 17–18.

77 'Michael Home', *Spring Sowing* (Methuen & Co., London, 1946), pp. 9 and 24; 'Michael Home', *Autumn Fields* (Methuen & Co., London, 1944), p. 37.

78 'Home', *Autumn Fields*, p. 38.

79 Phyllis Bottome, *Search for a Soul* (Faber & Faber, London, 1947), pp. 54–5. *Crockford's Clerical Directory* for 1900 shows Mr Bottome as vicar of Fawley 1884–7 and of Over Stowey 1887–90.

80 'Primrose', *A Modern Boeotia*, pp. 118–20 and 172–3.

81 Paley Marshall, *What I Remember*, pp. 6–8.

82 Barbara Stephen, *Emily Davies and Girton College* (Constable & Co., London, 1927), pp. 25 and 29–30.

83 Paley Marshall, *What I Remember*, p. 10.

84 Rita McWilliams-Tullberg, *Women at Cambridge* (Victor Gollancz, London, 1975), pp. 60–2; Paley Marshall, *What I Remember*, pp. 13–17.

85 Paley Marshall, *What I Remember*, pp. 20, 22 and 23.

86 Monica Wagner, *My Memories* (Northumberland Press, Gateshead, 1964), pp. 25–6.

87 *Journal of Emily Shore* (Kegan Paul, Trench, Trübner & Co., London, 1891), pp. 1–2 and 24.

88 *Journal of Emily Shore*, pp. 31–2.

89 *Journal of Emily Shore*, p. 28.

90 'Vanity Fair and Jane Eyre', *Quarterly Review*, LXXXIV (December 1848), pp. 176–7; see also M. Jeanne Peterson, 'The Victorian Governess: Status Incongruence in Family and Society', in Martha Vicinus (ed.), *Suffer and Be Still. Women in the Victorian Age* (Indiana University Press, Bloomington, Indiana, and London, 1972), p. 13.

91 Pamela Horn, 'The Victorian Governess', *History of Education*, 18, 4 (1989), 336; Annual Reports of the Governesses' Benevolent Institution at the headquarters of the GBI, Chislehurst, consulted by kind co-operation of the director and secretary, Mr R. W. Hayward; Wanda F. Neff, *Victorian Working Women* (Frank Cass & Co., London, 1966, 2nd edn), pp. 154–5. Advertisements in *The Times*, such as those for 2 September 1850 and 8 October 1879, mention that the would-be governess was 'a clergyman's daughter'.

92 McWilliams-Tullberg, *Women at Cambridge*, pp. 21–2.

93 Rosalie Glynn Grylls, *Queen's College, 1848–1948* (George Routledge & Sons, London, 1948), p. 113; Horn, 'The Victorian Governess', pp. 340–1.

94 Horn, 'The Victorian Governess', pp. 341–2; admission registers at Queen's College Library, consulted with the kind co-operation of the librarian, Mrs Fitzgerald.

95 Gaskell, *The Life of Charlotte Brontë*, pp. 139–40.

96 Winifred Gérin, *Charlotte Brontë: The Evolution of Genius* (Oxford University Press, Oxford, 1967, paperback edn), pp. 169–71.

97 Winifred Gérin, *Anne Brontë* (Allen Lane, London, 1976, paperback edn), pp. 133–4.

98 Gérin, *Anne Brontë*, p. 159.

99 Davidoff and Hall, *Family Fortunes*, p. 125.

100 Anthony Trollope, *The Vicar of Bullhampton* (Alan Sutton, Gloucester, 1986, Pocket Classics edn), p. 6. The book was first published in 1870.

101 Davidoff and Hall, *Family Fortunes*, p. 125.

CHAPTER 5 FARMING FAMILIES

1 These were the *Royal Commission on the Agricultural Interest (1879–82)*, under the chairmanship of the Duke of Richmond, and the *Royal Commission on Agricultural Depression (1893–97)*, chaired by Lord Eversley.

2 Jean Stovin (ed.), *Journals of a Methodist Farmer, 1871–1875* (Croom Helm, London, 1982), p. 29; K. D. M. Snell, *Annals of the Labouring Poor* (Cambridge University Press, Cambridge, 1985), p. 165.

3 Rex L. Sawyer, *The Bowerchalke Parish Papers: Collett's Village Newspaper, 1878–1924* (Alan Sutton, and Wiltshire County Council, Gloucester, 1989), pp. 35, 54, 65, 86, 101, 104 and 105.

4 Maude Robinson, *A South Down Farm in the Sixties* (Bannisdale Press, London, 1947 edn), pp. 51–2.

5 Richard Jefferies, *The Toilers of the Field* (Macdonald Futura, London, 1981, paperback edn), p. 32. The book was first published in 1892, but most of its contents had appeared in articles during the 1870s.

6 George Eliot, *Adam Bede* (Dent, London, 1976, Everyman's Library paperback edn), p. 183. The book was first published in 1858.

7 Eliot, *Adam Bede*, p. 81.

8 R. S. Surtees, *Ask Mama* (Alan Sutton, Gloucester, 1984, Pocket Classics edn), pp. 249–50. The book was first published in 1858.

9 H. St. G. Cramp, *A Yeoman Farmer's Son: A Leicestershire Childhood* (John Murray, London, 1985), pp. 42–3.

10 *General Report of the Board of Agriculture and Fisheries: Wages and Conditions of Employment of Agricultural Labourers*, PP 1919, vol. IX, Report on Cardiganshire, p. 412.

11 Mrs M. Silyn Roberts, 'The Women of Wales and Agriculture', *Journal of the Board of Agriculture*, 25 (1918–19), p. 818; David Jenkins, *The Agricultural Community in South-West Wales at the Turn of the Twentieth Century* (University of Wales Press, Cardiff, 1971), p. 78.

12 Reminiscences of Mr Arthur Clifford, now living in Sutton Courtenay, Oxfordshire, concerning his mother; interviewed 2 September 1987.

13 Barbara Kerr, *Bound to the Soil* (John Baker, London, 1968), p. 59.

14 Diary of Robert Bretnall for 1846–8, at Essex Record Office, D/DBs F.38.

15 *Reports of Special Assistant Poor Law Commissioners on the Employment of Women and Children in Agriculture*, PP 1843, vol. XII, 'Report by Mr. Alfred Austin on the Counties of Wilts, Dorset, Devon, and Somerset', p. 5.

16 *Reports of Special Assistant Poor Law Commissioners*, p. 5.

17   *Royal Commission on Agricultural Depression*, PP 1895, vol. XVI,
     'Report by Mr. A. Wilson Fox on Suffolk', p. 67.
18   *Royal Commission on Agricultural Depression*, 'Report by Mr. A.
     Wilson Fox on Suffolk', pp. 67–8.
19   Pamela Horn, *The Changing Countryside in Victorian and Edwardian
     England and Wales* (Athlone Press, London, 1984), pp. 81–2.
20   *Second Report of the Royal Commission on the Employment of
     Children, Young Persons and Women in Agriculture*, PP 1868–9, vol.
     XIII, p. 143.
21   Notes compiled by Mrs R. A. Winnington, formerly of Wem,
     Shropshire, at University of Reading Library, SAL.8.2.1.
22   George Sturt, *William Smith, Potter and Farmer: 1790–1858* (Caliban
     Books, Firle, Sussex, 1978 edn), pp. 17 and 174–5. The book was first
     published in 1919 under Sturt's pseudonym, George Bourne.
23   *Royal Commission on Agricultural Depression*, 'Report by Mr. A.
     Wilson Fox on Lincolnshire (excepting the Isle of Axholme)', p. 103.
24   D. Haworth and W. M. Comber (eds), *Cheshire Village Memories*
     (Cheshire Federation of Women's Institutes, County Office of the
     Cheshire Federation of Women's Institutes, Malpas, 1969), p. 124.
25   Charles Kightly, *Country Voices: Life and Lore in Farm and Village*
     (Thames & Hudson, London, 1984), pp. 84–5.
26   *Royal Commission on Agricultural Depression*, 'Report by Mr. A.
     Wilson Fox on Suffolk', p. 59.
27   Richard Jefferies, *Hodge and His Masters* (Macgibbon & Kee, London,
     1966 edn), vol. I, pp. 35–6. The book was first published in 1880.
28   R. J. Olney, *Rural Society and County Government in Nineteenth
     Century Lincolnshire*, History of Lincolnshire (History of Lincolnshire
     Committee, Lincoln, 1979), vol. X, p. 178.
29   Jenkins, *The Agricultural Community*, p. 79.
30   Jenkins, *The Agricultural Community*, p. 79.
31   *Royal Commission on Land in Wales and Monmouthshire: Minutes of
     Evidence*, PP 1895, vol. XL, Evidence of Miss Kate Jenkins, p. 78,
     Q.38,024.
32   *Royal Commission on Agricultural Depression*, PP 1894, vol. XVI,
     'Report by Mr. A. Wilson Fox on the Garstang District of Lancashire',
     p. 14.
33   *Royal Commission on Agricultural Depression*, 'Report by Mr. A.
     Wilson Fox on the Garstang District of Lancashire', p. 63.
34   *Royal Commission on Agricultural Depression*, PP 1895, vol. XVI,
     'Report by Mr. A. Wilson Fox on Cumberland', p. 28.
35   *Royal Commission on Agricultural Depression*, 'Report by Mr. A.
     Wilson Fox on Cumberland', pp. 28–9.

36 *1911 Census of Population*, PP 1913, vol. LXXVIII, pp. xlv–xlvi; *Board of Agriculture and Fisheries: The Agricultural Output of Great Britain in Connection with the Census of Production Act, 1906*, PP 1912–13, vol. X, p. 18 (for persons regularly employed on farms in England and Wales during the twelve months ending 4 June 1908).

37 Rev. J. C. Atkinson, *Forty Years in a Moorland Parish: Reminiscences and Researches in Danby in Cleveland* (Macmillan & Co., London, 1891), pp. 5–6.

38 Charles Kightly, *Country Voices*, p. 109.

39 Atkinson, *Forty Years in a Moorland Parish*, p. 14.

40 *Royal Commission on Agricultural Depression*, 'Report by Mr. A. Wilson Fox on Cumberland', p. 44, quoting evidence given in 1892 by Miss Barnes of Baurgh near Wigton.

41 Leonore Davidoff and Catherine Hall, *Family Fortunes: Men and Women of the English Middle Class, 1780–1850* (Hutchinson, London, 1987), p. 289.

42 *Reports of Special Assistant Poor Law Commissioners*, Evidence of Mary Rendalls, p. 113.

43 Reminiscences of Mrs Florence Davis (née Stowe) in the Bodleian Library, Oxford, MS.Top.Gen.c.40; Pamela Horn, 'The Daily Grind', *Limited Edition*, 35 (September 1989), p. 36.

44 Alison Uttley, *The Country Child* (Penguin Books, Harmondsworth, 1969), p. 56. The book was first published in 1931.

45 Uttley, *The Country Child*, p. 190.

46 Quoted in Ivy Pinchbeck, *Women Workers and the Industrial Revolution, 1750–1850* (Frank Cass, London, 1969 edn), p. 36. The book was first published in 1930.

47 Quoted in Olney, *Rural Society*, p. 60.

48 *The Works of George Eliot: Essays* (Virtue & Co., London, n.d., Illustrated Copyright Edition), pp. 197–8.

49 Gordon S. Haight (ed.), *The George Eliot Letters* (Oxford University Press, London, 1954), vol. 1, p. 31, letter to Maria Lewis, 4 September 1839.

50 Gordon S. Haight, *George Eliot* (Clarendon Press, Oxford, 1968), p. 28; Haight, *The George Eliot Letters*, vol. 1, p. 68, letter to Maria Lewis, 1 October 1840.

51 Pamela Horn, 'Problems of a Nineteenth Century Vicar, 1832–1885', *Oxford Diocesan Magazine* (October 1969), p. 16.

52 Olney, *Rural Society*, p. 61.

53 T. Carrington Smith, 'Fifty Years of Staffordshire Farming', *Land Magazine*, IV, 1 (January 1900), p. 50.

54 Davidoff and Hall, *Family Fortunes*, p. 273.

55 Stovin, *Journals of a Methodist Farmer*, p. 170.

56 Stovin, *Journals of a Methodist Farmer*, p. 7.

57 Diary of Martha Randall at University of Reading Library, ESS.3/2/1; census returns for Orsett, Essex, for 1851, H.O.107.1773 and 1861, R.G.9.1074 at the Public Record Office; registration of births, deaths and marriages at St Catherine's House, London; E. J. T. Collins, *A History of the Orsett Estate, 1743–1914* (Thurrock Museums Department Publication No. 2, 1978), p. 58.

58 Diary of Martha Randall, ESS.3/2/1, entry for 28 June 1858.

59 Registration of births, deaths and marriages at St Catherine's House, London; will of Martha Sackett at Somerset House; 1871 census return for Orsett, R.G.10.1654, and 1881 census return for Orsett, R.G.11.1754, at Public Record Office; trade directories for Essex.

60 Edward Hyams (ed.), *Taine's Notes on England* (Thames & Hudson, London, 1957), p. 131.

61 Vera Brittain, *Testament of Friendship* (Virago Press, London, 1980 edn), p. 19. The book was first published in 1940.

62 Winifred Holtby, *Anderby Wold* (Virago Press, London, 1981 edn), p. 91. The book was first published in 1923.

63 Brittain, *Testament of Friendship*, p. 13.

64 Brittain, *Testament of Friendship*, p. 14.

65 Jenkins, *The Agricultural Community*, pp. 79–80.

66 D. Parry-Jones, *My Own Folk* (Gwasg Gomer, Llandysul, 1972), p. 83.

67 Joseph Arch, *The Story of His Life Told by Himself* (Hutchinson & Co., London, 1898), p. 37.

68 *1911 Census of Population*, PP 1913, vol. LXXVIII, p. xlvi.

69 Mrs McIlquham, *The Enfranchisement of Women* (Women's Emancipation Union, Congleton, 1894), p. 4, at the British Library 8415.g.63(16). 'Every woman', declared Mrs McIlquham acidly, 'except the Queen, is politically non-existent.'

70 Davidoff and Hall, *Family Fortunes*, p. 286.

71 Haworth and Comber, *Cheshire Village Memories*, pp. 57–8.

72 George Eliot, *Scenes of Clerical Life* (William Blackwood & Sons, Edinburgh and London, n.d.), vol. 1, pp. 158–9. The book was first published in 1857.

73 Eliot, *Scenes of Clerical Life*, vol. 1, pp. 159–60.

74 J. Oxley Parker, *The Oxley Parker Papers* (Bonham & Co., Colchester, 1964), pp. 101–3.

75 Census returns for Sutton Courtenay at the Public Record Office: H.O.107.1688 for 1851, R.G.10.1266 for 1871 and R.G.11.1286 for 1881; tombstone memorials in Sutton Courtenay churchyard.

76 Registration of births, deaths and marriages at St Catherine's House, London, and Mrs Pullen's will at Somerset House, London.

77 Census returns for Sutton Courtenay at the Public Record Office: 1851, 1871 and 1881; registration of births, deaths and marriages at St Catherine's House, London; William Bobart's will at Somerset House.

78 H. S. A. Fox and R. A. Butlin (eds), *Change in the Countryside: Essays on Rural England, 1500–1900*, Institute of British Geographers, Special Publication 10 (Institute of British Geographers, London, 1977), p. 46; Leonore Davidoff, 'The Role of Gender in the "First Industrial Nation": Agriculture in England 1780–1850', in R. Crompton and H. Mann (eds), *Gender and Stratification* (Polity, Cambridge, 1986), p. 201.

79 Fox and Butlin, *Change in the Countryside*, p. 51.

80 See advertisements, for example, in *The Country Gentleman's Catalogue* (1894).

81 *Royal Commission on Agricultural Depression*, 'Report by Mr. A. Wilson Fox on Lincolnshire (excepting the Isle of Axholme)', p. 172.

82 *Royal Commission on Agricultural Depression*, 'Report by Mr. A. Wilson Fox on Lincolnshire (excepting the Isle of Axholme)', p. 173; will of Mrs Eliza Marfleet at Somerset House.

83 *Royal Commission on Land in Wales and Monmouthshire*, Evidence of Miss Kate Jenkins, Q.38,022–38,025. One Commission member confessed that he had 'never met a lady land agent before' (Q.38,171).

84 A. E. Fairhead, *The Fairhead Series*, 7 (Essex Record Office, 1973), p. 16.

85 Davidoff and Hall, *Family Fortunes*, p. 311.

86 Fred Kitchen, *Brother to the Ox* (J. M. Dent & Sons Ltd., London, 1963, paperback edn), p. 37.

87 Kitchen, *Brother to the Ox*, p. 46.

88 *Women's Agricultural Times*, Preface to vol. V (18 November 1904); minutes of the meetings of the Lady Warwick Agricultural Association at Reading University, WAR.5.7.1, meetings on 21 February 1899, 19 October 1899 and 7 November, 1901; Margaret Blunden, *The Countess of Warwick* (Cassell, London, 1967), p. 120.

89 Details of these two organizations are at the Imperial War Museum, LAND 3/1 and LAND 5/1/8.

90 K. B. Bagot de la Bere, 'Women as Agriculturists', *Land Magazine*, II, 7 (October 1898), pp. 496–7.

91 *Country Life*, 11 November 1899, p. 578.

92 *Royal Commission on Agricultural Depression*, 'Report by Mr. A. Wilson Fox on the Garstang District of Lancashire', p. 10.

93 *Royal Commission on Agricultural Depression*, 'Report by Mr. A.

Wilson Fox on the Garstang District of Lancashire', p. 9.

94　Kenneth Hudson, *Patriotism with Profit* (Hugh Evelyn, London, 1972), p. 117.

95　Pamela Horn, *Education in Rural England, 1800–1914* (Gill & Macmillan, Dublin, 1978), p. 257; Hudson, *Patriotism with Profit*, p. 119.

96　*Mark Lane Express*, 31 March and 21 April 1890. The *Mark Lane Express*, 2 June 1890, noted that nine institutions in England and Wales had received government grants, and £1,600 had been disbursed. The Bath and West Society had received £300 and the Eastern Counties Dairy Institute £250.

97　*Royal Commission on Land in Wales and Monmouthshire*, Evidence of Miss Kate Jenkins, Q.38,045.

98　Jenkins, *The Agricultural Community*, p. 84.

CHAPTER 6　DOMESTIC SERVICE AND WORK ON THE LAND

1　Calculated from the *1901 Census of England and Wales: Summary Tables*; Aggregate of Rural Districts, PP 1903, vol. LXXXIV, p. 220.

2　Charles Kightly, *Country Voices: Life and Lore in Farm and Village* (Thames & Hudson, London, 1984), p. 147.

3　Pamela Horn, *The Rise and Fall of the Victorian Servant* (Alan Sutton, Gloucester, 1986, paperback edn), p. 18.

4　*1871 Census of Population*, PP 1873, vol. LXXI, part I, p. xliv.

5　Mrs Isabella Beeton, *The Book of Household Management* (S. O. Beeton, London, 1861), p. 1,001.

6　Gertrude Jekyll, *Old West Surrey: Some Notes and Memories* (Longmans, Green, & Co., London, 1904), pp. 240–1. At no time did this maid earn £4 a year.

7　Jill Watt, *Grannie Loosley's Kitchen Album, 1860–1920* (Sidgwick & Jackson, London, 1980), pp. 8–9.

8　Dashwood (Buckinghamshire) papers at the Bodleian Library, MSS.D.D. (Bucks.) G.3/33/10b, letter from Grace Henley to Ellen Fane, 11 April [1851].

9　Typescript from the late Miss Lloyd Baker of Hardwicke Court, Gloucester, sent to the author in November 1974. The maid concerned was born on the Baker family estate and retired there in 1919.

10　D. Haworth and W. M. Comber (eds), *Cheshire Village Memories* (Cheshire Federation of Women's Institutes, County Office of the Cheshire Federation of Women's Institute, Malpas, 1969), p. 54.

11 Haworth and Comber, *Cheshire Village Memories*, p. 114.
12 Englefield House Servants' Book at Berkshire Record Office, D/EBy.A.130.
13 Englefield House Servants' Book D/EBy.A.130.
14 Notebook of Mrs Elizabeth Dashwood, later Lady Dashwood, wife of Sir George H. Dashwood, fifth baronet, at the Bodleian Library, MSS.D.D. (Bucks) G.4/1.
15 Photocopy of a letter in the possession of the author and sent to her in October 1974.
16 Mary Carbery, *Happy World. The Story of a Victorian Childhood* (Longmans, Green & Co., London, 1941), pp. 171–5.
17 Noel Streatfeild (ed.), *The Day Before Yesterday* (Collins, London, 1956), pp. 15–16.
18 Flora Thompson, *Lark Rise to Candleford* (Penguin Books, Harmondsworth, 1979 edn), p. 164.
19 Horn, *The Rise and Fall of the Victorian Servant*, p. 49; Englefield House Servants' Book, D/EBy.A.130.
20 Diary of the Rev. W. C. Risley at the Bodleian Library, MS.D.D.Risley C.I.3/39, entries for 21 September, 17 October and 30 October 1868.
21 Mrs James de Rothschild, *The Rothschilds at Waddesdon Manor* (Collins, London, 1979), p. 81.
22 Typescript from the late Miss Lloyd Baker.
23 The Marchioness of Bath, *Before the Sunset Fades* (Longleat Estate Company, Longleat, 1967), p. 17.
24 Horn, *The Rise and Fall of the Victorian Servant*, pp. 18–20.
25 *Within Living Memory: A Collection of Norfolk Reminiscences* (Norfolk Federation of Women's Institutes, printed at Stone Ferry, King's Lynn, Norfolk, 1971), pp. 92–4.
26 Information provided by Mrs Dorothy Brookes of Tetsworth concerning her mother; in correspondence with the author in October 1972.
27 Information provided by Mrs Dorothy Brookes.
28 *Second Report of the Royal Commission on the Employment of Children, Young Persons and Women in Agriculture*, PP 1868–9, vol. XIII, 'Report by Mr. Culley', p. 76. Hereafter referred to as *1868–9 Report*.
29 Horn, *The Rise and Fall of the Victorian Servant*, p. 108.
30 *Board of Agriculture and Fisheries: Report of Sub-Committee Appointed to consider the Employment of Women in Agriculture in England and Wales* (HMSO, London, 1919), p. 38.
31 *1871 Population Census*, p. xliv.
32 *General Report of the 1891 Census of Population*, PP 1893–4, vol. CVI, p. 40.

33 Reminiscences of hiring fairs at Museum of English Rural Life, Reading, D.68/53.

34 Letter from Kate Faggetter to Mrs Mary Dew, 3 September 1875, at the Bodleian Library, MS.Dew *24.

35 Thompson, *Lark Rise to Candleford*, p. 163.

36 Thompson, *Lark Rise to Candleford*, p. 158.

37 E. S. Turner, *What the Butler Saw* (Michael Joseph, London, 1962), p. 266.

38 Merlin Waterson, *The Servants' Hall* (Routledge & Kegan Paul, London, 1980), p. 94.

39 Quoted in Horn, *The Rise and Fall of the Victorian Servant*, p. 111.

40 *Board of Trade (Labour Department): Report by Miss Collet on the Money Wages of Indoor Domestic Servants*, PP 1899, vol. XCII, p. 25.

41 Servants' book of a north Oxfordshire housewife in the possession of the author.

42 *Thame Gazette*, 15 September 1888.

43 Servants' wages at Nuneham Courtenay, at the Bodleian Library, MSS.D.D.Harcourt e.3.

44 Thompson, *Lark Rise to Candleford*, p. 165.

45 See, for example, Thea Holme, *The Carlyles at Home* (Oxford University Press, London, 1965), p. 162.

46 *A Few Hints for Home Happiness and Comfort Addressed Chiefly to Village Girls on their Leaving Home* by A Lady (J. & C. Mozley, London, 1861, 2nd edn), p. 5. They were also told that 'dress beyond our station, is *wrong*, and shows bad taste and false notions' (p. 7).

47 K. D. M. Snell, *Annals of the Labouring Poor: Social Change and Agrarian England, 1660–1900* (Cambridge University Press, Cambridge, 1985), p. 65.

48 M. K. Ashby, *Joseph Ashby of Tysoe, 1859–1919* (Cambridge University Press, Cambridge, 1961), pp. 1–2.

49 *1868–9 Report*, 'Report by Edward Stanhope on Dorset', p. 4, and Evidence, p. 27.

50 *1868–9 Report*, Evidence, p. 297.

51 *1868–9 Report*, Evidence, p. 300.

52 Clementina Black, *Married Women's Work* (Virago Press, London, 1983 edn), p. 232. The book was first published in 1915.

53 David Jenkins, *The Agricultural Community in South-West Wales* (University of Wales Press, Cardiff, 1971), pp. 52–3; David W. Howell, *Land and People in Nineteenth-Century Wales* (Routledge & Kegan Paul, London, 1977), p. 135.

54 *1868–9 Report*, Evidence, p. 13.

55 *Third Report of the Royal Commission on the Employment of Children, Young Persons and Women in Agriculture*, PP 1870, vol. XIII, 'Report by Mr. Boyle on Monmouthshire', Evidence, p. 143; *1868–9 Report*, 'Report by Mr. F. H. Norman on Surrey, Wiltshire, Warwickshire, Worcestershire, and Herefordshire', p. 54.

56 *Sixth Report of the Medical Officer of the Privy Council for 1863*, PP 1864, vol. XXVIII, 'Report by Dr. H. J. Hunter on the Excessive Mortality of Infants in some Rural Districts of England', p. 456.

57 Celia Miller (ed.), *The Account Books of Thomas Smith, Ireley Farm, Hailes, Gloucestershire, 1865–71* (Bristol and Gloucestershire Archaeological Society, Bristol, 1985), pp. xxxiii, 138 and 171.

58 Munby Diaries, vol. 16, at Trinity College, Cambridge, entry for 6 October 1862, pp. 97 and 105.

59 Pamela Horn, 'The Education and Employment of Working-Class Girls, 1870–1914', *History of Education*, 17, 1 (1988), p. 80.

60 K. D. M. Snell, 'Agricultural Seasonal Unemployment, the Standard of Living, and Women's Work in the South and East: 1690–1860' *Economic History Review*, 2nd series, XXXIV, 3 (August 1981), pp. 413 and 425; Snell, *Annals of the Labouring Poor*, p. 56.

61 *Board of Agriculture and Fisheries: Report of Sub-Committee*, p. 28; Pamela Horn, *The Changing Countryside in Victorian and Edwardian England and Wales* (Athlone Press, London, 1984), p. 95.

62 Celia Miller, 'The Hidden Workforce: Female Field Workers in Gloucestershire, 1870–1901', *Southern History*, 6 (1984), pp. 145 and 146.

63 Miller, 'The Hidden Workforce', pp. 145 and 161; Miller, *The Account Books of Thomas Smith*, pp. xxxv, 131–2 and 171–2; Labour Book of Ireley Farm, Hailes, at Gloucester Record Office, D.2163/3.

64 Farm Labour Book of Wick Farm, Radley, Berkshire at University of Reading Library, BER.13.5.5; 1861 census return for Radley, at Public Record Office, R.G.9.732.

65 Farm Labour Book of John Butler of Tarrant Monkton, Dorset at University of Reading Library, DOR.5.3.1; 1861 census return for Tarrant Monkton, at Public Record Office, R.G.9.1334.

66 Farm Labour Book of Snowshill Farm, Stanway, Gloucestershire, at Gloucester Record Office, D.2267/A8. In 1890 Fanny Aston, for example, who had earned £1 15s. 10d. for the harvest, spent 7s. 3d. of it on lamb, hops and faggots for the fire.

67 Farm Labour Book of Wick Farm, Radley, BER.13.5.5.

68 Farm Labour Book of a farm at Little Wittenham, Berkshire, at University of Reading Library, BER.10/2/1; 1881 census return for

Little Wittenham, at Public Record Office, R.G.11.1293.

69 Farm Labour Books of John Butler of Tarrant Monkton, DOR.5.3.1 and DOR.5.3.2–3.

70 Miller, *The Account Books of Thomas Smith*, pp. 39–43 and 76–80.

71 Miller, 'The Hidden Workforce', pp. 144–5; Snowshill Farm Labour Book, at Gloucester Record Office, D.2267/A8.

72 Snowshill Farm Labour Book D.2267/A8.

73 Kightly, *Country Voices*, pp. 37–9.

74 Richard Jefferies, *The Toilers of the Field* (Macdonald Futura, London, 1981 edn), p. 88. The book was first published in 1892.

75 David Hoseason Morgan, *Harvesters and Harvesting 1840–1900* (Croom Helm, London, 1982), p. 141; Gertrude Jekyll, *Old West Surrey*, p. 183.

76 Jefferies, *The Toilers of the Field*, p. 89.

77 Arthur Randell, *Sixty Years a Fenman*, ed. Enid Porter (Routledge & Kegan Paul, London, 1966), p. 17.

78 Peter King, 'Gleaners, Farmers and the Failure of Legal Sanctions in England, 1750–1850', *Past and Present*, 125 (November 1989), pp. 125, 127 and 134; David H. Morgan, 'The Place of Harvesters in Nineteenth-Century Village Life' in Raphael Samuel (ed.), *Village Life and Labour* (Routledge & Kegan Paul, London, 1975), p. 58.

79 Jennie Kitteringham, *Country Girls in 19th Century England*, History Workshop Pamphlets No. 11 (Ruskin College, Oxford, n.d. [c.1973]), p. 50; *1868–9 Report*, Evidence, p. 448.

80 *1868–9 Report*, 'Report by Mr. F. H. Norman', p. 53.

81 *1868–9 Report*, 'Report by Mr. F. H. Norman', pp. 56–7.

82 Mary Lewis (ed.), *Old Days in the Kent Hop Gardens* (West Kent Federation of Women's Institutes, Tonbridge, 1962), pp. 22–5; *1868–9 Report*, Evidence, p. 43.

83 Lewis, *Old Days in the Kent Hop Gardens*, p. 20.

84 *Morning Chronicle*, 30 January 1850, p. 5; Lewis, *Old Days in the Kent Hop Gardens*, p. 22; *1868–9 Report*, Evidence, p. 61.

85 '"Merched Y Gerddi": A Seasonal Migration of Female Labour', *Folk Life*, 15 (1977), pp. 15–17, 19–20 and 21; L. G. Bennett, *The Horticultural Industry of Middlesex* (University of Reading: Department of Agricultural Economics, Miscellaneous Studies, No. 7, 1952), pp. 20–2 and 33; *1868–9 Report*, 'Report by Mr. F. H. Norman', p. 54.

86 Bennett, *The Horticultural Industry*, p. 22.

87 *Third Report of the Royal Commission on the Employment of Children &c. in Agriculture, 1870*, 'Report by Mr. Boyle on Monmouthshire', Evidence, p. 145, and 'Report by Mr. J. H. Tremenheere on Cardiganshire, Montgomery, and Merioneth', pp. 51–2.

88 Hiring agreements from Thornborough, Northumberland, at University of Reading Library, NORTHUM.2/2/1. The women supplied were both family members, in this case.

89 *Royal Commission on Labour: The Agricultural Labourer*, PP 1893–4, vol. XXV, 'Report by Mr. A. Wilson Fox on the Glendale Union', p. 128.

90 *Board of Agriculture and Fisheries: Report of Sub-Committee*, p. 117; Snell, *Annals of the Labouring Poor*, pp. 96–7.

91 Munby Diaries, vol. 21, entry for 31 August 1863, p. 240.

92 Munby Diaries, vol. 16, entry for 7 October 1862, pp. 123–30.

93 Kitteringham, *Country Girls*, p. 35.

94 Kitteringham, *Country Girls*, p. 35.

95 *Sixth Report of the Children's Employment Commission*, PP 1867, vol. XVI, p. v.

96 *Sixth Report of the Children's Employment Commission*, Evidence, p. 95.

97 *Sixth Report of the Children's Employment Commission*, Evidence, p. 103.

98 'Agricultural Gangs' [no author given], *Quarterly Review*, 123 (1867), p. 183.

99 *Sixth Report of the Children's Employment Commission*, Evidence, p. 53.

100 Calculated from statistics in the *Thirtieth Annual Report of the Registrar General of Births, Deaths and Marriages in England*, PP 1868–9, vol. XVI, pp. xiv–xv and 51.

101 *Sixth Report of the Children's Employment Commission*, 'Report by Mr. F. D. Longe on Agricultural Gangs', p. 8.

102 *Sixth Report of the Children's Employment Commission*, p. x; calculations from statistics in the *Thirtieth Annual Report of the Registrar General of Births*, pp. 51 and 67.

103 *Sixth Report of the Medical Officer of the Privy Council*, 'Report by Dr. H. J. Hunter', pp. 457 and 458.

104 Calculated from statistics in *Twenty-Ninth Annual Report of the Registrar General of Births, Deaths and Marriages in England*, PP 1867–8, vol. XIX, pp. 100–12.

105 *Royal Commission on Labour: The Agricultural Labourer*, 'Report on the Swaffham Union, Norfolk', p. 68.

106 Eve Hostettler, 'Gourlay Steell and the Sexual Division of Labour', *History Workshop*, 4 (Autumn 1977), p. 100.

CHAPTER 7   RURAL CRAFTS AND VILLAGE TRADES

1   Pamela Horn, 'Child Workers in the Pillow Lace and Straw Plait Trades of Victorian Buckinghamshire and Bedfordshire', *Historical Journal*, XVII, 4 (1974), p. 779; J. L. Green, *The Rural Industries of England* (Marlborough & Co., London, n.d. [1895]), p. 123.

2   Thomas G. Austin, *The Straw Trade* (Patrick O'Doherty, Luton, 1871), p. 18.

3   Joan Thirsk, 'Industries in the Countryside', in F. J. Fisher (ed.), *Essays in the Economic and Social History of Tudor and Stuart England* (Cambridge University Press, Cambridge, 1961), pp. 70 and 85–6.

4   *Reports of Special Assistant Poor Law Commissioners on the Employment of Women and Children in Agriculture*, PP 1843, vol. XII, p. 295.

5   S. Minwel Tibbott, 'Knitting Stockings in Wales: A Domestic Craft', *Folk Life*, 16 (1978), pp. 62 and 68–9.

6   Tibbott, 'Knitting Stockings', p. 63.

7   *Second Report of the Royal Commission on the Employment of Children, Young Persons and Women in Agriculture*, PP 1868–9, vol. XIII, 'Report by Mr. R. F. Boyle on Somerset', p. 12. He noted that in the Bristol area, where wages were higher, the women would 'hardly work out at all'.

8   Horn, 'Child Workers', pp. 779–80.

9   *First Report of the Children's Employment Commission*, PP 1863, vol. XVIII, Evidence, p. 257. This Report is hereafter cited as *1863 Report*.

10   *1841 Census of Population: Occupations*, PP 1844, vol. XXVII, entries under Bedfordshire and Buckinghamshire.

11   *1863 Report*, Evidence, p. 256.

12   *Second Report of the Royal Commission on the Employment of Children, &c. in Agriculture*, Evidence, p. 344.

13   Mervyn Bright, *Buttony: The Dorset Heritage* (The Old Button Shop, Lytchett Minster, Dorset, 1971), pp. 6–7; Pamela Horn, 'Women's Cottage Industries', in G. E. Mingay (ed.), *The Victorian Countryside* (Routledge & Kegan Paul, London, 1981), vol. I, p. 348.

14   J. G. Dony, *A History of the Straw Hat Industry* (Gibbs, Bamforth & Co. (Luton), Luton, 1942), pp. 86–7 and 91.

15   Jean Davis, *Straw Plait* (Shire Publications Ltd., Princes Risborough, 1981), p. 31; Horn, 'Child Workers', p. 796.

16   *Royal Commission on Labour: The Employment of Women*, PP 1893–4, vol. XXXVII, part I, 'Report by Miss Clara E. Collet', p. 29.

17   Charles Freeman, *Pillow Lace in the East Midlands* (Museum and Art Gallery, Luton, 1966), p. 20.

18 Horn, 'Child Workers', p. 796.

19 *Honiton Lace Industry*, PP 1888, vol. LXXX, 'Report by Alan Cole from the South Kensington Museum', p. 7.

20 These early attempts at organization are discussed by Geoff Spenceley, 'The Lace Associations: Philanthropic Movements to Preserve the Production of Hand-made Lace in Late Victorian and Edwardian England', *Victorian Studies*, XVI, 4 (June 1973), p. 438.

21 Midland Lace Association Letters, at Northamptonshire Record Office; letter from Mrs Brown of Moulton and Cash Book of the Association, also at Northamptonshire Record Office; Horn, 'Women's Cottage Industries', p. 348; Freeman, *Pillow Lace*, p. 21.

22 Midland Lace Association Letters: letters from Mrs Lovell, of Grendon. When taxed with failing to send lace to the association, she indignantly denied that she was 'selling my work to any one else . . . i have lernt a little girl to make lace'; clearly she found the pressure to work a great strain.

23 Spenceley, 'The Lace Associations', pp. 451–2.

24 Horn, 'Women's Cottage Industries', pp. 349–50.

25 Clementina Black (ed.), *Married Women's Work* (Virago, London, 1983 edn), pp. 236–7. The book was first published in 1915.

26 *Second Report of the Royal Commission on the Employment of Children, &c. in Agriculture*, 'Report by Mr. R. F. Boyle on Somerset', p. 131.

27 Pamela Horn, *Around Abingdon in Old Photographs* (Alan Sutton, Gloucester, 1987), pp. 8 and 45.

28 Pamela Horn, *The Changing Countryside in Victorian and Edwardian England and Wales* (Athlone Press, London, 1984), p. 149; Horn, 'Women's Cottage Industries', p. 350; Jennie Kitteringham, 'Country Work Girls in Nineteenth-Century England', in Raphael Samuel (ed.), *Village Life and Labour* (Routledge & Kegan Paul, London, 1975), p. 115.

29 *A Pattern of Hundreds* (Buckinghamshire Federation of Women's Institutes, Chalfont St Giles, 1975), pp. 20–1; Green, *The Rural Industries of England*, pp. 57 and 60.

30 Horn, 'Women's Cottage Industries', p. 349; *A Pattern of Hundreds*, pp. 94 and 99.

31 *1863 Report*, Evidence, p. 257.

32 *Appendix to the Second Report of the Children's Employment Commission*, PP 1843, vol. XIV, p. d.29. Hereafter cited as *Appendix to Second Report, 1843*.

33 *1863 Report*, Evidence, p. 258.

34 *1863 Report*, Evidence, p. 261.

35 *1863 Report*, Evidence, p. 259.
36 Quoted in Horn, 'Women's Cottage Industries', p. 344.
37 *1863 Report*, Evidence, p. 203.
38 *Appendix to Second Report, 1843*, p. A.13.
39 *1863 Report*, Evidence, p. 202.
40 Stock Book of Henry Horn, Plait Dealer, at Luton Museum, M/8/6; Bank Account of Messrs Gray and Horn, at Luton Museum, M/8/8/.
41 William Page and J. Horace Round (eds), *The Victoria History of the County of Essex* (Archibald Constable, London, 1907), vol. 2, p. 376.
42 Edwin Grey, *Cottage Life in a Hertfordshire Village* (Harpenden & District Local History Society, Harpenden, 1977 edn), pp. 88–9. The book was first published in 1934.
43 Henry Horn's Notebook and Stockbook for 1858, at Luton Museum. When Horn died at Luton on 4 December 1897, his estate was valued at £3,713 18s. 8d. At the 1871 Census (at the Public Record Office, RG.10.1566), Horn was shown as employed as a warehouseman, but a decade later he was again working as a plait dealer – as his records confirm.
44 László L. Gróf, *Children of Straw* (Barracuda Books, Buckingham, 1988), p. 95.
45 *The Church Family Newspaper*, 3 May 1901, preserved in a book of newspaper cuttings on the plait trade at Luton Museum.
46 *Royal Commission on Labour*, 'Report by Miss Clara Collet', p. 29.
47 Dave Thorburn, 'Gender, Work and Schooling in the Plaiting Villages', *The Local Historian*, 19, 3 (August 1989).
48 C. A. and P. Horn, 'The Social Structure of an "Industrial" Community: Ivinghoe in Buckinghamshire in 1871', *Local Population Studies*, 31 (Autumn 1983), pp. 10–11.
49 William Page (ed.), *The Victoria History of the County of Hertford* (Constable & Co., London, 1914), vol. 4, p. 253; Horn, 'Child Workers', p. 791.
50 David and Joan Hay, *Hilltop Villages of the Chilterns* (Phillimore, London and Chichester, 1971), pp. 176–7.
51 Clergy Visitation Returns for the Oxford Diocese, at Oxfordshire Record Office, MS.Oxf.Dioc.Pp.d.701.
52 Clergy Visitation Returns for 1854.
53 *Appendix to Second Report, 1843*, p. A.12.
54 Quoted in Horn, 'Child Workers', p. 791.
55 This ballad is preserved at Luton Museum.
56 Gróf, *Children of Straw*, pp. 55 and 101. I am indebted to my brother-in-law, Mr Ian Horn of Ivinghoe, for drawing my attention to the case of Deborah Rawlings.

57 *Morning Chronicle*, 5 April 1850, Letter XXXIV, 'Labour and the Poor: The Rural Districts', p. 5.

58 *Report by Alexander Redgrave, Inspector of Factories, for the Half-Year ended 30 April, 1874*, PP 1874, vol. XIII, p. 11.

59 Thorburn, 'Gender, Work and Schooling', p. 110.

60 See, for example, *Report of Alexander Redgrave, Inspector of Factories, for the Half-Year ended 30 April, 1875*, PP 1875, vol. XVI, Prosecutions, p. 54. An Ivinghoe straw factor was prosecuted for employing a child under eight and was fined 5s. 6d., with £1 4s. 6d. costs (p. 56).

61 Reminiscences of Mrs E. Turney of Great Horwood, obtained with the help of my sister-in-law, Mrs Margaret Horn of Ivinghoe.

62 Reminiscences of Mrs Wright, Church Row, Leafield, interviewed by the author on 15 June 1988.

63 Reminiscences of Mrs Howse of Leafield, interviewed by the author on 12 May 1988.

64 Horn, *The Changing Countryside*, p. 150.

65 Horn, 'Women's Cottage Industries', p. 349.

66 *Twentieth Annual Report of the Registrar-General of Births, Deaths and Marriages in England*, PP 1859, vol. XII, p. ix; *Sixty-third Annual Report of the Registrar-General of Births, Deaths and Marriages in England*, PP 1901, vol. XV, pp. 64–7.

67 Pamela Horn, 'Handicraft Communities in Victorian Oxfordshire and North Berkshire', in Stephen Jackson (ed.), *Industrial Colonies and Communities* (Conference of Regional and Local Historians in Tertiary Education, Liverpool, 1988), p. 57.

68 Stuart Seager, 'Hand-in-Glove with Tradition', *The Countryman* (Summer 1979), p. 113.

69 K. D. M. Snell, *Annals of the Labouring Poor: Social Change and Agrarian England, 1660–1900* (Cambridge University Press, Cambridge, 1985), pp. 289–94.

70 Pamela Horn, 'The Education and Employment of Working-Class Girls, 1870–1914', *History of Education*, 17, 1 (1988), pp. 80–1.

71 Flora Thompson, *Lark Rise to Candleford* (Penguin Books, Harmondsworth, 1979 edn), pp. 394–5. The census returns for Fringford show Mrs Whitton was born in the nearby village of Stoke Lyne. See also *Kelly's Directory for Oxfordshire and Berkshire for 1895* (Kelly, London) for women running blacksmiths' businesses. Census return for 1871 for Fringford at the Public Record Office, R.G.10.1445; will of John Whitton at Somerset House.

72 Flora Thompson, *A Country Calendar*, ed. Margaret Lane (Oxford University Press, Oxford, 1979), p. 15.

73　Will of Mrs Kezia Whitton at Somerset House; *Trade Directory* for 1899.

74　D. Haworth and W. M. Comber (eds), *Cheshire Village Memories* (Cheshire Federation of Women's Institutes, County Office of the Cheshire Federation of Women's Institutes, Malpas, 1969), p. 86.

75　Arthur R. Randell, *Sixty Years a Fenman*, ed. Enid Porter (Routledge & Kegan Paul, London, 1966), pp. 21–2.

76　J. A. Chartres, 'Country Tradesmen', in Mingay, *The Victorian Countryside*, vol. 1, p. 311.

77　*Post Office Directory of Bedfordshire, Huntingdonshire, Northamptonshire, Berkshire, Buckinghamshire and Oxfordshire for 1877* (Kelly & Co., London, 1877).

78　Barbara Kerr, *Bound to the Soil* (John Baker, London, 1968), pp. 137 and 142.

79　*Appendix to Second Report, 1843, Evidence*, pp. d.52–3.

80　*Appendix to Second Report, 1843, Evidence*, p. d.53.

81　*1901 Census of Population for England and Wales: Summary Tables*, PP 1903, vol. LXXXIV, 'Occupations in the Aggregate of Rural Districts', p. 223.

82　Samuel, *Village Life and Labour*, p. 202.

83　S. Minwel Tibbott, 'Liberality and Hospitality: Food as Communication in Wales', *Folk Life*, 24 (1985–6), p. 47.

84　'Deborah Primrose' [Mrs R. L. Ottley], *A Modern Boeotia* (Methuen & Co., London, 1904), pp. 8–9.

85　Rex L. Sawyer, *The Bowerchalke Parish Papers: Collett's Village Newspaper, 1878–1924* (Alan Sutton, and Wiltshire County Council, Gloucester, 1989), pp. 29–30.

86　Mrs J. M. Spinney and Mrs P. Genge (eds), *Romsey Remembers* (Lower Test Valley Archaeological Study Group, Romsey, 1979), p. 21.

87　*Second Report of the Royal Commission on the Employment of Children, &c. in Agriculture, Evidence*, p. 16.

88　Oxfordshire Reminiscences, Interview Transcript No. 24 at Oxford City and County Museum, Woodstock. The daughter herself did not do much laundry work until she was twelve.

89　Samuel, *Village Life and Labour*, pp. 180–2.

90　Samuel, *Village Life and Labour*, p. 194.

91　Reminiscences of Miss M. Tyrrell of Marcham, interviewed on 31 August 1986. Miss Tyrrell lived at Steventon before the First World War.

92　Fred Kitchen, *Brother to the Ox* (J. M. Dent & Sons, London, 1963, paperback edn), pp. 22–3 and 36.

93　Richard Curle, *Mary Anning, 1799–1847* (Dorset Worthies No. 4, published by the Dorset Natural History and Archaeological Society, Dorchester, n.d. [*c.*1960s]), pp. 2–3.

94 Horn, *Around Abingdon in Old Photographs*, p. 159.

95 The 1911 Census of Population shows that out of 15,821 female innkeepers, hotel-keepers and publicans, 7,918 were married and 3,201 were widows. PP 1913, vol. LXXIX, p. 19 (Aggregate of Rural Districts).

96 Leonore Davidoff and Catherine Hall, *Family Fortunes: Men and Women of the English Middle Class, 1780–1850* (Hutchinson, London, 1987), p. 299.

97 Quoted in Eric Richards, 'Women in the British Economy since about 1700: An Interpretation', *History*, 59 (1974), p. 351.

CHAPTER 8   PROFESSIONAL WOMEN: TEACHERS AND NURSES

1 Phil Gardner, *The Lost Elementary Schools of Victorian England* (Croom Helm, London, 1984), p. 115.

2 Lesley Hall, *Hygieia's Handmaids: Women, Health, and Healing* (Wellcome Institute for the History of Medicine, London, 1988), p. 7.

3 Maud F. Davies, *Life in an English Village* (T. Fisher Unwin, London, 1909), p. 95.

4 Mary Paley Marshall, *What I Remember* (Cambridge University Press, Cambridge, 1947), p. 2.

5 Rex L. Sawyer, *The Bowerchalke Parish Papers: Collett's Village Newspaper, 1878–1924* (Alan Sutton, Gloucester and Wiltshire County Council, 1989), p. 40.

6 Charles Kightly, *Country Voices: Life and Lore in Farm and Village* (Thames & Hudson, London, 1984), p. 100.

7 Flora Thompson, *Lark Rise to Candleford* (Penguin Books, Harmondsworth, 1979 edn), p. 136.

8 Queen Victoria's Jubilee Institute for Nurses: Rural District Branch, Hampshire Centre, Inspector's Report, 18 July 1892, at the Public Record Office, PRO.30/63/126.

9 Report by Inspector of Midwives to Somerset County Council Midwives Act Committee, 1 March 1907, at the Public Record Office, PRO.30/63/348.

10 Rebecca Fraser, *Charlotte Brontë* (Methuen, London, 1988), p. 210.

11 Pamela Horn (ed.), *Oxfordshire Village Life: The Diaries of George James Dew (1846–1928), Relieving Officer* (Beacon Publications, Sutton Courtenay, 1983), pp. iv and 57.

12 *Royal Commission on Secondary Education*, vol. VI, Reports of

Assistant Commissioners, PP 1895, vol. XLVIII, 'Report by Mr. and Mrs. Lee Warner on Norfolk', p. 414.

13 *Royal Commission on Secondary Education*, vol. VI, 'Report by Mrs. Armitage on Devon', p. 94.

14 *Reports of the Commissioners of Inquiry into the State of Education in Wales*, PP 1847, vol. XXVII, part II, 'Report on Brecknock, Cardigan and Radnor', p. 29.

15 Gardner, *The Lost Elementary Schools*, p. 179.

16 *Minutes of the Committee of Council on Education for 1845* (HMSO, London, 1846), p. 57.

17 Mary Smith, *The Autobiography of Mary Smith (1822–1889)* (Bemrose & Sons, London, 1892), pp. 16–19.

18 *The Autobiography of Mary Smith*, pp. 24–5.

19 Pamela Horn, *Education in Rural England, 1800–1914* (Gill & Macmillan, Dublin, 1978), p. 276.

20 Comment by the Rev. B. M. Cowie, HMI, quoted in John Hurt, *Education in Evolution* (Rupert Hart-Davis, London, 1971), p. 120.

21 In 1895, out of 4.3m children attending elementary schools, 2.4m went to the various voluntary schools (most of them Anglican) and 1.9m went to board schools.

22 See Admission Book and Quarterly Report Book of Students at Sarum St Michael, 1585/94, at Wiltshire Record Office.

23 Admission and Quarterly Report Book of Students at Sarum St Michael, 1585/94.

24 Pamela Horn, 'The Recruitment, Role and Status of the Victorian Country Teacher', *History of Education*, 9, 2 (1980), p. 129; Horn, *Rural Education*, pp. 188 and 193.

25 *Report of the Committee of Council on Education for 1862–63*, PP 1863, vol. XLI, 'Report by the Rev. F. C. Cook, HMI', p. 231.

26 'A Letter Addressed to the Members of the Council of the Whitelands Training Institute for Schoolmistresses by the Rev. Harry Baber, Chaplain and Secretary' (Whitelands College, 1850), preserved in the archives of Roehampton Institute: Whitelands College, London, pp. 7–8.

27 Pamela Horn, 'The Role of Women Teachers in Elementary Education 1840–1914' in John Wilkes (ed.), *The Professional Teacher* (History of Education Society, Leicester, Conference Papers for December 1985), p. 57; *Report of the Committee of Council on Education for 1862–63*, pp. 233–4.

28 Louisa M. Hubbard, *Work for Ladies in Elementary Schools* (Longmans, Green & Co., London, n.d. [1872]), p. 5.

29 T. J. Macnamara, 'The Village Schoolmistress', *National Union of Teachers Annual Report*, 1894, p. lxxxvi, in National Union of Teachers Library, London; Frances Widdowson, *Going Up into the Next Class* (Hutchinson & Co., London, 1983), p. 36.

30 Horn, *Rural Education*, p. 111.

31 Pamela Horn, 'Mid-Victorian Elementary School Teachers', *Local Historian*, 12, 3 and 4 (1976), p. 165.

32 Admission Book and Quarterly Report Book of Students at Sarum St Michael, 1585/96.

33 Letter from Katharine Hardy to Emma Hardy, n.d. [1882], written at Sandford Orcas, Dorset, where Katharine was then school head. Published with the permission of the Trustees of the Thomas Hardy Memorial Collection and preserved at Dorset County Museum, Dorchester; Michael Millgate, *Thomas Hardy* (Oxford University Press, Oxford, 1987, paperback edn), p. 351.

34 Edward Steward (ed.), *Salisbury Diocesan Training School* (Bennett Brothers, Salisbury, n.d. [c.1908]), p. 27, reminiscence no. 5.

35 E. M. Sneyd-Kynnersley, *HMI. Some Passages in the Life of One of H.M. Inspectors of School* (Macmillan & Co., London, 1910, 2nd edn), pp. 64–5, referred to the 'very green girl, fresh from the training college', whom he found in charge of many Norfolk schools.

36 *Report of the Royal Commission on Popular Education*, PP 1861, vol. XXI, part I, p. 641.

37 Macnamara, 'The Village Schoolmistress', p. lxxxiv.

38 Sandford Orcas School Log Book at Dorset Record Office, S.11/12/1.

39 Bramley School Log Book for 1864–85, at Hampshire Record Office, 63M70/PE2, entry for 25 April 1864, for example.

40 Drayton St Leonard School Log Book at Oxfordshire Record Office, T/SL.21.

41 Horn, *Rural Education*, p. 74.

42 Horn, *Rural Education*, p. 75.

43 Hurt, *Education in Evolution*, p. 125.

44 Horn, *Rural Education*, p. 70.

45 *Report of the Committee of Council on Education for 1885–86*, PP 1886, vol. XXIV, p. 321, for the situation in Oxfordshire, for example.

46 Thompson, *Lark Rise to Candleford*, pp. 189–90.

47 Thompson, *Lark Rise to Candleford*, p. 178. For details of Miss Holmyard's career see Pamela Horn, 'Country Teachers in Victorian Oxfordshire', *Cake and Cockhorse*, 10, 8 (Spring 1988), p. 206; returns under Cottisford, at Public Record Office, ED.7.101.

48 For the diocesan inspector's report see Cottisford School Minute Book,

at Oxfordshire Record Office, T/SM.6/ii.

49 Pamela Horn, 'Country Teachers in Victorian Oxfordshire', p. 209. For Tadmarton's long-term attendance problems see Pamela Horn, *Village Education in Nineteenth-Century Oxfordshire* (Oxfordshire Record Society, Oxford, 1979), vol. 51 [of Oxfordshire Record Society publications], pp. xxxvii–xxxviii.

50 Roger R. Sellman, *Devon Village Schools in the Nineteenth Century* (David & Charles, Newton Abbot, 1967), p. 110.

51 *General Reports of H.M. Inspectors of Elementary Schools for 1901*, PP 1902, vol. XXI, p. 95.

52 Sellman, *Devon Village Schools*, p. 139.

53 Information provided by the headmistress's daughter, the late Miss D. B. Dew of Lower Heyford, in communication with the author, March 1983. Miss Dew (b.1888) accompanied her mother to these meetings and demonstrated the exercises to other pupils at Lower Heyford.

54 Quoted in Horn, *Rural Education*, p. 252.

55 Horn, *Rural Education*, pp. 78–9; Horn, 'The Victorian Country Teacher', p. 134.

56 Horn, 'The Victorian Country Teacher', p. 135, for details of the high number of monitors employed in Devon and Oxfordshire.

57 Horn, 'The Victorian Country Teacher', pp. 135–6.

58 School records for Rydal, Westmorland, at the Public Record Office, Ed.7.129.

59 Pamela Horn, 'The Problems of a Village Headmistress in the 1880s', *History of Education Society Bulletin*, 26 (Autumn 1980), p. 17.

60 Letters from Miss Rose Knowles, at Northamptonshire Record Office, YZ.5541, letter undated [c.14 August 1888].

61 Horn, *Rural Education*, p. 112.

62 Sneyd-Kynnersley, *HMI. Some Passages*, p. 65.

63 Quoted in Hurt, *Education in Evolution*, pp. 140–1.

64 Horn, 'The Problems of a Village Headmistress', p. 19.

65 Horn, *Oxfordshire Village Life*, pp. 29–30; letter, dated 16 March 1868, from George James Dew to Mary Banfield, in the Bodleian Library, MS.Dew *23.

66 *Salisbury Training College Magazine*, Whitsun 1915, 'Appreciation of Lucy Lampet', at Wiltshire Record Office. Miss Lampet retired from Hursley school in 1906; she was 73 when she died.

67 Report by Inspector of Midwives to Somerset County Council Midwives Act Committee, 1 March 1907, at the Public Record Office, PRO.30/63/348.

68 Anne Summers, 'The Mysterious Demise of Sarah Gamp: The

Domiciliary Nurse and her Detractors, c.1830–1860', *Victorian Studies*, 32, 3 (Spring 1989), p. 371; Hall, *Hygieia's Handmaids*, p. 47.

69 Summers, 'The Mysterious Demise of Sarah Gamp', p. 371.

70 Brian Abel-Smith, *A History of the Nursing Profession* (Heinemann, London, 1960), pp. 5 and 23–4; Robert Dingwall, Anne Marie Rafferty and Charles Webster, *An Introduction to the Social History of Nursing* (Routledge, London, 1988), pp. 56–60.

71 *Report of the Departmental Committee on the Nursing of the Sick Poor in Workhouses*, PP 1902, vol. XXXIX, appendix: 'Return relating to the Sick in the Workhouses on 1 January, 1902, and of the Nurse and Pauper Attendants Employed in their Care', pp. 165–6.

72 Quoted in M. A. Crowther, *The Workhouse System, 1834–1929* (Batsford, London, 1981), p. 180.

73 Quoted in Abel-Smith, *A History of the Nursing Profession*, p. 46.

74 Dingwall, Rafferty and Webster, *An Introduction to the Social History of Nursing*, p. 67.

75 *Burdett's Official Nursing Directory for 1898* (Scientific Press, London, 1898), p. 141; Pamela Horn, *The Changing Countryside in Victorian and Edwardian England and Wales* (Athlone Press, London, 1984), pp. 153–4.

76 Horace Swete, *Handy Book of Cottage Hospitals* (Hamilton, Adams & Co., London, 1870), pp. 96–7.

77 Monica E. Baly, *A History of the Queen's Nursing Institute* (Croom Helm, London, 1987), p. 49; Mary Stocks, *A Hundred Years of District Nursing* (George Allen & Unwin, London, 1960), pp. 92–3.

78 *Report and Proceedings of the Jubilee Congress of District Nursing at Liverpool, May 1909* (D. Marples & Co., Liverpool, 1909), 'History of District Nursing in England and other Countries', pp. 39 and 45.

79 *Report and Proceedings of the Jubilee Congress*, p. 166; *Report of the Departmental Committee on the Nursing of the Sick Poor in Workhouses, 1902*, Evidence of Miss Broadwood, p. 122 (Q.3737–3740).

80 *Report of the Select Committee on Midwives' Registration*, PP 1892, vol. XIV, Evidence of Mrs Elizabeth Malleson, pp. 81–2 (Q.1123); Stocks, *A Hundred Years of District Nursing*, p. 99.

81 Stocks, *A Hundred Years of District Nursing*, p. 100.

82 *Report of the Rural District Branch of Queen Victoria's Jubilee Institute for 1893*, p. 2. The Report is in the British Library, Cup.401.i.3.

83 Stocks, *A Hundred Years of District Nursing*, pp. 93–5; Queen Victoria's Jubilee Institute for Nurses, *Conditions of Affiliation*, 25 March 1890, at the British Library, Cup.401.i.3; *Burdett's Official Nursing Directory for 1898*, p. 206.

84 *Report of the Rural District Branch for 1893*, p. 3.

85 Queen Victoria's Institute: Rural District Branch, Hampshire Centre: Inspector's Report, 18 July 1892, at Public Record Office, PRO.30/63/126.

86 See, for example, report of the Inspector of Midwives for Oxfordshire for final quarter of 1911, in Report of the General Purposes Committee, Oxfordshire County Council Reports, 1912 –13, 14 February 1912, p. 15, at Oxfordshire Record Office.

87 Appleby and Bongate Society to provide trained sick nurse for the poor, Reports, 6 November 1895 and 4 September 1897, at the Public Record Office, PRO.3/63/452. By 1897, perhaps significantly, 'Queen's Nurse' Pratt had taken over from Nurse Backer; she, too, lived in the lodge.

88 Stocks, *A Hundred Years of District Nursing*, p. 120; *Report of Queen Victoria's Jubilee Institute for Nurses for 1901*, pp. 9 –10.

89 Lincolnshire County Nursing Association, Report by E. F. Ross, Inspector of N.E Midlands, at the Public Record Office, PRO.30/63/267.

90 *Queen's Nurses Magazine*, I, 1 (1 May 1904), p. 4 – the Magazine is at the British Library, Pp.2707.kac; information from Queen's Nursing Institute in London.

91 *Queen's Nurses Magazine*, II, 2 (30 August 1905), pp. 67 –72.

92 *Queen's Nurses Magazine*, IV, 2 (31 August 1907), p. 59.

93 Queen Victoria's Jubilee Institute for Nurses: General Inspector's Report, January 1891, at the British Library, Cup.401.i.3. In this Miss Rosalind Paget, first general inspector of nursing, commented: 'Miss Nightingale has impressed indelibly on my mind that the District Nurse should not only be a *Nurse*, but a *sanitary reformer*. With a view to obtaining this result, Practical Hygiene is of all subjects the one most important to be studied by District Nurses.'

94 Minute Book of the Nailsworth District Nursing Association, at Gloucester Record Office, D.3548/1/1. p. 26.

95 General Rules of the Nailsworth District Nursing Association Affiliated to Stroud District Nursing Association, at Gloucester Record Office, D.3548/1/1.

96 Nailsworth District Nursing Association Minute Book, pp. 39– 41.

97 Jean Donnison, *Midwives and Medical Men: A History of the Struggle for the Control of Childbirth* (Historical Publications, New Barnet, Herts, and London, 1988), pp. 92 –3 and 114 –15.

98 *Report of the Departmental Committee on the Working of the Midwives Act 1902*, PP 1909, vol. XXXIII, Evidence of Mrs Elizabeth Miles, p. 172 (Q.5144 –5145); Donnison, *Midwives and Medical Men*, p. 130.

99 Quoted in Donnison, *Midwives and Medical Men*, p. 147.

100 Donnison, *Midwives and Medical Men*, pp. 146 –7.

101 Donnison, *Midwives and Medical Men*, pp. 163–4.

102 *An Act to Secure the Better Training of Midwives and to Regulate their Practice*, 1902, sections 1 (1–5), 2, 3 and 8 (1–7).

103 Hampshire County Council, Midwives Act Committee Minutes, meeting on 19 April 1909, at Hampshire Modern Records Office; *Report on the Work of the Central Midwives Board from its Formation to 31 March, 1908*, PP 1909, vol. XXXIII, p. 6.

104 Hampshire County Council, Midwives Act Committee Minutes, meeting 15 July 1907.

105 Hampshire County Council, Midwives Act Committee Minutes, meeting on 25 April 1910.

106 *Report on the Work of the Central Midwives Board from its Formation to 1908*, p. 9; *Report of the Work of the Central Midwives Board for the Year ending 31 March, 1909*, PP 1909, vol. XXXIII, p. 4.

107 *Report of the Departmental Committee on the Working of the Midwives Act*, p. 5.

108 Report by Miss Pybus on the Midwives Act, 1915, at Public Record Office, PRO.30/63/267; Somerset County Council: Midwives' Act Sub-Committee, Report on the Working of the Midwives' Act for the Year 1911, at the Public Record Office, PRO.30/63/348.

109 Report by Oxfordshire midwives' inspector submitted to the General Purposes Committee on 11 May 1910, p. 14, in Oxfordshire County Council Reports, 1910–11, at Oxfordshire Record Office.

110 *Report of the Departmental Committee on the Working of the Midwives Act*, Evidence of Mrs Elizabeth Miles, p. 173 (Q.5164–5168); Elizabeth Roberts, *A Woman's Place: An Oral History of Working-Class Women, 1890–1940* (Basil Blackwell, Oxford, 1985, paperback edn), p. 107; Donnison, *Midwives and Medical Men*, p. 181.

111 Donnison, *Midwives and Medical Men*, p. 181.

112 Hampshire County Council, Midwives Act Committee Minutes, meeting on 10 April 1911. On 7 October, however, the Committee decided that there was 'insufficient evidence' on which to prosecute three other women charged with 'illegal practice'.

113 Report by Oxfordshire midwives' inspector submitted to the General Purposes Committee on 10 May 1911, p. 157.

114 *Report of the Departmental Committee on the Working of the Midwives Act*, p. 29.

CHAPTER 9 EPILOGUE

1 Edith J. Morley, *Women Workers in Seven Professions* (George Routledge & Sons, London, 1914), pp. 37–8.

2 Quoted in Pat Jalland, *Women, Marriage and Politics, 1860–1914* (Oxford University Press, Oxford, 1988, paperback edn), p. 7.

3 Maud F. Davies, *Life in an English Village* (T. Fisher Unwin, London, 1909), p. 287.

4 G. E. Mingay (ed.), *The Vanishing Countryman* (Routledge, London, 1989), p. 28.

5 John Saville, *Rural Depopulation in England and Wales, 1851–1951* (Routledge & Kegan Paul, London, 1957), p. 56.

6 Mingay, *The Vanishing Countryman*, p. 4.

7 See, for example, Rollo Arnold, *The Farthest Promised Land: English Villagers, New Zealand Immigrants of the 1870s* (Victoria University Press, Wellington, New Zealand, 1981), pp. 127, 250 and 279.

8 *The Journals of George Sturt, 1890–1927*, ed. E. D. Mackerness (Cambridge University Press, Cambridge, 1967), vol. I, p. 39.

9 George Sturt, *Change in the Village* (Caliban Books, London, 1984 edn), pp. 160–1. The book was first published in 1912.

10 Michael Winstanley, 'The New Culture of the Countryside', in Mingay, *The Vanishing Countryman*, pp. 148–9; B. J. Davey, *Ashwell 1830–1914: The Decline of a Village Community*, Department of English Local History Occasional Papers, 3rd series, 5 (Leicester University Press, Leicester, 1980), pp. 56–7.

Index

277